THE BEST-HATED MAN

The Best-Hated Man

GEORGE MALCOLM THOMSON,
INTELLECTUALS AND THE
CONDITION OF SCOTLAND
BETWEEN THE WARS

George McKechnie

ARGYLL ✣ PUBLISHING

First published by
Argyll Publishing
Glendaruel
Argyll PA22 3AE
Scotland
www.argyllpublishing.co.uk

The author has asserted his moral rights.

British Library Cataloguing-in-Publication Data.
A catalogue record for this book in available from the British Library.

ISBN 978 1 908931 32 0 hardback
ISBN 978 1 908931 33 7 e-book

Printing: PB Print UK

For Jan, Scott and Craig

George Malcolm Thomson,
1930s

Contents

ACKNOWLEDGEMENTS

Special thanks are due to Dr Martin Johnes, Head of History and Classics in the College of Arts and Humanities at the University of Swansea, and to George Malcolm Thomson's son, Peter.

'The Best-Hated Man'

> It is time Scotland was re-discovered. The best-hated man in Scotland, the author of *Caledonia*, follows up his initial onslaught on the shortcomings of the Scottish people with a more detailed account of conditions in modern Scotland. Mr Thomson describes the methods by which the Irish invasion of Scotland is being carried out and the new and bitter problems it is creating. He goes down into the slums and tells what existence means in terms, not of death-rates, but of the lives of human beings. Modern Scotland in a score of phases comes under his penetrating gaze.
>
> Cover Sheet, *The Re-Discovery of Scotland*, (1928) [1]

IN AUTUMN 1928 the London publishing house Kegan Paul, Trench, Trubner and Company brought out *The Re-Discovery of Scotland,* a book focused on contemporary Scottish affairs and the second book written by a young Scottish journalist, George Malcolm Thomson. This was Thomson's sequel to *Caledonia or The Future of the Scots*, produced in October 1927. *Caledonia* had been a commercial success but its theme, a bitter condemnation of modern Scotland, received a critical response establishing Thomson as one of the most controversial and notorious of Scottish intellectuals and writers between the two world wars.

As the dust jacket blurb demonstrates, Kegan Paul did not hesitate to exploit the publicity potential of Thomson's newly acquired status. These polemical works, *Caledonia* and *Re-Discovery*, are the books which defined Thomson's interwar reputation. They are also the books which attracted the attention of the press baron, Lord Beaverbrook, a development which significantly changed the course of Thomson's life and career.

Thomson's notoriety at the time was based on his outspoken and almost exclusively negative views of his fellow countrymen. Few sections of Scottish society escaped his acerbic pen as he railed against national failure, defeatism, complacency, ignorance and dependency. Thomson's books represent a brutal economic, social and political analysis of a country experiencing industrial slump and national decline epitomised by large scale unemployment, mass emigration and hundreds of thousands of people living in some of the worst slums in Western Europe. His body of work from the period provides us with an insight into one individual interpretation of the major events and issues which had long-lasting consequences for Scotland throughout the remainder of the century.

In the period between the wars Thomson's Scottish work and activities were focused on one subject, the condition of the country, whether viewed from an economic, political, social, cultural, historical or identity perspective. Thomson established himself as a polemicist, propagandist, and one of the leading commentators chronicling Scotland's post-war decline.

In addition to his books he produced pamphlets, essays and news-paper articles and he emerged on the airwaves of the BBC Scottish Region as one of the first radio commentators broadcasting on political, social and cultural matters. Thomson was a brilliant commentator and columnist able to use popular and vibrant language in his polemics to inspire reaction and controversy. His strident and accusatory voice was planned and deliberate, reflecting his view that his journalism and polemic writing should be a vehicle for propaganda. Thomson not only believed in the power of words as a propaganda force, he revelled in their application and impact. His awareness and skills helped him to exploit the possibilities and opportunities afforded by the post-war growth and popularity of publishing, newspapers and broadcasting, and his use of these as propaganda tools.

Thomson's written and propaganda skills impressed Beaverbrook, himself a self-confessed enthusiast for and participant in the use of propaganda. In 1931 he was employed by Beaverbrook Newspapers, becoming later personal assistant and advisor to Beaverbrook; and as the chief commentator of the *London Daily Express* Thomson was the propagandist voice of the press magnate. Thomson was eminently qualified for the role.

One Scottish MP, Lachlan MacNeil Weir,[2] accused Thomson of making false and malicious statements and bringing disgrace on Scotland. Thomson, he said, 'had wielded a poison pen', was 'sensation mongering' and had deliberately set out to achieve notoriety. The leader of the Scottish literary revival, the poet Hugh MacDiarmid, writing under his real name, Christopher Grieve, said *Caledonia* was 'too pessimistic' and quickly produced his own book on contemporary Scotland, *Albyn or Scotland and the Future*, also published by Kegan Paul.[3] The unionist historians Robert Rait and George Pryde described Thomson's *Caledonia* as 'lurid' and Grieve's *Albyn* 'vitriolic' and assessed Grieve and Thomson together as 'discordant elements'.[4]

Yet Thomson had created the condition of Scotland genre which emerged as the dominant discourse in intellectual, social, political and cultural debate in books, pamphlets, essays, speeches and broadcasts between 1928 and the late 1930s. Leading intellectuals and writers like MacDiarmid, Lewis Grassic Gibbon, Edwin Muir, Andrew Dewar Gibb, William Power, Neil Gunn, George Blake and others followed much of the narrative of Thomson's polemics and while many did not always share his views or conclusions they contributed important critical commentaries to the public debates.

At the end of the 1930s the historian Agnes Mure Mackenzie recalled there had been a spate of books, articles, and pamphlets on Scotland's evil condition. 'Some were over-passionate with a startled horror,' Mackenzie wrote. 'A few, too clearly, were written by men delighted to find a good excuse for scolding the world. The sense of peril – and it was a peril increasingly huge and real – stirred men and women once again to face it.' [5] One contemporary literary critic described as 'remarkable' the number of books 'filled with bitter self criticism in which the new generation of writers had diagnosed the sorry condition of their country.' [6]

The modern historian Richard Finlay in his seminal essay *National Identity in Crisis: Politicians, Intellectuals and the 'End of Scotland', 1920-1939* (1994) said that for many intellectuals at the time all the indicators pointed to a nation in the process of terminal decline. Politicians and writers debated the state of modern Scotland, 'the early 1930s saw the publication of a number of books which linked economic decline with national decline'.[7]

George Malcolm Thomson was born in Leith in the final year of the nineteenth century, the eldest son of Charles Thomson, a journalist. He was brought up in a family dedicated to the sober and strict values of Scottish Presbyterianism, one which ensured that his education would be a priority. Thomson excelled at school and was the Dux pupil in his final year at Daniel Stewart's College, one of Edinburgh's leading fee-paying schools. When he graduated from Edinburgh University in the early 1920s he was politically a conservative unionist but culturally he was an active supporter of the emerging movement which called for a Scottish literary revival and which was bitterly opposed to any further Anglicisation of Scottish society. He entered the period enthused with optimism intent on playing his part in a national cultural reawakening.

Newly married, he moved to London in 1926 where he remained until his death seventy years later. All of his controversial Scottish material was written from desks in Hampstead, as was the prodigious stream of correspondence which he sent to Scotland on an almost daily basis in the early 1930s. Until the late 1930s Thomson continued to write and correspond on Scottish matters, but after World War II he concentrated on his work as a journalist and advisor to Beaverbrook. In later life he wrote histories and novels, some with Scottish themes and settings.

The issue which dominates and sullies Thomson's modern reputation is the campaign he waged in his books and other writings against Irish Catholic immigrants. Thomson claimed that an alien and minority Irish Catholic population was out-breeding the native Scots, thereby diluting the purity of the Scottish race, the consequence of which, he forecast, would turn Scotland into a little Ireland by the twenty-first century. [8]

In 2009 the literary historian Margery Palmer McCulloch said Thomson's treatment of Irish immigration and the influence of the Roman Catholic Church, 'brought him a notoriety which has lasted to the present day'.[9] In 2000, more than seventy years after the publication of *Caledonia*, another historian, Liam McIlvanney, said that in modern

Scotland his opinions would arouse horror. 'The kind of rhetoric practised by Thomson was used to underpin systematic discrimination and even to justify violence against a poor and often despised minority,' McIlvanney wrote. The book was 'nasty, a jeremiad'.[10] Keith Dixon described Thomson as a 'nationalist fringe intellectual' who proposed racial exclusiveness through 'strident orange racism' polemical writings.[11]

On the eve of the millennium, in his last column of the twentieth century, the commentator Alf Young chose Thomson's book with its dire and manifestly exaggerated race predictions to demonstrate the dangers of forecasting the shape of the future on the basis of prejudicial analysis of events and conditions in the present. Thomson's fears, Young said, spawned a virulent contempt for his fellow Scot and his 'forebodings of sectarian violence' were 'feverish hokum'. [12]

Finlay suggests that notions of race dominate all of Thomson's ideas, that Irish immigration had induced the Scots into a state of national lethargy, 'ultimately, he believed, this would lead to the collapse of Scotland as a nation.'[13] It is a view shared by Liam Connell who claims that nationalist accounts of the economic and social problems facing Scotland placed Irish immigration at the centre of their analysis.[14] James Mitchell said that Thomson's nationalism contained 'a strong element of anti-Catholic bigotry and anti-Irish racism.' [15]

Yet, as this book argues, Thomson should not be regarded purely as a negative, rebellious voice of dissent. Despite the controversies surrounding him, many writers and voices of the period were friendly with and admired Thomson, some praising the quality of his polemics and others the part he played in the Scottish literary revival by encouraging the cultural blossoming of new poetry, prose, and novels. His contemporary and friend, the poet Helen B. Cruickshank, said later that Thomson deserved credit for his courage, along with others, for launching 'on a shoe-string' the Porpoise Press in Edinburgh in 1922. 'Thomson's part in the so-called Scottish Renaissance is often overlooked in the face of C. M. Grieve's more spectacular role,' Cruickshank wrote.[16] In a letter to the novelist Eric Linklater, Cruickshank encouraged him to read Thomson's third polemic on the condition of Scotland, *Scotland,*

That Distressed Area (1935), declaring it 'the best book on Scotland for years'. [17]

It was a view shared by the poet, Edwin Muir who described *Distressed* as 'one of the best books that have been written about the Scottish question', adding 'probably the best'. Thomson's research, Muir said, defined clearly for the first time the economic state of Scotland. 'It is the state of a country slowly dying without having wakened to the fact. For Scotland it is a national domestic problem as well as an economic one. Thomson has tried to rouse Scotland to a realisation of its state.' [18]

When the playwright George Scott-Moncrieff returned to Scotland from London in 1931, T.S. Eliot gave him a copy of *Caledonia*, telling Moncrieff that the book underpinned the distinctive identity of the Scots and reflected the idea of the Scottish Renaissance. *Caledonia*, Scott-Moncrieff said later, was one of the books which led him to believe that things were happening in Scotland: 'I made my return full of high hopes in a cause'. [19]

The novelist Lewis Grassic Gibbon, a socialist and one-time communist, was opposed to Thomson's nationalism and right-wing unionist views. Yet he shared Thomson's analysis of the economic and social condition of Scotland in *Caledonia*, and confirmed his admiration of Thomson's work by dedicating to Thomson *Cloud Howe*, the second book of his *A Scots Quair* trilogy.[20] Grieve (Hugh MacDiarmid) described as 'remarkable' Thomson's Scottish home rule pamphlet *The Kingdom of Scotland Restored* (1931).[21] The pamphlet, outlining Thomson's plan for a Scottish parliament within a reconstituted union with England but retaining Scotland's position at the heart of the British Empire, was given public support in its introduction by four intellectuals: the journalists and authors, George Blake, William Power and Moray McLaren and the right-wing nationalist and law professor, Andrew Dewar Gibb.[22]

Thomson's involvement and contribution to the debate about the condition of Scotland deserves greater attention and analysis than an intellectual known only for his prominent role in a campaign against Irish Catholic immigrants. He was accurate in concluding that a century of industrial growth and success had ended and that Scotland faced a future in which it would be a poorer and dependent nation as financial and industrial power was centralised in London and the south of England. Although, today, this is regarded as self-evident, at the time many industrial and business leaders in Scotland rejected such pessimistic predictions, stubbornly maintaining the Scottish economy would recover.

Thomson's writings, speeches and his literary and political activities provide us with a remarkable insight into the psychological, emotional and personal development of one intellectual whose original beliefs and values and, ultimately, life and career choices were challenged, leading him to re-assess his view of his native country and his fellow countrymen. While Thomson deserves opprobrium from history for his invective against his country's Irish Catholic population he is entitled to positive recognition for his prescience in foretelling that the economic, political, and social issues of the period were shaping a dependent, less confident nation.

Thomson is a significant author, commentator, journalist and propagandist of the period. He played a pivotal and persuasive role behind the scenes in the events and discussions which led to the formation of the Scottish National Party (SNP) in 1934 and made an important contribution to the Scottish literary revival and was influential in defending and promoting Scottish culture and national identity.

By many historical measures George Malcolm Thomson's life is significant. He died in June 1996, aged 96, having lived a full twentieth century life which he started in Victorian Leith and ended in a wheelchair in leafy Hampstead, as an adopted and then fully-fledged Londoner. London was his chosen home for more than two thirds of his life. He was a controversial and influential intellectual and writer on Scotland between the wars with a notoriety which persists to the present day. He was the principal private secretary and advisor to Lord Beaverbrook, at the press baron's side when he served in Churchill's war-time cabinet, travelling with him on missions to Washington and Moscow.

He was the leading commentator, columnist and chief leader writer of the *London Daily Express*, and in his retirement he produced histories, biographies and novels, many of which were successful and well-received.

Yet no books, no single volumes, have been written specifically with Thomson as the subject; he does not merit a listing in the Oxford Dictionary of National Biography. Despite Thomson's controversial Scottish reputation between the wars and his lasting notoriety since, there has been no comprehensive examination of this period of his life encompassing both his written and spoken works and his relationships with contemporaries and writers. The only history in which he features is Alistair McCleery's *The Porpoise Press* (1988) as one of the founders of the Edinburgh publishing house in the early 1920s.[23]

This book seeks to put that right. Thomson's contribution and impact on interwar Scotland deserves attention across a series of connected themes. As well as his pre-eminent role in instituting the condition of Scotland debate, his literary and practical participation in the cultural revival, his influence on nationalism and the home rule movement, and the significance of his friendships, associations and collaborations with other intellectuals and writers form a notable part of Scotland's cultural history.

CHAPTER 1

The State of Scotland

AT THE TURN of the twentieth century the Scotland into which Thomson was born was a nation with an identity forged by modern industrialism, empire, and Presbyterianism, blended with proud and romantic notions of its history and traditions. It was wedded to the union with an unshakeable tenet that as Scotland served the union, so the union, in turn, would protect and provide for Scotland, not that the latter was necessary since Scotland, economically strong, consistently punched above its weight.

Prior to 1914 Scottish pride and optimism was solidly constructed on the belief that the Scots were pivotal in the founding and running of the British Empire. It provided a tailor-made outlet for the exhibition of all those qualities of virility, martial prowess and romanticism. There was no thought, or misgivings, at least in Scotland, that the Scots were the junior partner or were in any way inferior or dependent on England for economic success or stability. This was seen as a true partnership illustrated by the Scottish heavy industry conglomerates which supplied the empire and other major markets throughout the world. Glasgow, an industrial colossus on the Clyde, was, it was said, the second city of the empire.

But the self-regard of the Scot extended beyond the supply to the world of liners and locomotives, they saw their country as playing a leading part in the invention of almost every modern technique, from steam power to the telephone and in breakthroughs in medicine and the physical sciences. The journalist and author J.M. Reid recalled later: 'the simple Scotsman need do no more than look around him to see that his country was in the vanguard of what his age regarded as progress.'[1]

In the years between World Wars I and II this image of a successful nation began to disintegrate and with it the cosy sense of a shared

Scottish and British identity based on equality began to unravel. First the War had had devastating impacts on Scottish towns and communities, as it had elsewhere in the United Kingdom. The national pride in the Scottish regiments and their sacrifice remained but the losses took on a peculiar Scottish dimension evidenced by a determination to establish a separate National War Memorial, finally opened within Edinburgh Castle in 1927.

Many anticipated that the end of the War would herald a national re-birth in the political, social and cultural life of the country. It was a theme pursued by G.R. Blake in 1918 who hoped that the War would bring in its wake such a national re-awakening, but feared that misty-eyed failings in the Scottish national psyche, a reverence for 'long dead heroes' and [. . .] 'false ideals in history, art and sentiment' would prove a barrier to change. To achieve a new chapter in Scottish life the Scots had to reconcile the past and the present, Blake said, but he was pessimistic, 'for the present, at least, no such basis exists,' he wrote. Blake's book, *Scotland of the Scots* (1918), published before the onslaught of the social and economic difficulties, preceded the literary revival of the 1920s and proved remarkably accurate in questioning the Scots' obsession with the glorification of the country's history. [2]

If Scottish society in the years before 1914 had appeared one of political and social stability and economic success, of docile and well-ordered communities, the two decades before World War II brought massive structural and social changes which would influence Scottish society throughout the remainder of the century. The Scots, for the first time since the Union in 1707, faced the charge that without English subsidies their economic future was bleak: 'increasingly, politicians told the Scots that they were dependent on the English for economic survival'.[3] At the root of this bleak analysis of the Scots – a picture painted of a nation depressed, complacent, pessimistic, disillusioned and fearful – lay the stark statistics of an economy battered by events and a society in which a large proportion of the population continued to endure an appalling quality of life.

Large parts of Scotland's heavy industries collapsed, local control of numerous firms was lost through closures, mergers and rationalisations, and a procession of businesses were either removed to England or taken over by English companies. Four Scottish banks were taken over by English ones; the Scottish railways were subsumed into two large English companies leading to the end of locomotive manufacturing in Scotland; well known High Street retailers lost their Scottish independence; and a number of shipping lines disappeared or moved their headquarters to England.

It was, J.M. Reid wrote, 'an age of amalgamations with a growing tendency to rationalisation which usually meant concentration of work nearer headquarters and markets in the south.'[4] In 1931 Scottish industrial production was less than it had been in 1913, 'it seemed the nation was locked into a spiral of decline'.[5] What was unquestionable was that there had been a massive economic slump, partly due to structural weaknesses in the country's industrial base, but also, as was to become increasingly more apparent throughout the 1930s, Scottish business across almost all sectors had failed to match the growth rates achieved in other parts of the country. The stubbornness and complacency of Scottish elites and industrialists appeared to be matched by the response – at least until the mid-1930s – of the government which maintained that there was little that could be done until the international economy picked up.

Unemployment soared to unprecedented levels, over a quarter of the entire labour force; nearly 400,000 individuals were out of work in 1932. The extent of emigration was unprecedented. Between 1921 and 1931 more than 400,000 Scots left home, the vast majority to Canada, Australia, New Zealand and the United States. Another 63,000 migrated to England searching for work. 'The scale of the losses dwarfed the Highland clearances of the early nineteenth century. Most of the emigrants were young and with industrial experience. They represented over a fifth of the total working population.'[6] More than 70 per cent of the natural increase of the population was drained away by emigration, reaching its nadir in the years between 1921 and 1931 when for the first time in its recorded history there was an intercensal population drop of 40,000. A study confirmed that in the first thirty years of the century the total loss of people through emigration was ten times greater than the number of Scots who died in World War I. The Registrar General for Scotland later commented: 'As the migrants represent the flower of young manhood and womanhood, this continual drain, persisting over many generations, must have had a lowering effect on the reproductive potential of the country.' [7]

The established narrative that the interwar period was one of unremitting hardship and gloom was subjected to large scale revisionism by social historians in the 1970s and 1980s. The revisionists depict the period, particularly the 1930s, as one delivering important economic and social progress. In this scenario any hardships suffered in the west and north of Britain, including Scotland, should be balanced against increased prosperity in the Midlands and the south of England.

Two decades after World War II the unemployment rate of the era remained the dominant fact of memory whereas 'in the consumerist 1970s and 1980s the picture of the 1930s as the beginning of the contemporary economy came to dominate'. [8] Others support the view that because unemployment and hardship occurred in Britain at a distance from London it helps to explain what some regard as not only government indifference, but also the disinterest of intellectuals in London and the south of England: 'whether an economic radical or a conservative, London, Oxford and Cambridge were still a long way from Jarrow'. [9]

The view of the historian Angus Calder was that Scotland was 'traumatised' by a combination of the disproportionate casualties from the Great War and the effects of the post-war slump: 'as unemployment soared, people drained away. Skilled and enterprising emigrants left despair behind them.' A decade later the picture is one of a disunited people, depressed rather than oppressed, 'quick to resent any insult to Scotland but lethargically incapable of taking any action to stop its decline.' The people were both shocked and bitter. 'The Scots now had a grudge against history,' Calder wrote. 'This, not 1707, was the decisive watershed in Scottish attitudes. Boast gave way to whinge.' [10]

Modern historians seeking contemporary evidence to describe the condition and mood of Scotland between the two world wars are fond of reaching for Edwin Muir's book, *Scottish Journey*, an account of his personal odyssey in search of the identity of modern Scotland across the Lowlands and Highlands in the summer of 1934. Edwin Muir was one of Scotland's greatest twentieth century writers of prose and poetry. The book is a classic mix of history, geography, observation and commentary but it is Muir's brilliant, if mainly depressing, descriptions of the condition of Scotland at the time which establishes its historical significance. Muir's Scotland of 1934 reveals little of the optimism to be found in J.P. Priestley's *English Journey* of the same year. Priestley may have found 'three Englands' but even his regular bursts of doubt and cynicism, and his own nostalgic longings for a past then gone, cannot disguise the book's recognition that despite hardships in the north much of England appears a land of promise and plenty.[11] With rare exceptions this was not Muir's experience travelling through Scotland and neither was it his message.

'Scotland is gradually being emptied of its population, its spirit, its wealth, industry, art, intellect, and innate character,' Muir wrote, gloomily concluding, 'my deepest impression was one of emptiness.' [12]

Edwin Muir and Thomson had been near neighbours in Hampstead in the early 1930s when the north London suburb was, in Muir's words, 'filled with writing people and haunted by young poets despairing over the poor and the world.' Muir and his wife Willa lived three minutes away from the home of the Scottish writers Donald and Catherine Carswell and 'George Malcolm Thomson, an old friend of ours, was a little distance up the hill.' [13] *Scottish Journey* may be, arguably, the most quoted source, but it is only one of the library of books written in the 1920s and 1930s which looked at the condition of Scotland. In view of the economic and social hardships of the period it was inevitable that Thomson, Muir and others found little about which they could be cheerful.

Thomson found a spiritual and cultural emptiness: 'Scottishness,' he wrote, 'does not effectively belong to the age in which Scotsmen live.'[14] Thomson's friend Andrew Dewar Gibb said in *Scotland in Eclipse*, 'the national sentiment of Scotland is not healthy.' [15] George Blake was despairing of his fellow countrymen: 'they sit, curiously complacent, amid the ruins of their own civilisation.' [16]

The movement that became known as the Scottish Renaissance was launched through the early poems of Christopher Michael Grieve, writing in Scots as Hugh MacDiarmid, intent on igniting a modern intellectual quality into Scottish writing, scorning the sentimentality of the past, and drawing as inspiration the new and emerging nationalism of small European nations. Grieve, the movement's driving force, declared in 1926 that the Scottish Renaissance was 'a propaganda of ideas', ideas involving the modern movement of the arts that might be made to flourish in Scottish terms. [17] Reid later recalled that literary talent and patriotic feeling were waiting to be attracted by the idea of Scotland as a country with an active and lively culture of its own and a future equal to its past. Grieve's influence, he said, was immense. 'It had the effect of encouraging new generations of young men and women to write in and about Scotland.' [18]

The historical significance and importance of the literary intellectuals of the Scottish Renaissance between the wars is well documented and has been subjected to intense scholarly research, the weight of this heaping much praise on the poets, playwrights and novelists. General and literary historians have also sought to link the literary revival of the period with cultural developments in Scotland in the late twentieth century, and by extension with the role of culture in promoting national identity and ultimately political change. While the modernism agenda of the rennaissance movement did not achieve wider popular appeal, it did however bring a new dimension to the intellectual debates of the day. Its real significance has been its lasting impact on the advancement of a distinctive Scottish culture.

Intellectuals like Thomson wrote and broadcast beyond the Scottish literary revival, although many had a presence in both camps, as poets or authors and also, as in Thomson's case, by attempting to provide a specifically Scottish publishing outlet for indigenous writers. Many intellectuals believed that nationhood itself was threatened and this was a common view in their published books, essays, articles and broadcasts. If it was a message many Scots agreed with it was also greeted with scorn, particularly by Scottish elites, industrialists, and many politicians, but also by large sections of the professional middle class and the skilled working class. Accusations of radicalism and nationalism, or a mixture of both, were common currency but despite this the intellectuals, commentators and creative writers were successful in putting the state of the nation firmly on the political and social agenda.

This was reflected in the media coverage and the books created further platforms, in newspapers and radio, to which Thomson and others such as Blake and the nationalist author, Compton Mackenzie were regular contributors. Intellectuals are instrumental in writing the history of any period and in Scotland between the wars writers such as Thomson, Muir and MacDiarmid were prominent among those who observed and analysed the condition and mood of the nation and also raised important questions about national identity. They defined and defended these issues and gave expression to the changing society that was emerging from the debris of the era. Some were opinionated and prejudiced, often revealing a view of Scottish society and the Scottish people that was harsh and unsympathetic.

These interpretations and analyses of intellectuals and writers were all the more important as historical accounts of a period during which Scottish academia struggled to bring scholarly examination to major issues and events.

This paucity was noted by later historians, J.H. Burns in 1985 stating: 'neither in monography nor in works of synthesis, neither in established nor in the newer kinds of history was an adequate harvest of scholarship being garnered.' [19] George Hewitt in 1992 observed that the *Scottish Historical Review* had been forced to cease publication in 1928, 'leaving the nation with no scholarly historical periodical.' Along with other historians he concluded that the 'sterility of the interwar period' for Scottish history as an academic discipline had been adversely affected by World War I: 'in short, during these years Scottish historical studies, if not quite dead, were moribund.' [20]

CHAPTER 2

Formative Years 1899-1920s

I knew a very wise man who believed that if a man were
permitted to make all the ballads, he need not care who
should make the laws of the nation.

THE WORDS are those of the 'Scottish Patriot', Andrew Fletcher written
in 1704 and today one of twenty four text inscriptions – all chosen by
the people of Scotland – which adorn the Canongate Wall, the boundary
wall at the members entrance to the new Scottish Parliament building
in Edinburgh. The nationalist historian Christopher Harvie described
Fletcher as 'the most energetic champion of the doomed Scottish
parliament.' [1] Fletcher's passionate optimism was that poems and songs
are not only levers for the cultural identity of a nation but are the
foundations for the creation and preservation of wider national identity
and the nation itself.

Almost three hundred years later a retired senior civil servant, having
produced a history of the first hundred years of the Scottish Office,
pondered its future and concluded, like Fletcher, that it was in the hands
of the nation's cultural development: 'it depends more on the vitality of
Scotland's distinctive self-expression than her civil servants. Ultimately,
you might say, it all depends on the poet, not the politicians.' [2]

The proposition is that the culture of the people will eventually
underpin national identity and the political and social structures of the
nation. But it cannot be limited to the authors of ballads and poems. It
includes their input but extends across the life and soul of the nation.
'This is how culture works,' the social anthropologist Anthony Cohen
said when considering Scottish national identity. 'Even though these
items may be interpreted differently, it is on the sharing of them that the
sentiment of an attachment to the nation is predicated.' [3]

In the early 1920s George Malcolm Thomson's motivation and

passion was to be part of a revival of Scottish culture and to secure national identity. He would have been inspired by Fletcher's insight at the beginning of the eighteenth century and he would easily have identified with the conclusions of civil servants and scholars at the end of the twentieth. Modern historians regularly describe him as 'the nationalist George Malcolm Thomson', referencing his political nationalism of the early 1930s when Thomson supported home rule and was involved in developments leading to the formation of the SNP. But his entry into public life in the early 1920s was as a cultural nationalist.[4]

The literary revival which followed in the wake of the Great War excited and inspired him. He was eager to contribute to it and in his own way he did, as a literary publisher, author, playwright, and historian.

Thomson's beliefs were influenced by the religious devotion of his parents, his mother's work with the poor, and the example and ambition of his father's dedication to journalism and commercial success. They also bequeathed to him loyalty to Britain and the union and pride in his separate Scottish culture and identity. Thomson, the oldest son, was also moulded to succeed, an expectation he repaid with an outstanding academic record.

Leith, Family, Presbyterianism

George Malcolm Thomson was born on 2 August 1899 in a terraced flat at 7 North Fort Street, Leith, the eldest son of Charles Thomson, a journalist on *The Scotsman* newspaper, and his wife, Mary. He arrived in the world as Scotland was enjoying some balmy August weather while the news and commentaries in his father's newspaper provided comforting evidence for Edinburgh and Leith's middle-class readers that the economic, social and political condition of the country was strong, stable, healthy, successful and optimistic. In the final year of the nineteenth century Victoria remained on the throne, Britain was at the zenith of her imperial greatness, and by extension Scotland – believing itself a full partner in the Union and the Empire – looked back with exaggerated self-satisfaction on a century of glorious achievement.

The Scots were proud of their separate national identity and traditions but were equally loyal to the British state and to the institutions, customs and values they equated with the British part of a dual identity. Many of these, Scottish and British, were reported seamlessly in the columns of *The Scotsman* of 2 August. The opening of Cowes week on the Solent and the cricket match at Lords between the MCC and the visiting Australians were given equal coverage with the Scottish lawn tennis championships at Moffat, a national bowls tournament in Lanarkshire, and a new Agricultural Show at Dumfries. At the British parliament in London the House of Commons considered a new River Clyde Navigation Act and a telephone bill providing municipal powers for Glasgow Corporation.

The correspondent in Paris reported that letters had been published in which Captain Dreyfus proclaimed his innocence while in South Africa talks continued between the British government and the Boers over the new franchise laws in the Transvaal. *The Scotsman* gave its unequivocal support to the Government's policies in the Transvaal and the Orange Free State: 'The British government has proved its earnest wish to avoid war,' the newspaper declared, 'but it is going to carry its point. It will not be turned back. It will not be turned aside. Whether it is to be peace or war the Boers must choose.' They were convictions shared by most Scots who were as strongly wedded to the military might of Britain and the certainty of its colonial role as they were to the industrial and economic power to which, they boasted proudly, Scotland made a massive contribution.[5]

Thomson's parents embodied all of these things. They were staunch Presbyterian Scots dedicated to raising a family under the faith and guidance of the United Free Church and lived by a moral code that valued hard work, education, ambition and self-improvement but also virtues associated with a religious commitment to self-sacrifice and voluntarism. These were characteristics, behaviours and strengths taught by example to Thomson throughout his childhood and teenage years.

The sense of pride, loyalty and identity maintained within the Thomson family unit was recalled by Thomson when he was 65 years old; the memory of a seaside holiday at St Andrews on the eve of World

War I in August 1914. 'The weather was warm and sunny and the windows of our digs looked out on an open-air café with an orchestra. Every now and then the band, in an excess of patriotism, would play "God Save the King". The Thomson family would stand to attention round the landlady's bread-and-butter pudding, acknowledging by this homage their conviction that now Britain had gone to war, the Kaiser would swiftly be rounded up.'[6]

Thomson's father was born in Inverurie near Aberdeen and trained as a journalist in Peterhead before joining *The Scotsman* as its Leith reporter when he was 23 years old. He had also worked as a sub-editor at the newspaper's head office in North Bridge, Edinburgh gaining wide experience and knowledge of editorial, production and printing. In 1900, when Thomson was a year old, one of Leith's local newspapers, the *Leith Burgh Pilot*, was put up for sale when the owner was declared bankrupt.[7] Charles Thomson purchased the newspaper transforming himself overnight from journalist into the proprietor of a newspaper and a commercial printing business. One of his first initiatives as proprietor of the *Leith Burgh Pilot* was to launch a scheme to insure the lives of soldiers in the 5th Volunteer Brigade of the Royal Scots (Leith) who were part of the British army fighting the Boers in South Africa. Thomson's fund was well supported by the *Pilot's* readers and within weeks the lives of almost 60 local men were insured.[8]

A year after Charles Thomson purchased the *Leith Burgh Pilot* the family moved to a large terraced villa at 19 Dudley Terrace, Leith where Thomson would live until his marriage in the mid-1920s. Dudley Terrace was in a prosperous district of Leith but could hardly compare with more ostentatious Victorian villas to be found only a few streets away in Edinburgh's upmarket Trinity area.

If Leith provided Charles Thomson with the means of providing economic security for his family, the United Free Presbyterian Church in the burgh was its spiritual guide. Thomson, certainly until he entered his twenties, inherited from his mother a staunch support and commitment to Scottish Presbyterianism and particularly to the Calvinist, and evangelical approach of the United Free Church of Scotland formed in 1900 by the union of the United Presbyterian Church of Scotland and the Free Church of Scotland. It was opposed to any form of state interference in the Church and advocated a dedicated policy of voluntarism among its members. The Thomson family were members of the Junction Road United Free Church, established following the union.

Charles Thomson, whose printing works produced all of the literature and annual reports for the church, also served on several church committees but it was his wife who was the more active participant in church affairs. In 1906 she became a church visitor as a member of the Dorcas Society providing assistance to families in the poorer slum tenement streets of Leith, a role she continued into the 1930s following the reunification of the United Free Church with the Church of Scotland. She was also secretary of the Ladies Work Group which raised funds for the Church's Missionary Society and which re-directed its efforts during World War I to the Red Cross and the support and comfort of wounded soldiers and sailors arriving at Leith Hospital. In 1915 she reported that 700 parcels had been distributed, 'each accompanied by a copy of the new testament from the Minister'.[9]

The Church adopted a strict attitude towards the responsibility of parents to ensure that children attended church services and the Sabbath School. The minister, the Rev. James M. Scott also warned parents that sending their children to Sabbath School was not the end of their duties. 'If the young people do not form a habit of Church-going before they are thirteen they are practically lost to the church,' he wrote in the Annual Report of 1912, appealing to fathers and mothers to 'bring your children with you to the House of God'.[10] The church was also associated with an ancillary organisation, The Junction Street Church Band of Hope, its primary objective to promote total abstinence from all intoxicating drinks, particularly amongst the young – 'all office bearers and members of Society are pledged abstainers from intoxicating drinks and beverages'.[11]

Thomson's mother was a staunch supporter of the temperance movement within the church, a cause which Thomson opposed as an adult, although he remained sensitive and respectful of his mother's beliefs. When, in 1930, he wrote and published under the Porpoise Press imprint, the book *Whisky*, his literary homage to Scotland's national drink, he did so under the pseudonym of Aeneas MacDonald for fear of upsetting his teetotaller mother. Following its publication Thomson in a letter to the Highland author Neil Gunn asked him not to reveal his authorship of *Whisky*.

'Please keep my name out of *Whisky* if you don't mind. I have private reasons,' Thomson said. In January 1931 Thomson invited Gunn to visit him at his London home, but warned: 'My mother is coming down and she is an ardent TT (Good God!). You had better meet my wife, child and mother, for tea!!!'[12]

It was in this strict Presbyterian culture of religious observance and total abstinence that Thomson spent his childhood years. Education, however, was considered essential and after attending infant school in Leith, Thomson was sent to the fee-paying Daniel Stewart's College in 1909 when he was ten years old. Throughout his time at Daniel Stewart's, Thomson was a high academic achiever, and significantly many of the school prizes he won were for excellence in English and Literature; in 1915 while at the Intermediate Stage he collected the 'Thin' Prize awarded by the firm of Edinburgh booksellers, James Thin and also the Medal and books awarded by the Sir Walter Scott Club. In his final year, 1917, at the annual prize ceremony in the Hall of the Edinburgh Merchant Company in Hanover Street, Thomson was the School Dux and Gold Medallist, also picking up the main prizes for History, Geography, Mathematics and Latin and the Wallace Dunlop Testimonial Prize for English. He was also awarded the Daniel Stewart Higher Bursary of £80.00, amassing a grand total of seven major prizes.[13]

Thomson was one of the first batch of school Prefects, and as a senior prefect he took his turn with the other three senior prefects to read the lesson at morning prayers. He was also given the task of writing 'School Notes' for the School Magazine, the first public exposure of his enthusiasm for journalism and literature. He displayed his love of books welcoming with enthusiasm the opening of the School Library in late 1916, delighted that, at last, something he had always regarded as a myth had now become a reality: 'I wandered in and found several shelves crammed with the very books I had been seeking for years. I lost no time in grabbing one.'

Thomson's growing maturity and awareness of the changes in Scottish society, even in education, being brought about by the impact of World War I were revealed in his notes welcoming two new lady members of staff, one as assistant science teacher. 'Three years ago, none of us would have dreamed of seeing ladies filling these posts, but the war has banished many of the cobwebs of prejudice and conservatism, and has brought in train no more pleasant innovations than this.'[14]

In his words as he acknowledged the advance of measures bringing some degree of equality to women in professional life Thomson, perhaps for the first time, is also recognising that some of the certainties in Scottish society prevailing before World War I, would change in a post-war world. He enrolled at Edinburgh University in the autumn of 1919 writing in his matriculation form that his religion was Presbyterian but significantly taking the personal decision to add in brackets in capital letters 'UF' indicating that he was a member of the United Free Church.[15] In his late teens the Presbyterian influence of his parents and the Church remained strong. The subjects studied during his three years at university, indicate the wide range of his interests, particularly in literature, history and politics.

The Early 1920s: Literary Revival and the Porpoise Press

The young Thomson who emerged in 1922 from Edinburgh University was eager and ambitious, determined to make his mark as a writer and journalist. He embodied much of the certainty and purpose common to the well educated sons of the Scottish professional middle-classes, assured and confident in their own ability to achieve success in work and life. Throughout his school and university years Thomson had displayed high intelligence, an inquiring mind, and an eagerness to learn. But unlike most of his contemporaries who sought careers in well-established professions like the law, accountancy or public service, Thomson's intellectual powers were quickly focused on other areas of Scottish national life – literature, history and journalism – and embedded within all three a sense of his Scottishness and a passionate need to contribute to the growing cultural movement calling for a re-awakening and re-assessment of Scottish national identity.

His appetite to explore these issues was whetted by the spirit of change and improvement which fluttered across Scotland in the aftermath of the War. Thomson's main grasp of this was directed towards the world of literature, of letters and books, the means, he believed, to lead such a reawakening. If the events and aftermath of the war marked a historic point to create a break with the past, a re-awakening also presented an intellectual and literary opportunity to question the extent to which Scottish society had allowed itself to become dominated by English influences and its modern identity misrepresented in literature by the Kailyard school and other romantic notions of tartan and highlandism. Thomson believed that with the exception of George Douglas Brown's *The House with the Green Shutters*, published in 1901, no worthy literature had been produced in Scotland in the early twentieth century.

'This fine, terrible book,' Thomson wrote of Douglas's book, 'with its restrained, calculated art, written by a Fleet Street hack, is the best modern Scottish novel.'[16]

As for the rest, Thomson was scathing: 'The publishing of books has been dead in the country for a very much longer period, unless the issuing of brochures in tartan covers, containing coloured views of the Trossachs interspersed with excerpts from 'The Lady of the Lake can be dignified with the name,' he wrote.[17] In 1922 Thomson was inspired with a passionate desire to be part of this growing mood of national conscious-ness among writers, journalists and intellectuals. At one literary and professional level he was an aspiring author and journalist but he also believed that there was a dearth of publishers in Scotland to meet what he hoped would be an expansion of new Scottish literary works.

At the age of 23 Thomson, along with a fellow undergraduate, Roderick Watson Kerr, founded the Porpoise Press which they ran from a single room above a dairy in Stafford Street in the west end of Edinburgh. The initial capital of the Press was £20.[18]

Certainly his father's journalism and business acumen was a major influence on his eldest son's early career path encouraging him with the launch of the publishing project but above all instilling in Thomson the ambition to become a successful journalist.

Kerr later recalled that the company never made a profit, 'though an income tax inspector did his ingenious best to find one. He refused to believe that anyone could be such fools as we were.'[19]

Alistair McCleery, who produced a short history of the Porpoise Press in 1988, commented that 'from 1922 until 1926 the Press was based on their enthusiasm and energy rather than on sound finance or expertise.' When McCleery met him in 1983, Thomson, then aged 83 said that the notion of a small publishing house was the product of two agile and energetic personalities in interaction. 'Thomson saw the press as a national publishing house that would give expression to a renascent Scottish literary culture. The two partners seem to embody the moods of renaissance and reaction'.[20]

Thomson admired and respected Kerr, his older colleague who had served with the Royal Tank Corps in the War and had been awarded the Military Cross for bravery in the battlefield. Thomson himself had been commissioned in the final year of war, serving briefly in Belgium, prior to his enrolment at Edinburgh University. He was also conscious of Kerr's literary efforts which included a number of collections of war poems: *From the Line*, *The Corpse*, and *A Dead Man*, poems which had established Kerr's reputation.

Kerr, in turn, was enthused by Thomson's creative tendencies: 'I have never met a more witty, gay and lucid spirit than George Malcolm Thomson. We bubbled together in each other's company and out of the ferment came the Porpoise.'[21]

An alternative view of Thomson in these early years was given many years later by another undergraduate contemporary of both, Margaret H. Kidd, who made her own impact on Scottish society when she became the first women advocate to be called to the Scottish bar. She recalled Kerr as a 'warm, outgoing fellow who commanded admiration.' Her memory of Thomson was 'disparaging'. 'He appeared too clever by half.'[22]

Kerr himself, later in life, continued to regard his years with Thomson with fondness, a relationship rooted in the comradeship of 'good undergraduate friends' and he also praised Thomson's literary accomplishments. 'Those who read his brilliant book on the future of the Scots called *Caledonia* will appreciate his quality,' Kerr wrote in 1957.[23] Kerr admitted that the eventual achievements of the original Porpoise Press between 1922 and 1926 were small, but did include the issue of eighteen pamphlets of poems and the reprint of a series of Scottish classics. It attracted the interest of poets, authors and play-wrights, publishing contributions from Eric Linklater, Lewis Spence, George Blake, Robert Crawford, and Hugh MacDiarmid, and also from the English poet Walter De la Mare, for whom they produced a limited edition of the poem, *Thus Her Tale* in 1923. To some observers the acquisition of a De la Mare poem hardly fulfilled the Porpoise's stated intention of being both a vehicle for 'new' and 'Scottish' literature.[24] However, De la Mare was quickly followed by the publication of a translation from the Danish of Jans Peter Jacobsen's short story, *The Plague in Bergamo*.

Thomson and Kerr's determination not to be seen as provincial met with the approval of the Scottish press. The *Edinburgh Evening News* said such material would stimulate public taste for literature and poetry of the very best description: 'the Porpoise Press is not only serving a national interest, but is at the same time justifying more and more its existence as a medium of original expression in Scotland.' The *Glasgow Evening News* agreed, noting: 'the editors of the Porpoise Press are evidently not going to have it said that because they publish in Scotland, their aims are in anyway parochial.'[25]

Despite such plaudits, Kerr admitted that the 'pond or backwater' of Scottish literature remained fairly undisturbed in the years when the Porpoise Press took the plunge into the publishing business. 'It splashed about, more or less joyously, for a number of years, and gave a good imitation of a Firth of Forth monster,' he wrote. 'It took no money from any living poet and made none, but it caused stir. It showed London and other places nearer home that the spirit of Dunbar was still alive and that the Scots did not mean to sing dumb. The launching of the venture was a creative feat that deserves mention, however small, in the history of post-war Scottish literature.'[26]

Thomson and Kerr delivered little in the way of personal literary input to the Porpoise Press during its original Scottish years, mainly due to the priority of attempting to build the business, but also because they were both also intent in establishing careers in journalism. In 1924 Kerr contributed *Annus Mirabilis or The Ascension O' Jimmie Broon*, a poem written in Lowland Scots vernacular and published over eight pages in the imprint's Broadsheet format. The poem itself was a satire mocking much of the elite and political class of Scotland through one event, the installation of the Lord High Commissioner of the General Assembly of the Church of Scotland. *Jimmie Broon*, the erstwhile hero of the piece, was based on James Brown, church elder, a miner's leader, the Labour MP for South Ayrshire and the first commoner since the seventeenth century to rise to the lofty pedestal of High Commissioner. Brown had been appointed by the Labour Prime Minister, Ramsay Macdonald but Kerr, displaying little regard for political or class niceties, cleverly captured the confusion of pride and distaste of a working class hero finding himself amidst such pomp and ceremony.

> Lord kens, a'd sooner come on ass, in miner's claes, than so tae pass,
> Flunkey o' New Jerusalem, in glory tae bamboozle 'em!
> Altho' a'm thinkin', efter a', it's no' sae bad tae be sae braw!
> And mebbe it wad jist be pride, if a wisna so tae ride
> Thus pondering, rode he thro' the toon,
> O happy, happy Jimmie Broon![27]

The choice of an anti-establishment poem, a satire, as the first publication from either of the two main principals of the Porpoise Press reflected the concerns of both that one of their original objectives – to find and publish new satirical verse – had failed to materialise. Thomson and Kerr had a dream of reviving the intellectual tradition of eighteenth century enlightenment Edinburgh. The subject and target of Kerr's lampoonery was also an expression of the mischievousness of two young journalists and writers intent on prickling the sensitivities of the establishment. And although Thomson was not the author of the piece, the context of church, state and the certainty and comfort of the Scottish establishment was a constant feature of his writings in books, essays and broadcasts throughout the interwar period.

Within three years of the launch of the Porpoise Press Thomson's initial enthusiasm began to wane, partly because the project, while it had created interest and found support from within literary circles, had failed to meet the high expectations of both himself and Kerr that they would find an abundance of new Scottish writing. The daily grind of searching for new contributors and managing the business began to fall increasingly on Kerr as Thomson focused on developing his career as a journalist and writer.

He had also met the person who would have a major influence on his life, his Norwegian wife, Else. Thomson first saw his future wife in a painting, a portrait by the controversial artist, Eric Robertson, one of the leading lights in the Edinburgh Group of painters who emerged in the city after World War I. The group gained considerable celebrity, and notoriety for their post-war exhibitions, none more so than Robertson, married to the painter Cecile Walton whose parents considered him a philanderer and painter of decadent paintings. Robertson, Walton and others in the Group exhibited their work from the New Gallery in Shandwick Place in Edinburgh's west end only yards from the offices of the Porpoise Press.[28]

Else Ellefsen, from the ancient town of Tonsberg in southern Norway, arrived in Edinburgh in 1920 to take up a position as au pair with the family of an Edinburgh doctor. She was a slim, blonde Nordic beauty and in Robertson's painting her blue eyes are radiant and dominant. Robertson called the portrait simply, 'Miss Else Ellefsen' showing it as part of the New Gallery's Winter Exhibition in 1921. The art critic of *The Scotsman* noted solemnly that on this occasion Robertson's paintings were 'happily free from that decadent perversity in conception which has frequently marred his work in the past'. He particularly praised his portrait of Else Ellefsen: 'relationship to reality is clear and the design is simple yet distinguished. He has achieved a real success, and produced an admirably balanced picture.'[29]

A smitten Thomson purchased the portrait from Robertson and was also introduced to the model. 'My father fell in love with her from the start,' his son Peter recalled. 'He got the painting and he also got the model, my mother.' The story of the meeting and Thomson's determination to win Else was recounted frequently among family and friends at the Thomson's home in Hampstead in North London where the portrait was displayed prominently. After Else's early death in 1957 and Thomson's second marriage, the portrait remained in the house, then occupied by Peter and remains there today. [30]

Following their marriage in Oslo in September 1926 Thomson and Else moved to London where Thomson worked as a journalist and began working on the books which would establish his reputation in Scotland. Else's Norwegian background and culture became an influential factor in Thomson's political and nationalist thinking, when, as a journalist and author, he began to draw comparisons between Scotland and other smaller European nations, particularly in Scandinavia and the low countries.

Thomson also made efforts to interest London booksellers in a new series of Scottish classics and liaised daily with Kerr achieving some success in attracting new orders in both Scotland and London. However it was not enough and both Thomson and Kerr accepted that they were unable to devote their full time attention to the Porpoise. [31] In 1926 Kerr, who had been working on *The Scotsman*, accepted an offer to join the *Liverpool Post* as Chief Leader Writer while the Porpoise Press was passed into the hands of another *Scotsman* journalist, Lewis Spence, who had gained a reputation for his poetry and support for Scottish nationalism.

The reality was that by 1926 Thomson, in addition to career ambitions and marriage, had moved on. He had developed stronger views about the economic, political and social condition of Scotland. He remained committed to the revival of cultural Scotland but had become increasingly disillusioned and angry about the decline he witnessed as the optimism of the immediate post-war years gave way to industrial closures, large scale unemployment, mass emigration and increasing evidence that thousands of Scots remained hopelessly trapped in slums and poverty.

Thomson said later that when the Porpoise Press was launched his political leanings had been similar to those of Kerr whom he described as a 'typical Scotch Tory'. [32] Thomson's nationalism, at least then, related primarily to themes of culture, identity and the sense and pride in Scottishness he found in Scotland's history, particularly in the centuries before the union with England in 1707 and the later enlightenment years of the eighteenth century. In the early 1920s he reflected middle-class, professional Scotland: he was a conservative unionist, an empiricist, he was both Scottish and British, and, again, like most of his peers, believed that Scotland played a full partnership role in the union with England. His one major concern about England was the Anglicisation of Scottish society and culture, particularly in literature and the arts. He was, as McCleery wrote, a conservative in the tradition of Sir Walter Scott, wishing to preserve a unique culture within a British political framework.

Gradually Thomson's nationalist feelings took on a stronger political dimension, particularly when he became convinced that the Conservative and Unionist Party had failed to protect Scotland from the consequences of industrial collapse and had, he argued, watched from the sidelines as Scottish businesses were taken over by English firms and as the new vogue for rationalisation transferred production and jobs to the Midlands and the south of England. He became similarly critical of the Scottish establishment for its inaction and complacency over the appalling living standards and the deteriorating housing and health conditions he himself witnessed in Scotland's slums.

Disillusion and the Porpoise in London

Thomson believed the economic decline of Scotland since World War I marked the end of a chapter in the country's history, one of such significance that in historical terms it could be compared with the devastating loss of thousands of the nation's young men during the military defeat at the hands of the English at Flodden in 1513; or as devastating as the Famine was for Ireland in 1846; or for the English the change of the course of their history in 1066.

'Finis has been written to a chapter two hundred years long,'

Thomson said. 'A new chapter begins. There are grand dividing lines drawn in red ink across the history of all nations. The turn of the industrial tide in Scotland must inevitably be for the Scottish nation an event of such proportions.'[33] Thomson was convinced that a century of continuous progress and economic success was over. His words were echoed and borrowed later by the social historian T.C. Smout who called Thomson's description of a 'grand dividing line drawn in red ink' as 'entirely appropriate'. Smout said Scotland entered bleak years 'which seemed to Thomson to mark so decisive a break in national history', from a long period imbued with confidence and the expectation of further enrichment to one of despair 'and the assumption that, in the natural order of things, Scotland would always need special care and attention'.[34]

Smout's assessment mirrors the accepted view from history, one which, at the time, Thomson saw as a national humiliation, the prospect facing the country that it should accept the reality of its 'shamelessness', and 'content itself with being a beggar'. Thomson's sense of anger and disgrace was fuelled not only by events in the present but also by his research into the history of Scotland since the 1707 Treaty of Union.[35]

In 1930 he produced a chronicle of Scotland's rise to prominence from the eighteenth and nineteenth centuries in *Short History*. Thomson's book was more polemical than scholarly yet he was fired with a determination to bring new authority and freshness to the story of the cultural, social and economic development of Scotland. The book which ends with the outbreak of war in August 1914 was written in 1929. But armed with the living knowledge of events since 1918, Thomson could not resist finishing on a note of pessimism.

'Is the long and many-coloured chapter which she has added to the story of European civilisation to draw weakly and drably to a close?' he asked.[36] Thomson invoked an expectation of gloom, one that accurately captured the mood of a country disillusioned by its rapid transformation from a position of strength, influence and success to one of decline, weakness and dependency. The events and issues of the interwar period also produced a fundamental change in the consciousness of being Scottish – compared with the certainty, pride and optimism of the pre-war years.

Such was the context from which Thomson and other intellectuals began to debate the condition of Scotland. The narrative that encompassed industrial collapse and the movement southwards of decision-making power, contributed to the perception that decline also represented a threat to pride and confidence in Scotland's separate national identity.

Thomson was a pioneering voice linking the economic and social state with the spirit of the people and national identity itself. For him the latter represented an extension of his passion of the earlier part of the 1920s when he supported the call for a cultural awakening. The interface between the structural, material and health of Scotland and the strength of its cultural and spiritual sense of nationhood was a staple diet of Thomson's commentaries, as it was also for MacDiarmid and other writers who emerged from the restrictions of a culturally focused renaissance.

'There was general agreement that the health of a nation's culture could not be separated from the health of the nation as a whole,' Margery Palmer McCulloch wrote. 'This ideological position resulted in an unusually rich amount of critical, social, political and philosophical writing by the principal creative writers of the period.' [37]

The backdrop was not only the events and consequences of the period itself but the historical links going back two centuries reflecting a story of almost non-stop economic growth. J.M. Reid in the 1970s revisited his book *The Scots Tragedy* written in 1935 under his pen name, Colin Walkinshaw, and conceded that his words then had been a 'cry of alarm' intended to shake the complacency of his countrymen, many of whom believed that the economic depression was a passing phase and things would eventually return to the certainties of the Victorian years. Looking back Reid recalled that there had been a reaction against the undermining of the national structure and spirit, 'particularly strong among writers and political thinkers'. [38] Richard Finlay describes the period as one of 'dislocation', a recognition that the anxiety surrounding the meaning of Scottish identity had its base in the fractures of the previously accepted established order, one that had been a key ingredient of identity before World War I. In his analysis, because the economic and social problems of the era were so great, 'they seemed to be insoluble', the disruption and damage resulted in a 'crisis of confidence' in feelings of national identity. 'Politicians and intellectuals debated the end of Scotland and it seemed that the nation was caught in a spiral of terminal decline. For many history was all Scotland had left to prove her nationality and it had to be readapted to suit the changed circumstances of the interwar period.'[39]

These were the issues which underpinned the two books, *Caledonia* and *Re-Discovery*, both polemics, which Thomson published in the late 1920s and they were also the concerns which moved him towards political nationalism, a convert to home rule and support for the establishment of a parliament in Edinburgh. When both books were published Thomson was based in London although he was a regular commuter to Scotland to visit his mother in Leith and, as his reputation grew from the reaction to the books, as a public speaker on political platforms and also as a regular radio broadcaster on the burgeoning BBC Scottish Region.

He still maintained an interest in the Porpoise Press, but *Caledonia* and *Re-Discovery* were issued by the London publishing house of Kegan Paul, Trench, Trubner and Co. In 1927, when *Caledonia* was published, Thomson described the hopes of the Porpoise – 'one modest and short-lived attempt to create a national publishing house in Edinburgh' – as unfulfilled, a failure. It had been no more than a brief flash, 'the only, and probably the last, spark of dissatisfaction with the complete dependence of the country on English presses.' [40]

Despite his pessimism, in 1930 Thomson was reunited with the Porpoise Press when he agreed to act as joint editor of the imprint following its acquisition by the London publishers Faber and Faber who had moved almost all of its functions from Edinburgh to London. Thomson's fellow editor was George Blake whom Thomson had first met in 1923 when the Porpoise Press published Blake's play, *The Weaker Vessel: A Play in One Act.*

Thomson admired Blake's journalism, essays and books, praising him for his commitment to writing about modern Scotland as it was. Thomson said Blake, 'with his firm grip on realities, has looked this Scotland in the face and by doing so has created a place of his own in literature'. [41] Thomson's eulogy to Blake, published in *The Bookman* in 1928, co-incided with Thomson's own emergence as a controversial and critical commentator of the condition of Scotland. Blake, who had worked as a journalist in London since 1924, first with *John O' London's Weekly* and later *Strand Magazine*, and who, therefore, like Thomson in the late 1920s, wrote about the situation in Scotland from a distance of 400 miles, had played a key role in persuading Faber and Faber to purchase the Porpoise Press.

Thomson and Blake had other common interests. They both lived in Hampstead and in 1930 when Thomson was in the process of moving home, Blake put him up at his flat in Pilgrim's Lane. Thomson also made regular references to Blake in correspondence with his fellow right-wing Scottish nationalist, Andrew Dewar Gibb, letters which also indicate that Blake, in the early 1930s, shared with Thomson and Gibb sympathy for home rule. Thomson told Gibb that Blake had played an important part in persuading the Highland author Neil Gunn to take an influential role in the merger talks between the National Party of Scotland (NPS) and the moderate Scottish Party (SP) which led directly to the creation of the SNP. [42]

'Blake too must be put on the roll of honour. He did a good deal to bring Gunn round,' wrote Thomson. Blake was also one of four signatories to Thomson's, *The Kingdom of Scotland Restored*, the pamphlet in which he set out his case for the establishment of a parliament in Edinburgh, for home rule within a reconstituted union with England. [43]

Thomson and Blake agreed that, although now under English ownership, the Porpoise Press should remain true to its original mission of publishing, promoting and advancing the works of Scottish poets, playwrights, authors and writers. They also believed that it would have greater credibility and prove attractive to others if they were able to capture one major modern Scottish writer. The man they set their sights on was the highly regarded Neil Gunn.

Thomson, already in correspondence with Gunn on nationalist issues, told him in March 1930 that he and Blake had taken over the Porpoise Press, and that the Faber and Faber connection would provide the resources of a modern commercial publishing house. 'I want to interest you in this Gunn, because your name was one of the first we mentioned when we thought of taking another job. I should like to hear your views and especially any ideas you may have. You may have something provocative you want particularly to say. You may have a story.' [44]

Blake also wooed Gunn, travelling to see him at his home near Inverness. 'He was called to exercise all his powers of reassurance on Gunn, presumably learning in the process that a disproportionate amount of the publisher's time is spent soothing his authors, calming their fears and deflating their expectations.' [45]

Gunn's move to the Porpoise Press brought immediate success when his novel, *Morning Tide*, was selected as the Book Society's 'Book of the Month'. Thomson was ecstatic. 'I have just heard the great news. A thousand congratulations. I have been nursing the secret hope in my bosom for weeks. But I never dared think it would be so good. You have put the Porpoise Press on the map good and proper,' he told Gunn. [46]

Thomson also boasted to Gunn that the original print order for *Morning Tide* was 19,000, of which 14,000 were pre-ordered. When Porpoise published Gunn's follow-up book, *The Lost Glen*, in 1932, it announced that total sales of *Morning Tide* had surpassed 24,000, easily the most successful publication from the imprint, but also one of the best-selling Scottish books of the period.

'This is only the beginning Gunn,' he wrote. 'It makes it clear to all Scottish writers that they need have no fear of publishing through the Porpoise Press. For having done so much a grateful publisher salutes you.'[47] The second Porpoise pamphlet to appear under Thomson's own name, his bitter denunciation of the Presbyterian Church, *Will the Scottish Church Survive?* was published in the Spring of 1930, followed later in the year by his book, *Whisky*, written under the pseudonym of Aeneas MacDonald.

But despite their close friendship, their common interests in Scottish nationalism, their shared success in attracting Gunn to the Porpoise Press, and the mutual respect they had as journalists, broadcasters and authors, the joint editorship of Thomson and Blake was not a success. McCleery argues that Blake 'decided to take on the job of easing Thomson out', an objective fulfilled in 1933 when Thomson resigned saying that he withdrew 'with extraordinary reluctance'. [48]

In view of the part he played in establishing the Porpoise Press a decade earlier, plus his continued commitment to promoting Scottish literature, Thomson was, no doubt, disappointed not to retain a hands-on role. But the reality of his own personal position at the time was one increasingly dominated by his work with Beaverbrook Newspapers and particularly his direct advisory role with Beaverbrook himself. He had also become active behind the scenes as a supporter of Scottish home rule and was in regular contact with other nationalist figures in Scotland. In the early years of the 1930s Thomson also began research for *Scotland That Distressed Area*, published in 1935, and the only one of his three 'condition' books produced under the Porpoise imprint.

Blake, whose novel about the industrial slump, *The Shipbuilders*, was also published in 1935, but by Faber and Faber and not the Porpoise Press, was hardly enthusiastic about Thomson's book.

'It seems to mean a pamphlet or a half-crown book, but it will stand serious discussion, and without further comment I enclose the typescript herewith,' he wrote to a Faber executive. [49] Unlike Thomson's two previous 'condition' books, *Caledonia* and *Re-Discovery*, *Distressed*, priced not at 'half a crown' but at 3s6d net, was not ignored by the Scottish mainstream media and received positive reviews.

'Mr Thomson finds himself driven to the conclusion that Scotland is suffering from economic difficulties that do not beset her European neighbours. His book is marked by clarity of exposition, and should secure the attention of all interested parties,' said *The Scotsman*. [50] The book marked Thomson's last contact with the Porpoise Press whether as founder, manager, editor, author or contributor, and the imprint itself was eventually closed by Faber and Faber in 1939.

Thomson is likely to have found it ironic that *Distressed*, focused on the economic and social condition, was his swansong in the publishing house he and Kerr had launched with enthusiasm and optimism into the fledgling literary revival of the early 1920s. By the early 1930s Thomson believed there was a home rule solution to Scotland's decline, but increasingly he was convinced that a fixation on the economic arguments was futile, that efforts to make political capital out of economic misery would end in failure. Such a nakedly political approach, he believed, was likely to ensure that more people would leave Scotland, for Canada, or England. 'Scotland's decay is a matter of regret but a comfortable bank balance is a wonderful consolation to the exile.'

The alternative approach was to convince the Scots that nationhood is in itself something worth having, worth paying for, worth the sacrifice of economic interest. Thomson's plan was to expose economic problems and the social evils that followed in their wake and to connect them to a reawakened national consciousness. Nationalism, he argued, would only make headway when it was able to touch and ignite the spirit of the nation, to reach a consciousness of Scottishness. Thomson laid out his strategy more in hope than real optimism that the task was achievable: 'Scottishness is an extraneous thing which does not square with life as they see it. It is a luxury, and they cannot afford luxuries,' he said. [51]

It serves as a symbolic reminder of Thomson's personal journey through the Scottish experience of the 1920s and 1930s. At the beginning of the period Thomson was focused on cultural renewal; by the late 1920s, a reluctant but eventual convert to political nationalism, he was a bleak commentator of the condition of Scotland on the broader canvas of industrial, economic and social decline; and by the mid-1930s this transformation in Scotland's fortunes remained the dominant theme of the third 'condition' book, *Distressed*. In 1922 the Porpoise Press was a vision of youth, ambition, optimism and change. Thomson's last words for the Porpoise Press written in 1935 were filled with pessimism and gloom.

'If the life of the Scottish people is menaced at its economic foundations, then, in simple truth, the first act of a tragedy is being enacted,' he wrote on the final page of *Distressed*. [52] To emphasise his despair, as he saw it, 'the last act of the tragedy', Thomson borrowed from the Scottish medieval poet, William Dunbar. Dunbar's *Lament for the Makars* is a prayer of memory for fellow poets who had died, and a lost literature that has gone with them. The poem is grim and morbid, punctuated at the end of each verse by Dunbar's use of the Latin refrain *Timor mortis conturbat me*, or fear of death disturbs me.

> No stait in Erd heir standis sicker;
> As with the wynd wavis the wicker;
> Wavis this warldis vanite;
> Timor mortis conturbat me. [53]

Thomson found a literary metaphor from a fifteenth century Scottish poet to give meaning to his own distressed outlook on Scotland's future, at least as he found it in the years following slump and depression. It was a despairing summary from a cynic who saw a dark side and, although he still hoped for a spiritual revival, had little expectation of something better. The events of the 1920s altered Thomson's outlook and views of his native country: optimism gave way to pessimism; enthusiasm gave way to cynicism; and pride gave way to anger. He turned from cultural nationalism to political nationalism with its demands for home rule and economic and social change.

CHAPTER 3
The Condition of Scotland

1938 London, Moonlight Flitting
Scene: Effie Brownlie's tenement flat in a Glasgow slum

Andrew (Effie's ne'er-do-well uncle): Now if there was one spark of
national feeling left in the country.

Rob (Effie's lodger): National feeling!

Andrew: I say if there was one spark of national feeling. . .

Rob: A Scottish patriot, eh!

Andrew: And what if I am! What if I am! Tell me that! I'm Scotch, am I
no! And I'll remain Scotch will I no!

Rob: A nationalist, God help us!

Andrew: A nationalist, certainly. Listen mister, it's not every nationalist
that prances about Glasgow with a tail of spider-legged ladies
exposed by their kilts.

Rob: Och, awa to Bannockburn!

Andrew: If you have given half of the time you spent fighting one
election for Ramsay MacDonald and the next one against him to
pondering the history of your own people, you might have
chanced upon the Highland Clearances.

Rob: You and your clearances! I've read my history. Let the dead bury
their dead, I tell you. Here's St. Mungo. People living nine and ten
in a room. Babies dying when they could live if they were born
half-a-mile to the west. Women starving because they give to the
kids, and men wearing their boots out and their hearts out
trampling for work.[1]

UNEMPLOYMENT, poverty, squalor, emigration, immigration, socialism,
nationalism, identity, and the past; the predominant themes on the
interwar condition of Scotland played out in a midnight performance
at London's Whitehall Theatre in November 1938. At half-past two in the
morning George Malcolm Thomson was summoned by the audience

onto the stage to receive their applause for his play, *Moonlight Flitting*, his dramatisation of life in a Glasgow slum in the early 1930s. Thomson's appearance after several curtain calls for the play and its cast, also, symbolically, brought down the curtain on the pivotal and controversial role he played in opening up a public debate on the condition of Scotland in the 1920s and 1930s. [2]

Thomson effectively signed off – at least publicly – on Scottish affairs with *Moonlight Flitting*. The play had arrived in London following its launch in October 1937 in Glasgow at the Lyric Theatre in Sauchiehall Street, performed by the Curtain Theatre Company, an amateur group established to support the work of modern Scottish playwrights.[3] It was Thomson's attempt to dramatise the harsh realities and barren choices facing those who lived in the tenement slums of Glasgow in the period. Thomson's ego, no doubt boosted by the response of a London audience, would have been flattered further by two reviews, both of which compared his work with that of the renowned Irish playwright, Sean O'Casey.[4]

Like Casey, Thomson dramatised the impact of the issues of a period on the everyday lives of the impoverished, juxtaposing the consequences of major events – economic, political and social – on the ups and downs of human relationships. All of the action of the play takes place in one room of the tenement flat occupied by Brownlie, her uncle, her grandfather, and two lodgers. These characters and others representing various strands of slum life pass through the daily routine of the flat. These include a socialist with parliamentary ambitions; a Salvation Army member; a bookie's runner; a housewife from a nearby flat who thrives on drink and gossip; and a street corner loafer with poetical aspirations; and joining them, from the street, young hunger marchers. At the heart of it all Brownlie and her various schemes to avoid the threat of eviction from the dreaded factor's man, the rent collector, the villain of the piece who Thomson, mischievously, chooses to cast as an Irish Catholic.

> Effie: It passes me to understand why they would want to leave their lovely Irish Free State for a common Christian country.
>
> Andrew: Did you hear that? Intolerance! Religious intolerance! Man,

it dies hard. You would think that education would have confiscated
a' that sectarian blether. But na, na![5]

It is a story rich in chaos, a pre-occupation with religion, sport,
politics, and even laughter masking the permanent struggle against
poverty and the fight for survival. The narrative moves from socialism
to nationalism to capitalism, from the past, inevitably both glorious and
despairing; from patriotism to sectarianism and the Irish problem; and
amid the poverty and hunger there is humour and fanciful if unlikely
plans for a prosperous future. In the end, there is no money for the rent,
and Brownlie and the others arrange a moonlight flitting.

The Final Scene:

Outside there is a loud burst of cheering and a brass band strikes up
the Red Flag. Hunger marchers are singing the Socialist Anthem.
They go out, burdened and singing. Effie stops, looks round, a
careworn expression on her face. Then she disappears.[6]

Thomson's anger and compassion had been aroused by the
conditions he found in the slums, a symbol, he believed, of Scotland's
failure and disgrace. But *Moonlight Flitting*, no more than an allegory of
life in the slums, neatly captured Thomson's own mental flitting away
from concerns about the condition of Scotland, now, in the late 1930s,
relegated to a combination of pathos and embarrassed comedy in two
hours of drama.

It was far removed from Thomson's outrage only a decade earlier.
But in 1938 Thomson was the leading columnist and commentator on
the *London Daily Express* newspaper, his reputation and influence
greatly enhanced by his separate role as political adviser and confidant
of Beaverbrook. Within two years, installed as principal private secretary
to Beaverbrook, the Minister for Aircraft Production, Thomson was close
to the heart of Britain's wartime government.

In November 1938 his rapturous audience at the Whitehall Theatre
almost certainly included friends and colleagues from the London press
and political circles, many of whom – no doubt both intrigued and
appalled at the picture Thomson painted of Glasgow's poverty – would

have been unaware of Thomson's Scottish past when his exposure of the slums and the economic and social plight of Scotland in the 1920s had established him as one of the country's most outspoken and contentious writers and commentators.

The Economic Decline of Scotland

> Danny Shields: When you get the yard going again, you'll see me at the gate with the rest o' the boys, and as fit as a fiddle.
>
> Leslie Pagan: The yard will never be open again, Danny.
>
> Danny: Oh, my God!
>
> Pagan saw how circumstance had trapped him and Danny too. The working man knew better than most that there were times when trade was bad, but it had always been so for him; and now the older men were waiting in patience for the wheel to turn again. What they did not know, what they could never know, was that in any calculation of which the human brain was capable, at least one half of Scotland's shipbuilders were out of work forever.[7]
>
> George Blake, The Shipbuilders, 1935

Leslie Pagan, owner of Pagan's shipyard on Clydeside during the depression, breaks the news to his worker and friend, the riveter Danny Shields, that the yard had been sold and closed. The decline of Scotland's great industry was dramatised in George Blake's book, *The Shipbuilders*, published to great acclaim in 1935 and still regarded as one of the best Scottish novels of the twentieth century. The novelist A.J. Cronin wrote to Blake to congratulate him 'on a magnificent piece of work which moved me and impressed me tremendously'. The praise from John Buchan was even more effusive, telling him in a private note that *The Shipbuilders* was the most important Scottish novel published for many years. 'The book is brilliantly written, and what I specially like about it is its spirit – its real humanity and its love of goodness, not very common qualities these days.'[8]

The goodness identified by Buchan reflected the friendships and loyalties of relationships both within and between the classes as they struggled to adjust and face the consequences of industrial demise. For one class lay ahead the prospect of unemployment and enforced poverty, for another the humiliation of takeover and the end of a dynasty. Blake's book captured the social and economic consequences but also the sense of national failure and shame. It was said by one contemporary scholar to be 'a piece of fine and substantial creative literature' but ultimately in its time it was essentially 'brilliant topical journalism'.[9]

The journalism, the social commentary, the realism appealed to Thomson who had praised Blake as a new, modern writer determined to blow away the cobwebs from the old literature, literature that refused to acknowledge that there had ever been an industrial revolution or a slum in Scotland. Blake, Thomson said, saw modern Scotland as it is, 'with its cities and factories and vast special problems – that is the Scotland on which he fixes his eye steadily'.[10] Blake, the journalist, captured the agony and bleak future of one large part of Scottish society through a novel. Thomson's chosen route was the radical, angry and aggressive language of the polemic, deliberately partisan and unashamedly populist and propagandist.

'The head offices of shipping companies which once were crowded together in Glasgow no longer fly their house-flags in St Vincent Street. They are mostly transferred south of the border to London or Liverpool,' he wrote. Even before the Depression he claimed that the Clyde yards were being beaten by English and foreign rivals, they would never be able to regain their former dominance since the 'most highly skilled labour army in the world has been disbanded.' He mocked the leading shipbuilding magnate Lord Maclay who complained that Scottish industry was crippled because it was not Scottish enough and who protested against English control and interference in Scottish commerce. 'It is difficult to see what else his lordship can reasonably expect to find,' Thomson asked, 'when railways, banks and newspapers are directed from London.'[11]

Scottish businessmen he said 'are beginning to find that there is an awkward economic aspect to the intangible enthusiasm of the cranks, national consciousness.' Thomson was contemptuous of those who professed anxieties about rationalisation, take-overs and the transfer of the control of Scottish administration, commerce and industry to the south. 'The Scottish business man,' he wrote, 'shows a self-effacing readiness to be absorbed by large combines and multiple unit concerns.' An equally disastrous development for Scottish industry in the long run, he predicted, was the spectacle of commercial and industrial firms 'hurrying southward, especially to London, to open warehouses and factories.'[12]

Thomson wrote with a mixture of cynicism and concern, perceptions that permeated his accusations of complacency against the reaction of large parts of Scottish society to the consequences unleashed by economic and industrial decline. He compared the muted response of his countrymen to what would have been national outrage in England had emigration been at the same level as that of Scotland from where almost half-a-million had sailed since the end of World War I, four times the rate south of the border.

'The preservation of the people of England would be a political issue before which all others would sink into triviality,' he said. 'It is impossible to imagine anything else taking place in a self-respecting nation possessing the minimum amount of pride and conscience. Yet in Scotland there has been nothing of this, nothing but silence, indifference, and sullen acquiescence.' It was not, he said only the working class poor and unemployed who were leaving; there was a drain of educated, intelligent and energetic middle-class youths those, 'who would normally become the leaders of the commercial, political and intellectual life of the country'.[13]

Thomson believed that there was a large body of opinion that appeared to derive a 'macabre satisfaction' from these conditions, that it should be regarded as a matter of morbid Imperial pride that thousands of their fellow-Scots had been driven overseas. There was no organised or effective reply to the 'ceaseless and widespread' propaganda of emigration agencies such as the Canadian Pacific Railway offering inducements to would-be emigrants, 'the reiterated invitation to commit national suicide arouses no resentment, no indignant refusal,' he wrote. Thomson particularly pointed his finger of censure and blame at the country's political, business and religious leaders who had allowed a defeatist state of mind to demean the country's confidence. 'Scotsmen do not own their own country, they rent it on a short lease,' he said. 'The Scots are a nation waiting for the boat'.[14]

But if Thomson saw a generation of Scots condemned to a future waiting for a boat to take them to a better life overseas there was another group who were more likely to be found queuing for a train. The train in Thomson's gaze was *The Flying Scotsman* travelling nightly between London and Edinburgh bringing with it, he claimed, a culture and identity which was making Scotland one of the outer suburbs of London. Clambering aboard the train eager to embrace the power it brought were the Scottish members of parliament, 'enabled to forget the troubles of their native land in the wider excitements of governing an empire and being reported in *The Times.*'

Thomson saw *The Flying Scotsman* cast as a viceroy: 'there is no single factor of greater influence upon the moulding of Scotland today than the great train with the poetic name.'

This was a typical Thomson narrative of popular hyperbole, investing a train as the symbolic proof of Scotland's lost battle against the authority and control of London; endowed with such energy that it might overpower the national heritage lessons in the classrooms, the St Andrew's Society, the Burns Federation, Clan Societies, Caledonian Clubs and even burgeoning home rule bodies: 'there, where the rails lie silver at the platform's end, wreathed in bland steam, and hissing with a vast patience, stands the superb machine which will irresistibly turn that lesson into dust.'[15]

Thomson had added another dimension to his gripes about English influence on Scottish life and society which in the early 1920s had been focused on cultural matters and the threat this posed to national identity. The events of the decade widened and hardened his anti-English rhetoric even beyond his anger concerning Scotland's loss of control over its economy and industry. In the midst of his rants about the country's growing Irish Catholic population he warned that the English, also, were pushing the Scots out of their own country.

'Since the war,' he said, 'a strong tide of English immigration has flowed. English shops and stores have trebled since 1918. There are now more Englishmen living in Glasgow than there are Scots in that prostrate Scottish dependency, London.' Even at the time Thomson's all-encompassing complaints about Anglicisation might have been regarded as bizarre and incongruous since his words were written in Hampstead, the north London suburb where he lived and worked and which would be his home until his death seventy years later. But contradictions such as these appear commonplace as many of Thomson's observations and criticisms of the behaviour of his fellow countrymen did not, apparently, apply to his own choices in life and career.[16]

But if there was a smell of hypocrisy, Thomson was undaunted; he feared the worst for Scotland's future, 'a land in which both work and trade are destined to wither,' he wrote. Scotland was sinking slowly in an economic and racial quagmire, 'sinking steadily, in ignorance, an annex, half industrial, half sporting, of English civilisation.' In the face of these challenges Thomson finds a country taking refuge in the past, guarding jealously its patriotism, customs, religion, traditions and history, a response he dismisses as more related to a comfortable mid-nineteenth century view of the world and not the reality of the 'flustered, disillusioned, unscrupulous and out-at-the-elbows 1920s'.[17]

Here again Thomson presents one of the contradictions that pepper his narrative. He has committed a large part of his professional life in the 1920s to the protection and regeneration of Scottish culture and within this recognition of the nation's history, heritage and identity – these values were the very essence of the Porpoise Press – yet when they are wrapped up in beliefs he regards as a form of Kailyardism he dismisses it as pointless sentimentality. It is evidence of occasional confusion and inconsistency at the heart of Thomson's passion for cultural nationalism. He is also contemptuous of what he senses is the comfortable complacency and ignorance of the middle classes. He mocks up a caricature of what he regards as the modern Scot.

Thomson Attacks his Countrymen

His name is Mr Gillespie MacLean, he is middle class, he is a proud Scot, he is passionately British, and is particularly attached to the empire and is convinced that there is a Bolshevik conspiracy to break it up. MacLean believes that Scottish history only began with the Treaty of Union and is 'bewildered by all the fuss about Scottish literature and culture, about the national spirit and sentiment.' He wants Scotland to remain respectable, God-fearing and hard-working dismissing as frivolity ideas that the country should have a spiritual life of its own, 'with theatres and plays, publishing houses and art, and notions of a continental-style Sunday.'

In the character of MacLean Thomson embodies his version of the anglicised and provincial Scot, someone who willingly accepts English influences as superior and who rejects the idea that Scotland might reclaim her separate place in the world as 'the work of dangerous cranks'.[18] Scotsmen like the fictional MacLean have been centuries in the making, their comfort, acceptance and complacency ensuring that Scotland no longer counts among the nations. The proof of this, wrote Thomson, is that she does not make any original contribution to world culture, she is and has been without leaders and a conscious mass of opinion focused on Scottish affairs. 'The shrewd, proud, independent, patriotic Scot is a conception which can now be relegated definitely to mythology,' Thomson concluded. 'The Scotsman is a provincial English-man, and only by habit [. . .] does he call himself by a different name'.[19]

Mr Gillespie Maclean, the representation of a smug, self-satisfied and self-righteous middle-class Scot – apparently unconcerned by the declining condition of his country – was not alone in the dock of Thomson's reprobation. Sitting alongside was the well-fed and equally apathetic figure of that of a Church of Scotland parish minister, the public face of Presbyterian Scotland. Thomson, again, was scathing: 'The Scottish minister lives in one of the smarter suburbs of the town. He belongs to the golf club, he takes tea in the villas, and his children go to the best secondary school available. His descents on the crowded working class areas and the slums are in the nature of brief and hasty raids concluded with a relieved tram-ride back to suburbia.'[20]

In *Caledonia* he described a church mentally and spiritually bankrupt, scandalously complacent and tolerant when confronted with the social degradation of the mass of its flock. The more serious charge against the Scottish clergy, Thomson said, was their 'callous indifference' as they witnessed 'the steady submerging of the great mass of their people into slumdom and economic subjection.'[21]

He accused the Church of being too loyal an ally of 'rigorous capitalism' and associating low wages, wretched housing, and high death rates as the consequence of the sins of the poor. The calling they served was one laden with emoluments and privileges, not burdened by sacrifices or dangers, and tainted, Thomson said, by 'a faint, indescribably offensive air of patronage, of class consciousness.'[22]

This was a remarkable and vicious onslaught from a man who had been raised in a family committed to the social and compassionate values of the United Free Presbyterian Church, whose mother remained a church visitor in the working class tenements of Leith, and who himself, less than a decade earlier, had pointedly highlighted his faith and membership of the Church during his matriculation at Edinburgh University. The Kirk's vocal and very public campaign against Irish Catholic immigrants and its fears concerning the increase in the Irish Catholic population in Scotland – an issue to which Thomson devoted almost a third of *Caledonia* – failed to impress him or to restrain his criticisms. Instead he rebuked it for its failure to induce any government to take the Irish problem seriously and in an act of defiance designed to underline his contempt he wrote a 40-page pamphlet with the provocative title *Will the Scottish Church Survive?* published in 1930 by the Porpoise Press.

Thomson's timing was deliberate, intended to be controversial and cause affront only months after the Church of Scotland and the great majority of those in the United Free Church had reunited ending the Disruption that had torn apart the Scottish churches since 1843. More than 90 per cent of Scotland's Presbyterians were now under one church, an event which Thomson marked as 'historic' but only because there would be material benefits from pooling resources and economies from rationalisation. What was lacking from the new union he added with typical sarcasm were trifles such as 'courage, spiritual energy, passion imagination and brains.'[23]

Thomson's attacks were made at a time when, despite unification, the Church of Scotland was facing a crisis of identity. It was nervous about the spread of secularism and the forces of consumerism revolutionising society in music, film, radio, shopping and other leisure activities, and it had failed to develop an understanding and sympathetic response to the growing social and political awareness of the working classes following World War I. The latter – certainly at the higher echelons of the church – had been translated into a fear of socialism, which many connected with the growing support of the Catholic population for the Labour Party. This paranoia helped to feed its ultimately unsuccessful political campaign against Irish Catholic immigrants.

Thomson certainly agreed with the objectives of the church crusade but despite this he chose to compare its weakness in reaching out to the industrial masses with the success at a popular level of the Catholic Church. 'The simple fact is that the Roman Catholic Church is, all over, a more efficient organisation than the Protestant churches. The Church of Rome succeeds where the Church of Scotland conspicuously fails,' Thomson said. The Catholic priest, Thomson argued, could understand and sympathise with the working man in his flock who took a glass of beer and put a shilling on a horse. Thomson narrated a portrait of a church stuck firmly in the past, by instinct opposed to progressive social change, determined to hold the line against any suggestions that the Sabbath should be anything other than a day of prayer and rest.

'It corresponds to the needs and conditions of a dead age; it presupposes for its efficient working things about Scotland which are totally untenable.' He ridiculed the church's constant negativity and policies of prevention: shutting ice-cream shops on a Sunday, banning charabancs on a Sunday, opposing the opening of new pubs in previously 'dry' districts, its antagonism towards picture houses and dance halls. Thomson, the cultural intellectual and nationalist, saw this as part of the church's embrace of dreariness and repression, of a malign influence impoverishing the quality of Scottish life, its rejection of its culture and arts, its lack of colour and grace: 'this is no church but an organ of the narrowest bourgeois morality.'[24]

As he did with most areas of Scottish society Thomson revealed his frustration and disillusionment, a theme that resounds constantly in all of his public writings, speeches and broadcasts. There was a personal angst to his pessimism about the future of a church and Presbyterian Scotland that had strongly defined his own childhood and upbringing. He complained about a lack of leadership in the church, stating that the appointment to its highest office, the Moderator, was proffered like an annual compliment 'to some elderly parish minister of amiable character and undistinguished intellect.' It was, he said, a post that should be filled by the ablest and most far-sighted statesmen the Church can show, adding in an aside that was hardly likely to please his mother, 'It should be a full-time task, with no Dorcas Society or Mother's Meeting trivialities to distract its occupant's attention'.[25] As her son was accusing the Church of ignoring the plight of thousands trapped in poverty, Mrs Mary Thomson was as usual visiting the poor households in Leith as a member of the Dorcas Society of the Junction Road Church of Scotland.

In 1930, the year the pamphlet was published, his mother was appointed treasurer of the Dorcas Society, dedicated to helping the downtrodden and weak. Thomson, who went to great lengths not to embarrass his teetotal and temperance supporting mother by using a non-de-plume for his book *Whisky*, had no such qualms when he wrote a 10,000 word pamphlet which questioned if the Church to which he and his mother both belonged had, or even deserved, a future.[26]

Thomson was equally contemptuous of the legal profession, particularly the Faculty of Advocates who populated Parliament House in Edinburgh, 'the best Scotland can show in the way of an intellectual aristocracy,' he wrote dismissively. His central charge was that this was another establishment group primarily concerned with protecting its own vested interests and which paid scant regard to its wider role and responsibilities. The Scottish Bar was complicit in a corrupt relationship with the country's political leadership: 'the politics of Scotland are largely in the hands of Parliament House,' he wrote.

Whatever weaknesses, mistakes and exaggerations could be attributed to Thomson's provocative and controversial attacks on Scotland's civic, business and political establishments, at no point did he display a lack of courage. He frequently appears as a tiresome terrier determined not to let go of the bone, using the fearsome power of his words to prick and undermine the complacency and comfort of his targets. Scottish legal appointments from Sheriff Substitutes upwards, he said, were regarded as the spoils of office, 'the profits of a successful election and as the pay chest from which obedient party hacks will receive their reward.' It was a 'corrupt and detestable system' which ensured that politics in Scotland were more discredited, out of touch with national life, and a cause of popular cynicism.

'Scottish politics are rather dirty,' he observed. The evidence he presented for this was the haste in which he claimed large numbers of advocates had become converts to socialism following the rise to power in the 1920s of the Labour Party. 'What Karl Marx, Bernard Shaw and half a century of propaganda had been unable to do, was performed in a day or two by a change of master at Westminster,' he sneered, adding that fat briefs and comfortable offices under the Crown were irresistible to the inhabitants of Parliament House.

This cosy relationship existed to further the professional careers of a few 'quick-witted, glib and unprincipled young men lounging under the roof which once sheltered a nation's Parliament,' Thomson said. Today Parliament House stood for all that was 'dishonest, futile and disgusting in the political life of the country. Where Scotland has a right to turn for leaders she finds only pushful nonentities scrambling round a paymaster.'

Thomson's public denunciation of the Edinburgh legal profession and its political masters was delivered almost undercover in a little known journal, the *Library Review*, established in 1927 to provide an academic forum for librarians and researchers. The editors accepted Thomson's controversial article as relevant to the *Review* on the basis of his comments on the new National Library of Scotland, established by Act of Parliament in 1925 and made possible by the transfer of the books and manuscripts from the Library of the Faculty of Advocates. Today the accepted historical memory of this event is that by the 1920s the upkeep of such a major collection was too great for a private body and the Faculty of Advocates presented the library to the nation, albeit with the help of an endowment of £100,000 from the Edinburgh biscuit tycoon, Sir Alexander Grant.[27]

In Thomson's version the Faculty had 'allowed their library' to become a national possession, but they would retain their monopoly of the library: 'the only difference would be that the state and Sir Alexander Grant would maintain it', and when Grant provided funds for a new building it would be 'on a site most suitable to the convenience of the Faculty'. Grant, who is credited as the man who invented the digestive biscuit, gave a further £100,000 – his combined donations valued at about £6million in today's money – and a new building was erected on George IV Bridge, only 100 yards from Parliament House and the Advocate's Library.

Thomson's attack on the upper echelons of Scotland's legal profession reflected his conviction that its privileged position in Scottish society – like that of the Church jealously cherished and protected since the union – also came with a responsibility to represent the highest standards of fairness, honesty, trust, and example; not to prioritise its own vested interests. 'The condition of the Scottish Bar would not matter a tinker's curse to anyone but the unfortunates who are compelled, or the misguided who are induced, to litigate, if it were not for the fact that a great deal in Scotland derives in tone and temper from the Parliament House in Edinburgh,' he wrote.[28]

Thomson was no more respectful to the third institutional pillar preserved by the union – Scottish education, rejecting the established boast of most Scots that they were the best schooled and informed nation, with a learning legacy stretching back more than 500 years. He dismissed this as pretentious nonsense.

'Its educational institutions are one of the wonders of the modern world. The people is notoriously one of the best educated on earth,' he mocked. 'An extraordinary amount of intellectual activity ferments among them; the love of good literature and high thinking is widespread, but is balanced by a strain of harsh practical wisdom [. . .] the vigour of its mental life and the academic glories of its universities.' Thomson's truth was that Scottish education and its much vaunted ancient universities were devoid of ideas and if there were any they were likely imported, there was no intellectual community 'capable of producing the friction of minds from which ideas are generated. It is a land of second-hand thoughts and second-rate minds.'

Again Thomson bites the hand of his own upbringing, one that made it possible for him to emerge as the Dux of one Edinburgh's best schools and a graduate of its university, the epitome of a classical and successful Scottish education. But such grandiose reminiscences he now regarded as 'undiscriminating adulation' from people who should know better. Scottish education he saw as cheap and too easy to access even if it was the case that in population proportionate terms there were four times as many students at Scottish universities as there was in England. He was unimpressed: 'no number of half-wits will make an educated nation, though they be decked out in a veritable rainbow of degree-hoods and can marshal whole alphabets after their names.' It was a system geared to producing graduates who sought only security and respectability, 'with no strong ambition to beauty or danger or the adventures of the mind'; to them knowledge was a series of subjects 'to be carefully written down in notebooks, swotted up for examinations, and eventually passed out of and obliterated.'

To Thomson, the cultural historian and enthusiast, the much admired education system was not equipped or interested in providing platforms for creative students thereby ensuring the 'unpopularity' of subjects such as English literature which did not lend themselves to 'verbatim reporting or to brainless cramming'. Thomson conjured a picture of students as dreary plodders, second rate, lacking original thinking and real ability, where any creative intelligence was sacrificed on an altar of 'quiet, dogged determination to get there'.

The gloom which enveloped Thomson's conviction that Scotland was losing its capacity for innovation, inspiration and ultimately its genius was not confined to shortcomings and failures across civic Scotland and its great institutions. He argued that the dull and secure approach of the universities extended into the emergence of a risk-adverse business community. Entrepreneurial instincts had been sidelined by economic failure and decline, making this an unattractive prospect for a new generation of young Scots, particularly those from the middle and professional classes. They preferred to seek sanctuary in the safe havens of accountancy and the civil service.

In this climate, Thomson claimed, feelings of contempt had grown for the man whose part in commerce was creative and not administrative. 'Profits are without honour; salary is the god,' he said. He detected a new snobbery to add to those of birth, wealth and intellect, 'a snobbery of undistinguished security'. In this analysis one class of Scots was able to take cover against economic decline, an option not available to another, the skilled working class, but again, Thomson showed no sympathy, accusing them of listlessness and of embracing pessimistic defeatism.

'Among the working classes,' he said, 'the old pride of craftsmanship is dead, replaced with a lazy, shiftless and physical degeneracy: 'they make no strenuous attempt to find a footing for themselves in a country they believe to be doomed.'

These criticisms were in keeping with one of the major planks of Thomson's assault on the condition of modern Scotland, one that went beyond economic and social decline; his sense that it had also lost its verve for living and for thinking. He pronounced as 'dead' the spirit of adventure he boasted was at one time an integral part of Scottish nature; replaced by a resentful country submerged under a tide of harsh blows and events. Scotland, he wrote, was 'a land of working men and petty tradesmen, a land, that is, in which both work and trade are destined to wither. She is sinking slowly in an economic and racial quagmire, sinking steadily, in ignorance.'

His constant references to 'second class minds' appears at odds with the inspiration he had personally drawn from contemporary renaissance writers and poets, many of whom were, like him, products of the system he was berating. The cultural revival, started in a wave of national consciousness following the War, had little popular appeal in a society where the majority were bereft of the spiritual functions of art, intellect, conscience and consciousness. The blame for this, he believed, was not a failure on the part of the renaissance or a phenomenon of the 1920s; it lay much further in the past.[29]

The Scottish Cultural Betrayal

Thomson's study of Scottish history convinced him that cultural decline was rooted in the changes that engulfed Scottish society in the years following the Union of 1707 and the transfer of its parliament to London. To those who dismissed such thinking and pointed to the evidence of the post-union Scottish enlightenment of the eighteenth century Thomson argued that the seeds for the flowering of cultural and intellectual life were sown before the union. He had no misconceptions that the Edinburgh Parliament ended in 1707 had been one adorned with illustrious traditions, but what had been lost, he claimed, was something much more important than a mere legislature, 'she had lost for example a capital with all the elusive but intensely real advantages which derive from it.'

In his view the important literary and artistic efflorescence was organically linked with the relics of Scotland's pre-union development; in education, the universities, the law courts, and its social traditions. It was these that made Edinburgh 'a capital city of the mind, [. . .] a city which did not in a day forget that it had been the home of a Parliament and the head of a nation.' Scotsmen, Thomson believed, had undergone a subtle 'psychological metamorphosis', one that was more emotionally than intellectually driven and the transformation had been essentially negative. 'Their political development as a nation was arrested at the beginning of its most interesting experiment.'[30]

Here, yet again, we find the contradictions or inconsistencies in Thomson's beliefs and thinking. He is an admitted supporter of the union, he celebrates Scotland's part in the development of the empire, yet when he considers perhaps the major event in modern Scottish history, the union with England, he reveals a hardly disguised sense of regret and loss, that ever since, part of the nation's nationality had been slowly seeping away. It is, admittedly, a personal depression steeped more by his sense of cultural loss than that of political deficit, but Thomson's feelings are abundantly revealed when he takes on the mantle of would-be historian, providing ample evidence that his controversial views in *Caledonia* and *Re-Discovery* may be addressing the problems faced by modern Scotland but that much of the demise and decline have roots reaching back to previous centuries.

In his *Short History* he acknowledged that in economic terms Scotland was inextricably linked with England but bemoaned that this factor dominated all political considerations, effectively reducing to the sidelines matters of culture and the intellectual spirit of the Scots. He took some consolation that, despite the economic focus, a separate Scottish nationality had persisted, if not expressed as a political entity, at least still burning in other modes of Scottish life, in philosophy, literature, art and religion.

'Scottish culture,' Thomson wrote, 'was a more brilliant thing than the Scottish state had ever been.' But even such embedded brilliance struggled, he argued, to survive, faced as it was with the overpowering influence of Anglicisation and the emergence of a new class of elites in Scottish society who showed no interest, even displaying an ingrained aversion, to the notion of a separate Scottish culture and intellect.

In Thomson's eyes the cultural deficit he identified had several layers and many causes, chief among them a class of leaders who sought and embraced an English education and culture, often at pains to minimise their Scottishness in accent and behaviour. Industrialism also brought power, wealth and influence to men with mindsets formed in the harsh and unforgiving school of Scotland's Presbyterian Calvinism, 'whose traditional attitude to the arts was one of austere and unconcealed contempt.' The centralisation of cultural life with its dependence on London also drew from Scotland professionals whose families would have been expected to display interest and patronage towards the arts. Such cultural emptiness, Thomson believed, ill served a nineteenth century society in which a great mass of the people were plunged into wretchedness and squalor, 'where the higher pursuits of the mind could have no possible meaning'.

To those who would have challenged such a gloomy analysis of the previous century by directing his attention to the works of Sir Walter Scott at one end and Robert Louis Stevenson at the other Thomson had little sympathy. 'It was rare indeed,' he argued, 'for a Scottish man of letters in the nineteenth century to be a man who could devote himself wholly to literature.' The circumstances Scottish society found itself in were draining the leisured classes away from the country or were building a wall between them and its national life. Scottish literature, such as it was, displayed 'a certain slipshodness and haste of thought and expression'; in Thomson's opinion it betrayed the circumstances in which it was created.

'Men wrote quickly and not too well, or else with a careful eye to the easiest public, and the largest return.' And in a barely concealed contempt for the writers of the Kailyard books and plays he accused them of deliberately ignoring or criticising the realities of urban and rural life choosing instead to exploit an imaginary Scotland for the pleasure of foreign palates, eager readers and audiences principally found in England and North America.[31] He was not unique in his condemnation of the literary culture of the Kailyard; he joined a raft of intellectuals stretching back to the years before World War I but given greater force by the leadership of Hugh MacDiarmid.

Some of Thomson's strongest language was reserved for the negative impact of the Kailyard on theatre, relegating Scottish drama to something marked for export only, hardly blessed with quality or reflecting Scottish life but with undoubted commercial success. He termed it the Arms and the Manse School of drama, 'the arms are those of Bathos, the strumpet, into which the authors fall with rapture and frequency.' It was an invented, insipid, trivial and unreal vision, a false representation of rural Scotland, far less that of urban poverty, and Thomson scorned it with brutal invective.

'Amid the mingled odours of Sabbath and saccharine, maundering ministers, grim but kind-hearted elders, gimlet-tongued 'managing' beldams, and doctors who never ask for their fee, live and move and are by turns pawky, dour, and canny. It is all very quaint, very sad and sweet and Scotch, and it has led to many a good cry which would not otherwise have been there to give pleasure. But it is not so much drama as diabetes'.[32]

Scottish culture, he said, had been plunged into a variant of English as a 'debased coin of the same currency, a Birmingham product, cheap, facile, and brazen'. The commercial and fake identity success of this brand of Scottish literature was assisted, Thomson claimed, by the absence, in Scotland, of an educated nucleus of critics and intellectuals to judge such works in a Scottish cultural context. 'After all,' he said, 'a culture is not so much a mass of work or a list of names as a type of human society.'[33]

Thomson sneered at Scottish literature's obsessions with past glories and tragedies, a genre more interested in pratings about claymores and Culloden than events such as the Highland Clearances and the fate of the deer forests. 'These have infinitely more significance for the Highlands than the incident of the '45, and provide infinitely richer material for the novelist.' The same literature also ignored the existence of shipyards on the Clyde and Irish immigrants in Lanarkshire slums and suggested that there was nothing in the Highlands but clansmen 'filled with a morbid desire to die for the Stuarts'. All of this, Thomson argued, made modern Scottish literature insignificant, its denial of the main issues of national life reflecting an intellectual and spiritual disease, 'a central cowardice of the soul'. If the existing literature was an art form it was difficult to take it seriously while it said nothing about the fundamental conditions of Scottish life, appeared to believe that the industrial revolution had never happened and 'has never had the elementary honesty to look the huge fact of the slums [. . .] in its hideous face.'[34]

These are the thoughts and words of Thomson at the end of the 1920s emphasising not only his frustration with the country's cultural past but also his personal disillusionment over the failure earlier in the decade of the Porpoise Press and his misgivings, at least in the late 1920s, about the impact of the so-called literary revival.

The formation of the Porpoise Press provides evidence of action by deed to accompany Thomson's personal crusade for a new, modern literature in Scotland and also establishes his credentials as one of the early proponents and participants in the Scottish Renaissance. He welcomed the agitation for a cultural revival and also approved of the name it borrowed.

'To mariners weary of the well-buoyed fairways of letters the name has an instant charm,' he wrote; 'it suggests that in those stagnant, rarely-visited shallows where the Scottish genius lives there may be sights to see and sounds to hear worthy the eyes and ears of the most fastidious explorer.' In Thomson's eyes it was an attempt to revive Scottish letters and with it a requirement to reflect back to the people a narrative based on the development of modern Scotland.

But if Thomson could easily adorn the cloak of the romantic optimist when he considered Scotland's cultural past he was also a realist. While he could convince himself that in some parts of Scottish society there were signs of 'a re-orientation of the Scottish spirit' he also accepted that this was matched by widespread scepticism. Thomson was on the side of the line which urged caution mixed with a large dose of pessimism. He was conscious that beyond intellectual and literary circles the revival movement had only attracted slight attention and even less support among Scottish people in general.

'As far as the masses are concerned, the re-awakening has not got beyond the stage of a prolonged yawn,' he concluded.[35] Thomson remained committed to the renaissance but believed that it extended beyond a cultural agenda; it required the renewal of the national spirit and a revival of the nation's intellectual vibrancy. It also implied the regeneration of the economic heart of the country but at the tail-end of the 1920s Thomson had no sense or optimism that his fellow countrymen understood the connections. 'Having thrown up the sponge of culture,' he wrote, 'the Scots, we have noticed, are now divesting themselves of the control of their economic life, [. . .] and are impotent in the face of grave social problems'.[36]

Thomson's anger dominates his polemics. It might be masked with his cynicism, even his sarcasm, but at its roots is his disillusion and anger.

When Thomson wrote *Caledonia* and *Re-Discovery* he was still in his twenties but between his early twenties and late twenties a profound transformation had taken place in his view of his country and his fellow Scots. This had taken him from a mindset which believed that Scotland was on the brink of a national re-awakening led by a cultural revival to one which was steeped in pessimism where he feared that rather than regeneration of its spirit and identity it was moving in the opposite direction, mired in a sense of defeat, helpless against the economic forces eating away at the foundations that had delivered a century of uninterrupted economic growth.

But decline had also starkly revealed to him the other side of industrial success, the slums, the health inequalities, and – in Thomson's eyes – the arrogance and indifference of an establishment that preferred not to see such things. The same complacency was now being adapted to ignore the realities of an economic slump that was turning Scotland into a nation without self-sufficiency and dependent on English subsidies.

The Slums

> We ventured into a tenement close. Our sensitive young nostrils told us the squalor was there. The odour hung in the air, a repelling, cloying smell of decay that got into your nose and made your throat choke with the musty sweetness of its unseen touch. This evil thing sent us running back to the street, holding our noses until we were in the fresh air.[37]
>
> George Gladstone Robertson *Gorbals Doctor*

George Gladstone Robertson, recalls here a moment as a boy when he and friends entered a tenement in the Gorbals district of Glasgow in search of a lost football. It was, he later wrote, his first experience of conditions in the slums, but, despite his youth, he recognised that life in the teeming tenements could not be ignored.

'The squalor would be out in the open and the world would know of the pitiful conditions endured by those who had to live there because they had no other place to go,' he wrote.

The Gorbals would dominate Robertson's life, his teenage experience being repeated almost daily after he graduated as a doctor in 1923 and practised as a GP in the heart of the Gorbals throughout the 1920s and 1930s. He described as typical a visit to one slum tenement, home for thirty six houses: 'I climbed the worn steps, usually to answer some call in the hollow early hours of a long, dark winter's night. I would creep through the shadows and hear the sounds of snoring, children crying or screaming. Over two hundred people were crowded together in this miserable and hellish tenement.'[38]

The Gorbals became the synonymous symbol of Scotland's slums, ultimately as notorious for violence as it was for deprivation and poverty. It and similar slum districts in Glasgow and other Scottish cities and towns reflected the misery and hopelessness which caricatured not only the reality of life for thousands of Scots but gave to the wider world an image suggesting a second division country struggling, unsuccessfully, to keep up with the economic and social progress of other European nations. Robertson's experiences and vivid descriptions closely mirrored those of Thomson, even if his exposure to life in the slums was not as a doctor but as a visitor and journalist.

The slums were a world apart from the easy and comfortable life Thomson had led in Edinburgh, and if he shared with many of his fellow Scots a sense of anger and disgust, unlike the majority at the time, he chose to express his frustration very publicly. Thomson regarded it as outrageous that the main Scottish intellectuals and writers of the 1920s had written and said so little about the slums. The anger, he claimed, had been left to others.

'The only book on Scottish slums with any imaginative power and passion in it is the work of an Englishman,' he wrote.[39] The Englishman in question was the author and journalist, William Bolitho, who, in 1924, had written a devastating report on Glasgow's social conditions describing these through the title of his book as the *Cancer of Empire*. Bolitho claimed that in Glasgow, with a population of almost 1.1 million people, almost 600,000 were living in houses below the official standard set by Government Health Boards. There were, he said, 40,591 families living in one-roomed homes, 112,424 families living in homes made up of a room and kitchen, 'more than 13,000 of these 'homes' were officially condemned by the Medical Officer of Health, and all but a round hundred of them are at present occupied.' The Clydeside MP James Stewart told Bolitho that Glasgow was 'earth's nearest suburb to hell'. Bolitho's report was used as ammunition by Stewart and other Scottish MPs to demand urgent government action but the impact of the book itself was lessened because Bolitho argued that grievances on the Clyde had the potential to inflame a socialist revolution that could engulf the rest of Britain and the Empire, enabling his critics to brand him as a radical socialist.[40]

Thomson, still an enthusiast for conservatism, union and empire, did not subscribe to this thesis, but he admired the skills Bolitho displayed in his acquisition and use of statistical evidence to substantiate his arguments. Thomson's polemics were controversial, but he prided himself, almost to the point of arrogance, that he argued with the support of research and factual information. He also shared with Bolitho his contempt for those who preferred to ignore the problems. Thomson sensed that in some quarters of Scottish society the slums might rouse despair, but not real horror. There was, claimed Thomson, 'a conspiracy of silence'. The objective was to stop the truth about the slums from leaking, there was no other subject which the average Scot wanted to forget, the slums were a taboo issue in respectable Scottish circles. 'A vague impression prevails throughout the country that if the slums are only left alone they will right themselves by mysterious natural laws, that they are, in fact, improving, and that in any case, they ought not to be talked about.'

Thomson scorned his fellow countrymen who espoused a 'pleasing determination to smile the slums away'.[41] He dismissed the self-satisfying notion of many Scots that the social problems of Scotland were no worse than those existing in England, referring to official statistics which revealed that 45 per cent of Scots lived more than two in a room compared with only 9.6 per cent in England. 'It is ludicrous to pretend [. . .] that their country is at the same level of prosperity and civilisation as England,' Thomson said. 'They are a malignant disease affecting the whole body of the nation. Two million people live more than two in a room.' In Thomson's view if the slums had become no more than commonplace to his fellow countrymen to many Englishmen they were a 'wild exaggeration' since London, also, they claimed, had districts with poverty and bad housing.

'They have not,' was his reply. 'There is nothing in Europe to compare for vastness and vileness with the slums in Scottish cities.' He supported his argument with the story of a wealthy English manufacturer tempted by his curiosity to visit a Glasgow slum. His horror was highly diverting. 'I emptied my pockets of money,' he said, 'and went back to my hotel for more. What else could one do? These children were like animals.'

In *Caledonia* and *Re-Discovery* Thomson intended to shock. He employed angry, vicious and emotive language and description in both books as he painted a gruesome panorama of poverty, filth and disease. He did not confine his own personal research to the Gorbals or Glasgow recounting what he had personally witnessed in slums in Wishaw and Coatbridge in the heart of industrial Lanarkshire: 'a visit to one of those dwellings is needed to fill in the colours,' he wrote.

'There in a backland tenement [. . .] a family of eight people sleep in one bed in a room into which daylight never penetrates. An unspeakably foul odour permeates everything – the famous slum smell, to the making of which centuries of filth, damp, soot, bad air, and decay have gone.' He finds doors with small labels with a number, signifying that the house is 'ticketed' and liable to search at any time by sanitary officials. Thomson remarked cynically: 'The Scotsman's home is for sufficient reasons not his castle.' He finds shrivelled children peering round corners; stunted, decrepit and hopeless men slouch in passageways; women, hair hanging down uncombed, curse their offspring, 'deformed and unwashed'. And then Thomson, 'the abominable, inescapable stench in his nostrils', turns and escapes to the open air.

Thomson's experience in Lanarkshire mirrors in all its horrendous details that of the family doctor, Robertson, in the Gorbals. But if Thomson physically escapes the slums he barely allowed his audience any escape from his anger and fury. The words, the phrases seem never-ending. Half of Scotland is slum-poisoned, he claimed; the taint of the slums permeates the nation's blood and mind giving birth to a new race of barbarians. 'Rickets and other infantile diseases, tuberculosis, venereal disease and various disgusting blood disorders abound in an appalling degree [. . .] The slum is to be regarded not so much as an area of bad housing but as a deadly plague.'

Unafraid of describing any aspect of human life in the slums, Thomson accounted as commonplace women giving birth to children on newspapers spread out beneath them, 'two inches of coal-dust covers the floor'. A Dundee doctor, struggling in a city with the highest infant mortality rates in the United Kingdom, admits the scale of the social and health failure: 'We kill off the weak ones, so those that are left can stand anything.'[42]

Thomson dismissed the view of Stanley Baldwin, the Prime Minister, who had said that although he had been previously anxious about slum conditions he was now confident that Scotland, in time, would overcome the arrears which faced her.[43] On 30 September 1925 when he was in Glasgow to receive the Freedom of the City Baldwin paid an unofficial and unheralded visit to the slums. Although appalled by what he saw, he urged Glaswegians not to despair, holding up to them as an example of an ideal citizen, the knight from Rembrandt's famous painting, 'ready with spear to attack what is evil, and with shield, to defend the weak'.[44]

Thomson was unimpressed, sneering at the nation's political leaders with a combination of rude cynicism and factual evidence. 'It has become almost indecent, a breach of good manners,' he wrote, 'to hint that anything Mr Baldwin may say is not quite in accordance with all the facts. The omniscience as well as the honesty of the Prime Minister is one of the fixed points round which arguments and opinions gyrate.'

Thomson was well aware that calling the Prime Minister a liar in any form of public print, whether newspaper article, essay or book would be considered unacceptable across most of Scottish society and would only serve to add to the negativity surrounding his newly established notoriety. But, he insisted, the evidence available in official statistics and government reports, told a different story. In 1911 47 per cent of Scots lived in houses of only one or two rooms – the corresponding figure in England was seven per cent – but by 1921 the Scottish figure had risen to 56.7 per cent. 'In that year no fewer than 2,661,853 Scots were living in slum conditions,' wrote Thomson. In 1917 a Royal Commission reported that Scotland needed 235,000 new houses immediately, the annual demand for new homes was estimated at 20,000. This had fallen to 10,000 annually because of mass emigration. But even taking the lower figure as the basis, 355,000 houses should have been built by the end of 1927. Thomson said the official figures revealed that only 65,000 new houses were erected during that period, 'so that the slums of Scotland, worse in 1911 than in 1861, and worse in 1921 than in 1911, were, at the end of 1927, worse by 35,000 unbuilt houses, than in 1917. The slums of Scotland are growing each year vaster and more evil,' he added.[45]

Thomson's conviction and contention in both *Caledonia* and *Re-Discovery* that large parts of the Scottish establishment preferred to wish away the reality of the slums and to insist that accounts of life in the slums were overblown was supported by the evidence of numerous public pronouncements, not only from politicians and business men, but leaders of the Presbyterian Church in Scotland. Much of their critical denials were concentrated on the damage to the reputation of Glasgow and Scotland as a whole and there was also a tendency for parts of the establishment to stick together and praise the efforts of other bodies and organisations.

Sir John M Macleod, a Glasgow chartered accountant told the annual meeting of the Glasgow Benevolent Society that the city's reputation as one of the blackest spots in the United Kingdom was 'a great exaggeration'. MacLeod resented the large numbers from the south who came to Glasgow and then went elsewhere and shouted as if they had uncovered something entirely new. 'Some people speak as if Glasgow is all slums and nothing else. It is not true and it is unfair,' he pleaded.[46]

Like MacLeod, leading clergymen also often used the cover of meetings of voluntary groups to defend the Scottish establishment, including the church, against outside attacks. The Rev. Dr George Morrison, moderator designate of the United Free Church, speaking at the annual meeting of the Orphan Homes of Scotland, said that the press had been 'unfair' in their criticism of Glasgow, describing 'peripatetic visitors' subsidised by London newspapers who come north and in an incredible short space of time explore our slums and go back and write articles headed 'Glasgow'. Morrison did not expect them to flatter or praise but begged that 'these flying visitors' should keep a sense of perspective and a balance of judgement. He claimed that no other authority in the country, including Manchester, Liverpool, London and Leeds, had addressed itself to the slum problem with greater courage, vision, tenacity and faith than Glasgow.[47]

A second leading clergyman, the Right Rev. Dr. John White, moderator of the General Assembly of the Church of Scotland, argued that social conditions only appeared to be worse because modern society had acquired a greater 'social conscience'. Speaking at the annual meeting of the Scottish Christian Social Union White said that the social problems of the day had not arisen because there had been social retrogression. 'Social conditions are better and not worse today and the poor are not poorer. Unconsidered and unmeasured attacks, for instance, on the slums of Glasgow conveyed a false impression that things were worse, whereas they were better in Glasgow,' White declared. Like Morrison he praised the work of Glasgow Corporation, and also, like Morrison he was critical of outsiders 'who visit the city for a few hours and come to a final judgement'.[48]

Intellectuals, Politicians and the Slums

Thomson's isolation – at least in a literary sense – did not extend into the 1930s when other influential writers emerged pursuing and confirming that his views were not merely commentaries made at a moment in time, or observations drawn from a chapter of Scottish life unique to the late 1920s. When Edwin Muir revisited Glasgow during his *Scottish Journey* expedition in 1934 he described Glasgow as a city 'where decay flourishes in a genuinely impressive luxuriance'.[49]

For Muir this was a trip down memory lane, recalling for him a time before the War when as an office boy in a law office he saved money by walking to work each day through the slum areas on Glasgow's south side: 'there was no way of getting [. . .] to the city except through slums. These journeys filled me with a sense of degradation: the crumbling houses, the twisted faces [. . .] the ancient, haunting stench of pollution and decay, the arrogant women, the mean men, the terrible children daunted me, and at last filled me with an immense, blind dejection.'

Muir, eventually, trained himself to treat the slums as an ordinary road to work, to ignore the pain in the faces he passed: 'I shrank from reading them and quickly learned not to see.'[50]

Edwin Muir's admission that he had once attempted to shut himself off from the realities of miserable lives may have given him a special insight into some of the reasons why many Glaswegians chose to ignore the slums, but he was unsympathetic. He concluded that the life of an average member of the city's respectable classes was a direct fight against the slums, adding dryly: 'and in that fight suppression and insensibility are invaluable weapons'. He found an attitude based on reprobation, that all slum dwellers were incurably depraved, they were 'outside the human pale'. Thus the 'respectable' people could ignore the slums since 'they were irrelevant to ordinary life'. Muir understood, even if he could not condone it, that those who turned their eyes and minds away from the slums did so because they were filled with a sense of disgust. But like Thomson he was aware that 'disgust' could not be so forgotten or easily washed away in a sea of denial; the slums and poverty they brought, he argued, could poison the life of the community beyond their own environs. They penetrated 'the lives of all classes in Glasgow, affecting their ideas and emotions, [. . .] but also sent out a dirty wash into the neatest and remotest suburbs and even the surrounding countryside, so that it is possible for one to feel that the whole soil for miles around is polluted.'[51]

The novelist Lewis Grassic Gibbon had struck up a friendship with Thomson when Thomson contacted him after reading *Sunset Song* (1932), the first part of Gibbon's trilogy *A Scots Quair*. Gibbon, in turn, was aware of Thomson and his controversial social views, having read *Caledonia*, and had pointedly drawn the attention of his old schoolmaster to the book.[52] Gibbon had been exposed to the slums when he worked as a journalist in Glasgow for a short period of one year and was in sympathy with Thomson's descriptions and his criticism of the muted response of Scottish society. Gibbon poured irony on the bourgeois of Kelvingrove in Glasgow's west end who, he claimed, had a view that the slum dwellers did not appreciate how well off they were.

'Free education, low rents, no rates, State relief – half of them, in fact, State pensioners. Besides, they enjoy life as they are – damn them, or they ought to. Always raising riots about their conditions,' he mimicked. But despite a common concern about the slums Gibbon did not share all of Thomson's analysis and prescriptions for improving the condition of Scotland. He may have dedicated *Cloud Howe*, the second book of his trilogy to Thomson, but he cared less than Thomson did about English influences in Scotland and, also, again in contrast to Thomson, he deplored the fixation of intellectuals on a cultural revival sensing that they were prioritising these issues at a time when the focus should be on social conditions.

Thomson campaigned both for social improvements and a cultural renaissance whereas Gibbon, happily casting himself as a 'complete philistine', said there was nothing in culture or art that was worth the life and happiness of even one of the thousands 'who rot in the Glasgow slums'. Culture had become the 'motif' word of conversation in intellectual circles, he said, 'ancient Scots culture, future Scots culture, culture *ad. lib.* and *ad. nauseam* and it was totally irrelevant to the fate of the people of the slums. 'It is no more than the chatter and scratch of a band of apes, seated in a pit on a midden of corpses.'

In his essay *Glasgow*, written as part of Gibbon's collaboration on contemporary Scotland with the poet Hugh MacDiarmid for their book *Scottish Scene*, he declared that he would welcome English suzerainty over Scotland until the end of time, the end of Scottish culture and history, and even live under the heels of a Chinese army of occupation 'if it could cleanse the Glasgow slums and give a surety of food and play to those people in the abyss'.[53]

The nutritional physiologist John Boyd Orr, knighted in 1936 for his ground-breaking work on poverty and diet, had little in common with literary figures such as Thomson, Muir and Gibbon. His intellectual world revolved around science and medicine and although he had a well established reputation for speaking bluntly to politicians on the evils of vitamin deficiencies in the diets of the poor he was not renowned for making social commentaries. As a student in Glasgow at the turn of the century Orr had, in his own words, 'prowled' the city to see the slums, leaving him with 'permanent impressions which have affected my whole life'. When he graduated he was sent to teach at a school in the Glasgow slums, in an overcrowded room with ill-clad children the majority of whom were suffering from malnutrition and hunger: 'one could see the lice crawling on their heads and on their clothing'.

Orr later admitted that the experience made him physically sick and depressed, and having concluded that there was nothing he could do to relieve the misery of the children he resigned.[54] If Orr failed to cope as a young graduate teacher, his subsequent lifetime commitment to the abolition of hunger, poverty and squalor was rooted in his intense hatred for all of these miseries he encountered in the Glasgow slums.

A decade after Thomson produced *Caledonia*, Orr's research revealed that whereas in 1900 the infant mortality rate in Scotland had been 15 per cent below that of England, in 1937 it was 50 per cent higher. He agreed with the description his former student colleague and lifelong friend, the unionist politician Walter Elliot had given to the slums: 'the heaped up castles of misery', places where human beings were huddled together under conditions where the income is insufficient to purchase enough food to rear healthy children.[55]

Orr estimated that almost one third of all Scottish children, even in the late 1930s, were born into slum homes. He accepted that across many sections of Scottish society living standards had been rising and rising faster than in any previous decade but he disagreed with those who maintained that it was only 'fanatics and fussy busybodies' who continued to demand a new and better Scotland. In Orr's view progress was moving more rapidly elsewhere, not just in England but in many other European countries, particularly those with national schemes to improve the living standards of the poor. The persistence of the slums, Orr maintained, meant that 'we cannot regard Scotland as prosperous while these conditions last'.[56]

Orr's negative analysis in the mid-1930s, like those of Thomson almost ten years earlier, reflected the shortcomings of official measures to deal with the health and housing problems emanating from slum conditions. Thomson's angry commentaries also reflected the views of many health professionals. In 1925 a Board of Health Inquiry was opened into a proposal by Glasgow Corporation for a slum clearance scheme in a northern area of the city centre leading the following year to one of the most devastating reports from a public body on the slums. The Inquiry Report said that it was impossible to draw any picture which could adequately describe the conditions under which it found human beings living in practically all of the houses inspected. It said:

> The houses are a hunting ground for vermin of every description. Fleas, of course, abound, but we found also that practically every property was absolutely bug-ridden. The tenants complained that they could get no peace from these pests, which drop upon their faces and crawl over their persons and beds at night, and which fall into their food during the day. We found evidences of a perfect menagerie of animal life, including lice, rats in great numbers, mice, cockroaches, snails and even toads. Neither adults nor children have much chance of health. Tenants gave repeated information of having lost one, two or even three children.[57]

The picture of mass poverty, disease and death painted by the Report confirmed the findings and warnings of doctors and health inspectors. It also provided official support for the statistical evidence Thomson had employed, at least in relation to slum conditions and their impact on health and mortality. His exaggerated use of language and the rage embodied in his words and descriptions may have been a more complex issue but his facts were accurate and justified by the official narrative.

However even such a critical analysis from the Board of Health failed to have any meaningful impact on government health or housing policy and it barely registered outside of Scotland. Glasgow and slums was, or so it appeared, an old story meriting little further discussion or attention beyond the city. That this was the case was shown in July 1927 when the Report was the subject of a Debate in Parliament. James Stewart, the Labour MP for Glasgow St. Rollox noted that as he spoke there was not one English MP present in the Commons. His colleague, David Kirkwood, the Labour MP for Dumbarton District Burghs, commented that if the debate concerned India, Egypt, Russia or any other country over the sea the benches opposite would be filled. 'But because it is Scotland the benches opposite are only scantily occupied. No one takes any interest in it.' Kirkwood accused Sir John Gilmour, the Secretary of State for Scotland, of doing nothing and having no intention of doing anything to mitigate the 'terrible conditions which prevail' and of being afraid to raise his voice in Cabinet on behalf of Scotland. 'If it was his own class, the rich class in Scotland, I am satisfied that the representatives of Scotland in this government would so their best to meet the case, but because it is the working class, the poor people, they do nothing,' Kirkwood said.[58]

If the anger of Labour MPs to slum conditions was both justified and predictable, they found in Walter Elliot, one Tory politician who shared their passion for action and reform. In 1930 when Labour was in power he conceded that slum clearance programmes of the 1920s were inadequate, that the situation remained grave, that Scotland could not regard itself as a civilised country while such conditions persisted. 'For a State to call itself civilised when children are kept awake by vermin is not a proper use of the word civilised. A State which allows walls to be built in front of windows so that it is impossible to see the light of day, where people have to burn gas throughout the whole 24 hours, is not sensible let alone civilised,' he said.[59]

Thomson asserted in *Caledonia* and *Re-Discovery* that the social problems, particularly in health and housing were far graver than those existing in England: 'it is impossible to consider them as divisions of the same subject [. . .] Compared with the Englishman, the Scot lives like a savage,' he wrote. The official figures he researched revealed that a child living in the slums was five times more likely to take measles as a child living in a decent Glasgow working class home and twenty times as likely to die from it. He compared Glasgow against Birmingham. The English industrial city 'was not the sort of place to which a father would choose as a health resort for his child,' he wrote. Yet the death-rate among Birmingham children contracting measles was only one-third of the death-rate in Glasgow. In *Re-Discovery* Thomson reveals little optimism that any real progress is being made in dealing with the horrors of the slums, he sees only a continuation of such life for almost half the people.

'From scenes like these auld Scotia's grandeur, in its present battered condition, springs', he wrote. 'From [. . .] this empire on which the sun never rises [. . .] from the filth, despair and promiscuity of the slums the latest generation of Scots is emerging.'[60]

Elliot would have rejected the crudeness of Thomson's language yet almost a decade later he himself stood in the Commons and declared that conditions in Scotland were far worse than those in England. 'The under housing in Scotland is something to which there is no parallel in England,' Elliot said. He had looked up the figures for cities and counties in England with apparently equally poor conditions, not the wealthy cities of the south of England or even Birmingham. In Liverpool which had the same immigration, industrial conditions and 'very much the same depression' 7.4 per cent of the houses were overcrowded, in Glasgow it was 30 percent; in Durham, a depressed area, overcrowding affected 12 per cent, in Lanarkshire it was 37 percent. Elliot added, 'for Scotland as a whole 23 per cent of houses are overcrowded, as against 3.8 per cent for all of England and Wales.'[61]

Elliot's public admissions of an apparent failure of policy and his personal frustrations may also have masked his inability to find sympathy with Cabinet colleagues who, by the late 1930s, had grown weary of Scottish grumbles. In any case Scottish realities were easily blurred in the context of a national view taken in Whitehall. 'The Ministry of Health tended to disregard the health statistics of Scotland: while the infant mortality rate in England and Wales was on average down to 58 deaths per 1000 live births in 1937, it was still at 80.3 in Scotland, 104 in Glasgow. That is an awful lot of dead babies,' noted the social historian, Stephen Constantine.[62]

In the late 1930s John Orr was commissioned by the Department of Health in Scotland to undertake research on the levels of nutrition and health but because of World War II his subsequent report was not published until 1943. Orr found that Scotland had the worse infant mortality rates in Europe, apart from Portugal and Spain, and 30 per cent above England and Wales. The rates for vitamin deficiency in all areas of diet correlated with overcrowded housing in which 23 per cent of all Scots lived compared with four per cent in England.[63] In 1951 48 per cent of Glasgow's population continued to live in houses of two or less rooms, the corresponding figure for Birmingham was 2.0 per cent, Manchester 2.0 per cent and Liverpool 3.4 per cent. In Glasgow 37.5 per cent of the city's households shared a water closet and in one district, Dalmarnock the figure was 75.5 per cent.

R.A. Cage, reviewing Glasgow's twentieth century health and housing experience, concluded that in terms of housing density measured by persons per room, Glasgow's was the worst in Britain. It was beyond doubt, he said, that an infant born into a one room dwelling faced the highest chance of dying within infancy than if born into a larger dwelling. In 1952 an infant born in Glasgow was more likely to die during its first year than if born in any other British city. 'Glasgow's single-ends were death traps, and as long as they existed, medical advances were unable to provide further reductions in infant mortality rates. Such was a fact of life, and death,' wrote Cage.[64]

Slum housing remained a constant reminder of Scotland's shame as late as the 1960s. In the 1920s Thomson's vision of the slums was as observer, reporter and commentator. What he saw, what he found was synonymous for him with his conviction that Scotland was a second-rate country, not only because of the existence of such conditions, but particularly by what he viewed as a lack of real resolve to tackle them. It was the same complacency, he argued, that existed across other parts of Scottish society, from its refusal to acknowledge the extent of economic and industrial failure, its indifference towards the Anglicisation of Scottish culture and the threat these and other issues posed to national identity. Thomson saw a host of inter-connected lines all pulling Scotland in a downward spiral. The slum problem in Scotland was of such a magnitude that it deserved special government action. There was no indication that this was happening. Some improvements with limited slum clearance schemes had started in Glasgow and other cities and towns but progress was slow and new house-building was well behind the numbers of homes needed. In 1927 Thomson wrote that in Scotland the slums aroused no horror: 'if occasionally there is despair, the most prevalent attitude is apathy and a vehement desire to say and think as little as possible about an unsavoury topic.' Of the response from Westminster he said that the gulf between England and Scotland was not a division of poor and rich relations, 'but rather that between coolies and white exploiters'. He was deliberately provocative, using exaggerated language in his rage as he apportioned blame against both the Scottish and London establishments.[65]

Thomson's criticisms of the slums and the complacency he encountered only added to his contentious reputation at the time. But it was his attacks on another part of Scottish society, its Irish Catholic population, which would create his long-lasting notoriety.

CHAPTER 4

Irish Catholics,
Immigration and Population

The first fact about the Scot is that he is a man eclipsed.
The Scots are a dying people.

George Malcolm Thomson, *Caledonia* [1]

IN HIS ACCLAIMED history of Scotland, *The Scottish Nation 1700-2007* (2006), the eminent Scottish historian Tom Devine accords Thomson the rare compliment of referring twice to this quotation from *Caledonia*. In the first the words are used in the context of the impact of the Depression and economic decline. The second reference, three hundred pages later, is used in relation to the mass emigration of Scots in the 1920s. [2] Thomson's words are emotive, structuring a vision of a country and a nation on the wane, the precise sentiment Thomson sought to arouse.

But while emigration and industrial slump were in Thomson's gaze his words had a more basic purpose in mind, an intent steeped in racism directed at Scotland's minority population of Irish Catholic immigrants. The Scots were 'eclipsed' and 'dying', wrote Thomson, because they were being replaced by a 'people alien in race, temperament, and religion, at a speed which is without parallel in history outside the era of the barbarian invasions.'

Thomson was well-regarded by his peers for his efforts in support of Scotland's arts and his contribution to the literary revival. Today he is only occasionally recalled for his cultural inputs. His modern Scottish reputation is grounded almost exclusively on his obsessive campaigns against Irish Catholics.

Caledonia is a small blue book of less than one hundred pages, a third of which Thomson allocated to the Irish Catholic issue, the final 25 pages the substantive conclusion of his narrative, that within a century Scotland would be a Catholic state, his imagined apocalypse of *The Future of The Scots*. Thomson's purpose was to shock, an exaggerated attempt to paint a future in which the native Scot – mainly Protestant Presbyterians – would be overtaken by the unstoppable march of a Catholic mass slowly, but steadily, reaching out from its heartlands in the west of Scotland to engulf the entire country.

'Certainly there is nothing in modern times,' he wrote, 'to compare with the ousting of one population by another [. . .] which is going on with undiminished momentum.' He unashamedly invoked populist phrases as a form of 1920s style human interest journalese writing: 'Today every fifth baby born in Scotland is a little Irish Catholic,' and, 'In Glasgow in 1924, 28 per cent of the children born saw the world through the windows of an Irish Catholic home.' [3]

In Thomson's bleak scenario the distorted picture of multitudes of little Irish Catholic boys and girls dominating the urban landscapes was symptomatic and justified. In similar vein he claimed that a third of all crimes committed in Scotland were the work of Irishmen, 'most sinister and significant of all,' he wrote. He stated that in 1926 out of 15,728 persons sent to prison or other penal institutions in Scotland 3591 were born in Ireland, and if Scottish-born Irishmen are included the number rose to 4500. Armed with these figures Thomson concluded that the 'Irish colony' of 650,000 'is perpetrating the same amount of crime of a graver kind as would be found in a population of 1,350,000 Scotsmen.' [4]

There were villages that were entirely Irish, towns that were predominantly Irish, and in Glasgow the largest Christian communion was Roman Catholic. The inevitable consequence was that 'already revolvers have been drawn and blood has been spilt in the feuds of Orange and Green,' and Thomson again had no doubts regarding the guilty party, citing an image of brawling Irishmen. 'Donnybrook is an institution that the Irish take about with them as the Jews did the Ark of the Covenant.' As the Irish moved in the native Scots would leave, he maintained. 'The Scottish lion and the Irish bull will not lie down together.'

He left little doubt that he regarded Catholic and Irish as synonymous. For all practical purposes they were interchangeable terms, although he took care not to include in his acrimony Scotland's minority native Roman Catholic population which had, he said, legitimate links stretching back to the Celtic clans of the Highlands and south west Scotland. Such an observation only served to confirm the racist nature of his anti-Irishness.

Thomson was torn between blaming immigration or the 'greater fertility' of the Irish already settled in Scotland for his absolute certainty that the Catholic population had and would continue to increase. However when he accused Catholic bishops and priests for exerting pressure by issuing warnings against the 'grave sin' of birth control he admitted that native working class Scots were, likewise, unlikely to use any preventive measures. He acknowledged that a comparison made in one mining district in 1922 revealed that the Scottish birth-rate was higher and that Aberdeen, 'a purely Scots city', had a higher birth rate than Dundee which was one-fifth Catholic.

Thomson, the man who prided himself as a journalist and researcher on the rigour of his evidence-based analysis, was not prepared to let factual contradictions or inconsistencies interfere with the substantive thrust of his thesis. 'The essential facts are that the present Irish Catholic population is about 650,000 out of a total of 4,880,000, that the Irish have doubled their numbers in the last forty years,' he states. Thomson also attempted to make a direct link between mass emigration from Scotland in the 1920s and migration to Scotland from the Irish Free State. 'It is this that gives its peculiarly sinister aspect to the Irish inundation,' he claimed, suggesting that similar events in America would have sparked a race war. [5]

When he wrote this Thomson deliberately ignored the reality of population movements in Scotland. The 1921 census showed that there were in Scotland 415,000 persons of non-Scottish birth: 70,623 born in the Irish Free State; 88,397 in Northern Ireland; and 189,385 in England. In the four Scottish cities, only in Glasgow, did the Irish-born population outnumber the English-born, 65,658 against 49,296, and that was achieved only by combining both Catholic and Protestant born Irish from the Free State and Ulster. Aberdeen had fifteen times as many English-born persons than Irish-born, Edinburgh six times, and Dundee three times. The Irish-born total of 159,000 in 1921 compared with the total of 175,000 recorded at the 1911 census, a reduction of 16,000. [6]

Following the formation of the Irish Free State no official records were maintained for Irish immigration to mainland Britain but the figures prior to 1920 reveal that the high point of Irish immigration to Scotland – with the notable exception of the decade following the Famine of the mid-1840s – occurred in 1876 when almost 9,000 arrived. By 1881 this had dropped to 5,000 and after 1906 when there were 2,000 immigrants the numbers never again exceeded 1,000 a year. In 1913 only 238 arrived and after the war in 1919 and 1920 the numbers were 230 and 113 respectively. [7] In the 1920s as the Scottish economy contracted and unemployment rose steadily the numbers arriving from Dublin at Scottish ports was reduced even further to a level described later by the *Glasgow Herald* newspaper as a 'mere trickle'.[8] In 1933 the Census Office in Edinburgh officially confirmed that Irish immigration to Scotland had fallen consistently since the turn of the century and, perhaps more revealingly, that between 1921 and 1931 it was likely to have been outweighed by the numbers of those with Irish origins who were part of the mass emigration from Scotland in the same decade. [9] However in 1927 and 1928 Thomson ignored the statistical facts that did not support his argument and armed himself with figures designed to convince his Protestant readers that their very nationhood was under threat from Irish Catholics in their midst.

His use or misuse of fictional data perhaps reached its nadir in his follow up work to *Caledonia, Re-Discovery* in which Thomson claimed that during the previous fifteen years – the period from 1913-1928 and which included the War years – 150,000 immigrants had settled in Scotland. He presented no evidence or source for this figure opting instead to concentrate on an imagined significance since in the years between 1922 and 1926 the total population of Scotland had fallen by 700. [10]

Had Thomson seriously investigated the numbers he would have found that between 1913 and 1920 the total number of immigrants from

Ireland, including Ulster, was only 3566. The Irish historian James Edmund Handley later commented, 'Such a manifest absurdity absolves the reader from the obligation of paying serious attention to Mr. Thomson's views on immigrants.' [11]

In *Re-Discovery* Thomson pursued his offensive against the immigrants, resorting to a mixture of analysis, judgements and prejudices of social conditions and statistics mostly drawn from alleged anecdotal evidence, real or imagined, to create an exaggerated caricature of Irish infiltration into the depths and soul of Scottish society. One of Thomson's favourite tactics was to employ a fictional character as a third person storyteller, a supposed narrator of truth, someone whose persuasive testimony could be regarded as reliable and believable and because he brought real-life experience and knowledge, he could be presented as 'the best authority on the subject'.

In *Re-Discovery* the subject, again, was the Irish Catholic population and the authority a man Thomson meets in a Glasgow tea-shop: 'he was a tall, lankily-built fellow of about thirty, with gloomy, twitching brows, a sprout of disagreeable red hair, thin, long cheeks, and, in contrast, full petulant lips.' Thomson quickly assured the reader that he has never met this man before, adding an almost fictional sense of drama and colour to the proceedings when the man says, 'MacDonald sent you to me, did he?', while at the same time 'grasping an éclair in his uncompromising way'.

Reading this today one wonders if Thomson expected anyone to accept the scenarios and characters he described, even if his narrative was feeding the racial and religious bigotry of many, who, at the time, desperately wanted to believe such prejudice. No such misgivings are visible, however, as Thomson allows the man in the Glasgow tea-shop, 'his West country accent thickened', ten pages of *Re-Discovery* to share his experiences living with the 'Irish problem in Scotland'; encounters with Irish Catholics as a steward on the ferries between Dublin and Ardrossan, as an apprentice in a Clyde shipyard, living in an Ayrshire mining district, even as a tramp wandering round Scotland.

He chronicles a network of alliances and arrangements which

smooth the path of the Irish immigrant; from the boat to the priest, to the community, to the workplace, and all of it organised to the disadvantage of and as a threat to the indigenous Scot. At the heart of conspiracy sits the priest. 'The priest is all-powerful in Irish Scotland to-day and he will take care that his people do not change their ways of living or thinking [. . .] There was going to be no mixing of the holy Irish blood with the polluted Scottish [. . .] The priest is steadily becoming the master of Scotland [. . .] The priests have their people in the hollow of their hands.' [12]

In essence through his ventilation of unfounded and popular prejudice, Thomson was no more than the 1920s' equivalent of a modern author, commentator or columnist both famous and infamous for publicly expressing extreme opinions but with the certainty that they would be eagerly consumed by a substantial section of the popular mass. In Thomson's case that mass included not only Church leaders and the inevitable groups of Protestant activists but influential figures across the Scottish establishment. Thomson's rage in *Caledonia* and *Re-Discovery* did not single him out as the lone voice of racial and sectarian intolerance and bigotry. But the convictions of Thomson and others were not held across all of Scottish society.

In 1926, a year before *Caledonia* was published, a leading article in *The Scots Independent,* the self-proclaimed organ of Scottish nationality, criticised churchmen and others who had popularly styled immigration as the 'Irish Menace'. 'The use of the term tends to arouse feelings of bitterness, the supposition of a clear racial distinction between the Scots and Irish that is, in fact, non-existent.' [13]

The term the 'Irish Menace' became common currency in the 1920s following a notorious report, *The Menace of the Irish Race to our Scottish Nationality,* published in 1923 by the Church and Nation Committee of the General Assembly of the Church of Scotland. The very name of the report was a clear indication that, although the product of a leading group of Protestant churchmen, it was less concerned with matters ecclesiastical and was directly aimed at emphasising so-called racial differences between the Scots and the Irish, but only the Catholic Irish. The report levelled many accusations against Catholics, including criminality, immorality, conspiracy, subversion, taking jobs away from 'native' Scots, and being an economic burden on Scottish taxpayers and ratepayers, and 'undermining the purity of the Scots race'.[14] A conservative interpretation of the report could only conclude that the Irish and the Catholic religion were to blame for all of the social problems facing Scotland. The report specifically excluded any criticism of native Catholics along with Irish Protestants from Ulster with whom Scottish Presbyterians shared a common religion and who belonged to 'the same race as ourselves'.[15]

The Kirk hierarchy, led by a group who were unionists, anti-Labour and anti-Irish Catholic, unsuccessfully petitioned the government to stem the flow of Irish immigration, claiming: 'They cannot be assimilated and absorbed into the Scottish race. They remain people by themselves, segregated by reason of their race, their customs, their traditions, and above all, by their loyalty to their Church, and gradually and inevitably dividing Scotland, racially, socially and ecclesiastically.' [16]

Incongruously the Rev. John White, who led the group, maintained that the Church considered it a racial and not a religious question and in a letter to Sir John Gilmour, the Secretary of State for Scotland he described Irish Catholics as 'an inferior race'. The attacks were carried to the pulpits from where some ministers warned that the emigration of Scots would eventually lead to an Irish Roman Catholic majority in industrial working class areas.[17]

Although sectarian tensions existed in other parts of the United Kingdom, such as Liverpool, religious issues in Scotland became aligned to concerns about Scottish identity and, in some quarters, the very future of the Scots as a race. The 1918 Education Act which gave equal rights plus separate state education to Catholic children aroused resentment in many Protestant establishment circles which regarded the concession 'the inroad of the death-watch beetle in the fabric of their religion'. [18] While radical Protestant organisations such as the Orange Order naturally welcomed and supported the Church's crusade, the sense that the Irish Catholic minority posed a threat to Scottish nationhood permeated other parts of Scottish society.

Sir John M. Macleod, a Glasgow chartered accountant, reflecting the views of some parts of the city's professional class, pinned the blame for the existence of slums on Irish Catholics. 'These conditions are not due to "our ain folk", but are largely caused by the great and continuous immigration that has been going on year after year by those of alien blood,' he said. Those aliens, their children and grandchildren may have become naturalised Scots and Glasgow people, 'but have always retained to the full their alien blood and outlook.' [19]

MacLeod's remarks, addressed to the annual meeting of the Glasgow Benevolent Society held in the rooms of the Religious Institute, were more typical than unique. A speaker told the Glasgow Philosophical Society that emigrant Scots were being replaced by 'inferior' Irish who exploited the inactions of politicians and 'live at ease and comfort on the bounty of our laws'. They were also responsible for serious crime, the slums, rent strikes, violence and fomenting revolution. [20]

Further evidence that the Kirk's 'Irish Menace' report was taken seriously, even in academic circles, emerged during the 12th International Geographical Congress held at Cambridge University in 1928. Alan G. Ogilvie, Reader in Geography at Edinburgh University referring to the report said: 'The evidence is overwhelming that the Irish in Scotland will increase while the Scottish race decreases, raising concerns that emigrant Scots were being replaced by Irish immigrants.' Ogilvie claimed that new Catholic Churches were springing up across the mining and industrial villages of central Scotland, and similar developments were appearing in the cities. 'This sign of the penetration of Protestant Scotland is viewed with alarm by many of her people, not so much on account of religious prejudice, as because of the social implications. Scotsmen value above all their nationality and traditions.' [21] Ogilvie's concerns were echoed by the eminent figure of Sir John Russell, ex-President of the Geographical Association, who referred to the 'curious change' coming over the west of Scotland. 'A large foreign population, chiefly Irish, is taking possession, ousting the Scotsmen and doing by peaceful penetration what no previous invaders were ever able to do by force. What the end may be no one can tell,' warned Sir John. [22]

Commentaries such as these had been entered into the common narrative in the early to mid-1920s, years before Thomson ensured that his own name would be forever identified with the bigotry and racism of the period. In 1922 one leading churchman won applause from the General Assembly when he claimed that not only were Roman Catholics of Irish origin alien to the Scots in both religion and race but that their presence was part of a sinister conspiracy to bring Scotland under Roman domination. The Rev. Duncan Cameron, who had a parish in the mining town of Kilsyth north of Glasgow, said Irish Catholic men were seducing innocent Scottish girls into mixed marriages 'to betray the faith of their fathers and their country'. The presence of these aliens, he predicted, would soon bring racial and sectarian warfare to Scotland. [23] Five years later, in 1927, Cameron remained steadfast in his condemnation of the Irish immigrants prophesying that in the industrial areas the majority of working class people would soon be Catholics, a position from which they would be able to assume both local and national political power. [24] In a contemporary climate in which divine oracles from the established church were regularly forecasting a cataclysm for native Scots, Thomson did not hesitate to don the mantle of prophet and conjure his own vision of Scotland in the twenty-first century.

Thomson Predicts the End of Scotland

Thomson, ever conscious of literature and history, of his own personal ambition to add the label of historian to his credentials, plus an opportunity for a mischievous display of his own cleverness, borrowed from the nineteenth century historian and politician, Thomas Babington Macaulay, when he answered his own question 'What will be the Future of the Scots?' Again he employed the use of a fictional character, on this occasion an invention from the future. His star witness from Scotland in the year 2027 is an intelligent young New Zealander called Mr Macaulay who 'drops out of the London-Reykjavik-Tokio express somewhere over Edinburgh.' [25] Neither his name nor country of origin was plucked randomly. Thomson chose the name and character – presumably believing it provided him with historical legitimacy and inspiration – from the misgivings and warnings about the strength and endurance of the Roman Catholic Church issued by Macaulay in an essay written in 1840 for the *Edinburgh Review*. [26]

Thomson would have been enthralled to place himself and his use of the New Zealander at the end of a line of historical narratives reaching from the eighteenth through the nineteenth to the twentieth century with prophesies of what he would likely find in the twenty-first century. Whether Macaulay would have shared Thomson's passionate contempt for Irish Catholics in modern Scotland seems unlikely; but the New Zealander in the future who might have found London in ruins now finds himself, in Thomson's version, transposed to twenty-first century Edinburgh, witnessing not a sea of rubble but a vision of Catholic supremacy. He witnesses 'an ecclesiastical procession, with many crucifixes and thuribles' as the Archbishop of Edinburgh and his clergy pass him on their way to the magnificence of a new Cathedral dedicated to St Patrick rearing 'its glittering white spire two hundred feet over Princes Street'.

Later, in a Glasgow hotel, Macaulay meets an elderly man, 'of somewhat shabby and melancholy appearance', who tells him he is in the 'Irish Belt', the Irish element of the population is the stronger, although the total population of Scotland has fallen by about a million since 1927. Through his characters Thomson depicts a country riven by racial and religious civil wars, of riots and sieges; 'revolvers had been freely used' and English armoured cars brought in to establish military law in Lanarkshire. The racist tone persists as he refers to the 'repugnancies' implicit in the incompatibility between the Scots and the Irish: 'it is as obscure as the hostility between one germ and another which at times leads to the cure of one disease by the onset of another.'

And even as he admits to the absence of scientific knowledge or evidence he cites as a phenomenon 'the sociological failure of mixed marriages between the two races'. Such partnerships, Thomson claims, result in a cross-bred type which unites the bad qualities of both stocks, 'and bred, in addition, a strange nullity, an abnormal lack of character and vigour'.

In the unfolding calamity Thomson predicts for Scotland, the mass emigration of the 1920s continues unabated throughout the twentieth century. Gradually 'the Irish' gain control of large swathes of industrial and urban Scotland, including Glasgow; and the historical alliance of two centuries with England is loosened. Scotland is no longer the faithful and trusted ally and as the Irish encroach on Scottish political life the spiritual union separates, the country ranks itself alongside the Irish Free State.

'Young men [. . .] look to Dublin as their spiritual home and to her artists and writers as their exemplars,' he prophesises. Too late England awakes to the dangers of Irish immigration and when a semi-military Scots nationalist league is formed it is suppressed by English troops: 'the last revolt of the Scots against their tragic destiny'. As the native Scots abandon the country and resettle in Canada, Australia, and even Siberia, Thomson notes that in Dublin the debate has begun about a 'Greater Ireland'.

He envisages a scenario in which Canadian Scots raise two million dollars to move and rebuild Burns Cottage in Toronto. In Thomson's bleak future he compares the destiny of the Scots with that of the Jews. They would die and enrich mankind, and the ripples the Scots made in the racial pool would grow fainter until they were no longer to be seen. 'The Scot was dead, dead with the dinosaur and the Bushman and the Dodo, and buried in the necropolis of the not-quite-good-enough. What did it matter anyway? Who cared?' [27]

It is a deliberate spectre of grimness and joylessness, the dark fantasies of a young writer who, while witnessing economic decline and social problems and accurately calling to account sections of Scottish society for their failures, chooses to fixate both his own and the fear shared by countless countrymen on one minority community. The anxieties he displays, if real, are grossly exaggerated; and assessed eighty years on it is difficult not to conclude that Thomson well understood that he was constructing a deliberate exaggeration of the future and did so with the calculated intention of stirring up racial and religious tensions. His prophecy was written in 1927 in the midst of an industrial slump, mass emigration and population decline. Like many of his fellow intellectuals Thomson was disillusioned by the failure of post-war promises, his optimism of the early 1920s had largely evaporated giving way to an anger which *Caledonia* and *Re-Discovery* exude.

His diatribes against Irish Catholics were not supported by the facts, and, again, Thomson must have been aware of this. Yet he pursued his campaign relentlessly, and if some parts of the Church and the Protestant establishment might have wished to distance themselves from his harsh language and dialogue, and above all the Armageddon he predicted, many remained passionately committed to maintaining the case against Irish Catholics into the 1930s. And like Thomson they remained unmoved even as the evidence accumulated against their cause.

Thomson's denial of the statistical evidence remains one of the enigmas of his anti-Irish crusade. He regarded himself not only as a journalist, but a skilled researcher and increasingly as a historian, following up *Re-Discovery* with *Short History* completed in 1929. All of these vocations required professional attention to detail and a disciplined approach to factual accuracy, yet Thomson continued to justify his Irish convictions on the basis of discredited information.

His campaign, and more crucially that of the Presbyterian churches, was convincingly undermined by the *Glasgow Herald* newspaper in a series of articles, 'The Irish in Scotland: An Inquiry into the Facts' published over six days between 20th and 25th March 1929. The newspaper's detailed investigation considered all aspects of the Irish Catholic issue from the historical background, the views of the Scottish Churches, benefit payments to the Irish, the question of Scottish nationality and popular concerns about the future. The newspaper's examination confirmed that immigration from Ireland had reduced to a trickle and that large numbers of Irish Roman Catholics were now part of the exodus from Scotland to the United States and the dominions.

In one Parish Council in Glasgow out of 58,000 persons receiving poor relief only 90 were Irish Catholics who had been in Scotland for less than six months. It also concluded that the faster increase in the Irish Catholic population was due to a higher birth count and lower infant mortality rates; immigration had had no impact on the figures. In an editorial, the newspaper stated that the Churches' demand for immigration controls could no longer be effectively pressed warning that this should be recognised before the Churches' campaign brought racial and sectarian warfare to Scotland. [28]

From the Church's position the conclusions of the *Glasgow Herald* investigation could not have been more damaging. It was the newspaper of the commercial and professional classes in the west of Scotland. Like the Kirk leadership at the time it was staunchly right-wing and unionist, and a supporter of Scottish Protestantism. It could hardly be accused of some pre-ordained favouritism towards the Catholic community; it was free of accusations of bias.

Handley later noted: 'The outcome of the investigation refuted the allegations of the numerous writers on the subject in its letter columns throughout the 1920s, and no future commentator on the Irish in Scotland could afford to ignore the results of its exploration if he hoped to secure an intelligent audience for his observations.' [29] The *Glasgow Herald* investigation was also the subject of a separate inquiry by the Scottish Office which supported the newspaper's conclusions. [30] However as Thomson's private correspondence with others in the 1930s confirmed, he remained unmoved by the wave of evidence which dismantled his arguments.

He was not, however, a lone voice, as other leading figures in business, politics and intellectual circles persisted with demands for immigration controls and issued further warnings about the spread of the Irish Catholic community in Scotland. During the Scotland Debate in Parliament in November, 1932 some well-known and established political figures argued that Irish Catholics were a threat to native born Scots.

John Buchan, the popular author and respected Unionist MP for Scottish Universities, joined this chorus when he voiced concerns that the mass emigration of the 1920s had taken away some of the best Scottish stock. But instead of questioning the economic and social conditions that had driven hundreds of thousands of Scots to emigrate Buchan chose to focus on an alternative issue and target. 'Their place is being taken by those who, whatever their merits, are not Scottish. I understand that every fifth child born now in Scotland is an Irish Roman Catholic,' he said. When David Kirkwood, the Labour MP for Dumbarton Burghs asked him to provide evidence for his statements Buchan replied, 'I am not responsible for it; but it was given to me by a careful inquirer.'[31] Since Buchan's phrase was identical to that used by Thomson in *Caledonia*, it is reasonable to assume that Buchan accepted Thomson's words at face value. [32]

In the same debate Buchan's fellow unionist colleague, Lord Scone, the MP for Perth, pursued a similar racist doctrine claiming that the Irish population had not been assimilated into the Scottish population. 'It is not my purpose to discuss now whether the Irish culture is good or bad, but merely to state the definite fact that there is in the West of Scotland a completely separate race of alien origin practically homogeneous whose presence there is bitterly resented by tens of thousands of the Scottish working-class.'

Again Kirkwood challenged the statement claiming that the truth was that many of the students at Glasgow University came from Irish parents: 'I mean poor parents – who have struggled and starved in order to send their boys and girls to a university. Surely that is assimilating what we consider to be our outstanding Scottish characteristic.'

Scone dismissed this and refused to withdraw his remarks. 'I do not think any such assimilation is proved merely by the fact that they have sent a large number of their sons and daughters to our universities.' [33] Scone was one of the most vociferous voices against Irish Catholics within the unionist Protestant establishment, making his public position abundantly clear when he agreed to become Honorary President of the Scottish Protestant League, an aggressive movement founded in 1920, 'exclusively concerned with No Popery themes, the evils of the confessional, convent horror stories and escapes, the power and secrecy of the Jesuits, and priestly immorality.' Scone refused to bow to the wishes of the Scottish unionist leadership which preferred to defuse the Irish Catholic issue. [34]

When the government set up a committee of inquiry into Vagrancy in Scotland, Scone asked the Secretary of State to add to its terms of reference specific instructions to ascertain the percentage of vagrants, 'and other persons of the wayfaring classes' who were of Irish birth and those, who although Scottish born, had Irish parents. The under secretary of state Noel Skelton rejected the proposal but Scone persisted claiming that the population of poorhouses in Scotland at certain times of the year was often comprised of 75 per cent of persons born in the Irish Free State. 'Does he not think that requires some investigations?' [35]

Skelton again refused insisting that it was up to the committee to determine if it should consider the nationality of vagrants. Scone's blatant bigotry and racism, however, did not prevent his rise through the Scottish establishment after he succeeded to the House of Lords as the Seventh Earl of Mansfield. He was later appointed as the Queen's Lord High Commissioner to the General Assembly of the Church of Scotland and also, again by Royal appointment, as Lord Lieutenant of Perthshire.

In 1934 the distinguished Oxford historian and former Liberal politician Herbert A.L. Fisher specifically raised the Irish situation in Scotland in his foreword to Rait and Pryde's new modern history, *Scotland*. To avoid any doubts about Fisher's own prejudices he described the Irish as 'malcontents' who had demanded home rule in contrast to Scotland which before the War Englishmen had regarded as a 'happy hunting ground, rich and prosperous and firmly rooted in the Liberal faith'. He quoted directly and sympathetically from the 'imposing Scottish deputation' that had gone to Sir William Joynson-Hicks, the Home Secretary, demanding that Irish immigration should be checked or prohibited. It was urged, Fisher wrote, that unless something were done the balance of creeds and races would be upset 'and that Scotland would lose her ancient character of stalwart self sufficiency and descend in human scale.' One eighth of the population was already 'alien in race, mode of life, and religious creed', a dangerously high proportion and likely to become higher still 'under priestly influence'. [36]

The sectarian tone of Fisher and other scholars to the Irish question, even as late as the mid-1930s, provides us with incontrovertible proof that although the government had rejected demands for legislation, and surveys showed there was no problem with Irish immigration and that the Irish community in Scotland was not a threat to the dominance of the native Protestant Scots, racism and bigotry persisted. Thomson's words reflected much of this back to Scottish society of the time, even if he expressed it in inflammatory, distasteful and exaggerated language.

Scotland in Eclipse, largely inspired by Caledonia and Re-Discovery, and equally culpable in its use of extreme and offensive language against Irish Catholics was published in 1930. It was written by Andrew Dewar Gibb, who was then a law lecturer at Edinburgh University, and who, in 1934, took up the post of Professor of Scots Law at Glasgow University. Gibb had served as adjutant to Winston Churchill during World War I, stood twice, unsuccessfully, as a unionist candidate and prior to the Glasgow appointment had lectured on Scottish law at Cambridge University. Today he shares with Thomson the reputation of the sacrificial bogeyman of racism and bigotry from the period, most of the reprobation of modern Scottish historians being based on ten pages of anti-Irish Catholic vituperation in Eclipse. [37]

Tom Devine described Gibb's language as being 'even more vitriolic' than that of Thomson and another scholar wrote that Gibb had remarked that dealing with the Irish had all the constructive merit of spreading manure on a concrete floor. Gibb, commented another, had gone one step beyond displaying his hatred of the Irish, believing that it was necessary to purify the Scottish race and condemning any racial mixing, even among neighbours. [38]

No such denunciations greeted Gibb's book when it was published in 1930 or interfered with his ascent to the influential Glasgow Law Chair. The appointment was approved by King George V on the recommendation of Sir Godfrey Collins, the Secretary of State for Scotland and subsequently announced in the Appointments Column of the The Times. The Scotsman newspaper noted that the new Law Professor at Glasgow having fought two elections as a unionist was now a Scottish nationalist and described the content of Eclipse as no more than a 'review of Scottish affairs'. [39]

Thomson's prediction to Gibb that Eclipse would land him in 'a hell of a row' and that they were both 'burning their boats' appeared to be far-fetched at least in respect of Gibb's legal and academic career.[40]

Thomson and Gibb had developed a close personal, professional and political friendship in the late 1920s and by 1930, when *Eclipse* was published, were in regular correspondence and met regularly in London and Scotland.

Their association had three major elements to it: their shared anger about the economic and social decline of Scotland; their conviction that the Westminster Parliament and Scottish unionism had failed to respond to the crisis; and a joint belief that nationalism or home rule should not be the sole province of left wing radicals in the National Party of Scotland. But they were also joined by their prejudiced obsession that the future of the native Scottish race was threatened by Irish Catholic immigration and the expansion of the Irish population in Scotland. The charge against them from history is that they were racist bigots, and on the evidence of their words from the time they are both guilty as charged.

Gibb's invective against Irish Catholics was not confined to *Eclipse*. A few months before the book was published he wrote to Stanley Baldwin, the leader of the Conservative Party urging him to develop a 'defining Conservative policy for Scotland' in connection with Irish Catholic immigrants. Gibb claimed that there was a new spirit in Scotland, one that was alive to the Irish menace. 'Any man who tackles the grave problem of the Irish in Scotland will be rewarded for his courage. The Conservative Party is restive and would appreciate action.' Gibb described the Irish population of 700,000 out of a total of almost five million as 'immense'. 'They are a poor type of citizen, constantly on the increase, hostile to Scottish ideals in religion, politics and domestic life and mainly responsible for Scottish crime, slums and socialism.' The very least Gibb wanted was legislation to change the Poor Laws to allow 'Irish pauper immigrants' to be returned to the Free State. Gibb's racism was underlined by his final message to Baldwin that his demands did not apply to Protestant Irish immigrants from Ulster. 'They are an asset and not a curse to Scotland,' he wrote. [41]

Gibb's private entreaties to one of the giant political figures of the day – and one who had written a personal letter of support to Gibb when he stood as a unionist candidate – had no more success than had the various appeals for legislation made by the leaders of the Church of

Scotland. Gibb had convinced himself that the Conservative Party wanted to do something about the Irish problem but 'was afraid to attempt a solution'. If it was anxious to endear itself to Scottish voters it should announce clearly and unequivocally 'a policy for the de-Hibernisation of Scotland'.

In *Eclipse* Gibb conjures a veritable feast of racist insults exposing him to accusations not only of narrow-minded sectarianism but an anti-Irish fanaticism bordering on loathing and hatred. He calls the Irish Catholic presence in Scotland 'a national evil'; they are 'low-grade immigrants' from the wilds of Kerry and Limerick and the slums of Cork and Dublin; their breeding is not merely unchecked but 'actually encouraged by their own medicine-men'; and they squat and breed in such numbers that within a hundred years they will gain predominance in Scotland.

Gibb repeats Thomson's doomsday prediction, and like Thomson, does so in defiance of the available statistical evidence. He choruses Thomson's allegations about the Irish and crime suggesting that without them Scotland would be the most law-abiding country in the world. He identifies the Irish with knives and razors, sneak thefts and mean pilfering, dirty acts of sexual baseness, and prowling the east end of Glasgow attacking the police and strangers. Their priests maintain a rigorous grip, warning of 'a standing threat of hellfire' if they marry Protestants or use contraceptives. It means, Gibb wrote, that in the heart of the native Scottish race there is another 'immeasurably inferior in every way' and who 'at the behest of obscurantist magic-men' obstinately refuse to mingle with the people whose land they are usurping. [42]

If Gibb's nauseating extremism ruffled few feathers in Scottish academia and the unionist establishment in 1930, James Edmund Handley later described his words as 'a venomous outpouring of prejudice against the Irish in Scotland without any attempt to weigh the evidence or offer a balanced judgement'. Handley's renunciation of Gibb and by association, Thomson, written from an Irish Catholic perspective, was the first critical scholarly assessment of their sectarian attacks. His judgement, made in 1947, has become the predominant assessment of modern historians. [43] As a self-regarding historian Thomson's position may have been that history must judge and he made no attempt, at least in print, to explain or revise his interwar views on Scotland's Irish Catholic population, or to defend his prophecies that Scotland would have a Catholic majority in the twenty-first century.

The social historian Tom Gallagher, in 1987, adopted a softer and modified interpretation casting Thomson as little more than a journalist who reflected popular unease about the 'Scoto-Irish' and used his pen 'to magnify the ill-effects of their presence'. Thomson, interviewed in 1982 by Gallagher, said that he 'regretted' his anti-Irish outbursts adding that he had not sufficiently thought through his 'exact views' when he was active in nationalist politics during the 1920s and 1930s. Gallagher, charitably I believe, accepted this, writing later that Thomson's work as Beaverbrook's chief assistant had taken him outside the interwar Scottish environment. 'It is no coincidence,' Gallagher wrote, 'that Thomson, the able journalist, considerably modified his views about the Irish in Scotland after rising in Fleet Street during the 1930s.' [44]

There are difficulties with Thomson's repentance of 1982 and Gallagher's apparent acceptance that Thomson, the Anglo-Scot, had been rescued from his anti-Irish sectarianism by his exposure to London and the prospect of a glittering career. Firstly, in *Caledonia* Thomson made no connection between Irish immigration, the Irish community in Scotland, and Scottish nationalism, although he did later argue, in private correspondence, that the NPS and subsequently the SNP should adopt anti-Irish Catholic policies, believing, wrongly, that this would prove electorally popular.

The evidence suggests that at the time *Caledonia* was published Thomson was in the process of developing his thinking about modern unionism, home rule and nationalism. The NPS, the catalyst which sparked Thomson's active political nationalism, was not formed until 1928, a year after *Caledonia*. Thomson's anti-Irish Catholic prejudices were more likely, I contend, to be associated with his strong Presbyterian background, the public campaign by the Church of Scotland against Irish immigration, and also a conception that since such views were commonplace in contemporary Protestant Scotland his fictional account of a doomed future would add weight to popular opinion.

The only charitable interpretation is that Thomson was misguided and alarmed that Scotland was losing tens of thousands of its people each year through emigration, and falsely conjured a simplistic vision in which an educated Protestant left the country to be replaced by a poor and unskilled Irish Catholic. But the most damning evidence against the suggestion that Thomson had a 'road to Damascus' conversion in London is his private correspondence with Gibb throughout the 1930s. At the time when he was emerging as a major commentator on the *Daily Express* and advisor to Beaverbrook, Thomson persisted with his agitation about the Irish problem, as he continued to describe it, and on several occasions put forward proposals to deal with it.[45] The views Thomson expressed to Gibb were in sharp contrast with those he exchanged during the same period with the nationalist author, Neil Gunn.

Thomson Claims he Likes the Irish

Thomson's correspondence and subsequent friendship with Gunn was based on their interest in Scottish nationalism and Thomson's desire to persuade Gunn to publish with the Porpoise Press. In 1930 Thomson denied that he was anti-Irish and challenged Gunn when he accused him of 'personal vindictiveness' towards Irish Catholics, claiming in one letter that he 'liked' the Irish. [46]

In dealing with Gunn, Thomson found that his words and reputation had gone before him. Gunn, a committed and influential member of the NPS, shared with many fellow nationalists and other figures in the Scottish literary revival an affinity and sympathy with the Irish Free State and welcomed the integration of immigrants into Scottish society. He had raised the Irish issue with Thomson, telling him that he admired the Irish and that because of his published views he had doubts about meeting him. Thomson's response was to send Gunn a copy of his book, *Short History*, a tactic designed to affirm both Thomson's literary credentials and, more particularly, his sympathy and belief in Scottish nationhood. Thomson believed that *Short History* represented the first nationalist history of Scotland, a claim he often made to figures within the NPS. [47] He was convinced that Gunn would be persuaded. 'I am glad that the first half of my history removed the lingering doubts in your mind about the desirableness of meeting me – I hope the second half doesn't renew your worst suspicions,' he wrote. [48]

In *Short History*, well researched and equipped with a bibliography and detailed index, Thomson ambitiously attempted to sketch over three hundred pages a potted history of Scotland up to the outbreak of the Great War. Having established his reputation as a journalist, publisher and commentator, he aspired to add the sobriquet of historian to his accomplishments. In respect of Scotland's Irish Catholic population Gunn found in *Short History* a more circumspect and restrained Thomson, one still concerned about the growth of the Catholic population, but evincing in terms of the known history a more understanding and sympathetic view of Irish immigration and the Irish community in Scotland. He still maintained, in calmer language than that found in *Caledonia* and *Re-Discovery*, that the numbers of Irish Catholics was alarming to those 'who had the preservation of the native Scottish stock at heart'. He conceded that the immigration rush of the mid to late nineteenth century had been instigated by Scottish capitalists seeking cheap labour and that Irish workers were frequently subjected to attacks from Scottish workers angry that they had taken their jobs and undercut their wage rates. They were also mostly to be found living in the slum districts of the west of Scotland yet, wrote Thomson, 'they suffered, perhaps, more than any other classes from them'.

Indulging the time span of his history Thomson acknowledged that the Irish Catholic issue was disturbing the Presbyterian churches in the present but omitted any reference to anti-Catholic rhetoric from a wider spectrum of Scottish society, including his own contribution. He restricted comment on the contemporary situation by noting that the Scottish churches did nothing to discourage the original importation of Irish workers or to condemn the motives behind it. [49]

Gunn's response to Thomson was to ask him how he would respond to the simple statement, 'I like the Irish'. Thomson declared himself staggered that he should have any doubts. 'How completely you misunderstand me,' he wrote, 'For, of course, I like the Irish. Some of my best friends now are Irish – north and south.' He did, however, admit that he liked the English more than he liked the Irish. 'Yet neither of these things prevents me detesting the twin menaces to Scotland of English culture and Irish population.' Again, unconvinced, Gunn accused Thomson of having a 'personal vindictiveness' against the Irish and that he was encouraging the NPS to pursue anti-Irish policies. Gunn had the evidence of Thomson's own words to support the accusation, not only from his polemics, but also his journalism and public speeches.[50]

At a meeting of the NPS in Edinburgh Thomson had controversially announced that one of his main reasons for his refusal – at that time – to join the party was that it was not Scottish. He said it was absurd that the party had taken Ireland as its model for a new Scotland, 'Are we to change the English hegemony for an Irish one?' he asked. There was no parallel between the two countries; Ireland had been a conquered nation. 'Let us not dress up the campaign for Scottish nationalism in the cast-off clothing of Irish intransigence.' [51]

Thomson again maintained that he was innocent of Gunn's charges. He did believe, however, that the extent of Irish immigration confirmed that Scotland had lost control of its own destiny. 'I say the immigration is *prima facie*, easily the best argument for home rule there is but I don't say we should kick 'em out, exterminate 'em or anything else. Why do the nationalists shirk this best of all arguments? Why should they denounce the English and never the Irish? I like them as I like the English, and I hate the dangers that both of them are bringing to Scotland.' [52]

Thomson pursued the same arguments in correspondence with another nationalist activist, George Dott, dismissing as 'fascinations' Dott's comparisons between the enthusiasm of the Irish for home rule with the poor response of the Scottish people, insisting that Irish Catholic immigration to Scotland was a more burning issue. 'I look forward to a national party to face a national problem and at least admit that it is there,' he told Dott. [53]

Gunn, by raising his concerns about Thomson's campaigns against Irish Catholic immigrants and extending the interpretation to a wider meaning, that Thomson was also anti-Irish, suggesting a racist undertone to his writings, was reflecting views across much of Scottish society. His reticence at the time to engage too closely with Thomson – they later developed a friendship based on their publishing interests and Thomson's eventual enthusiasm for home rule nationalism – was based on the notoriety Thomson had achieved following the publication of *Caledonia* and *Re-Discovery*.

Thomson, however, as is clear from his responses to Gunn's challenges, continued to defend his position on Catholic immigration, and in the years that followed, even when faced with official statistical evidence that he was wrong, did not relent or alter his views. His stubbornness was borne from a personal dislike of the Catholic Irish, the Catholic Church and the very existence of an Irish Free State, an uncompromising stance hardly softened by the contradictions and inconsistencies he revealed by his words and actions.

He claimed, mostly with evidential justification, that his commentaries on the economic and social state of Scotland were supported by official reports and statistics, yet chose to deny the meagre and declining Irish Catholic immigration figures. He also claimed – the letters to Gunn are typical – that he was not anti-Irish yet until the mid-1930s he continued to act and manipulate within the nationalist movement for policies designed to send Catholic immigrants back to the Free State.

In the 1920s when anti-Irish Catholic feelings were at their peak in large parts of the Scottish Presbyterian establishment Thomson's words – even if the language was often repugnant and exaggerated – was the hard-edged reflection of a common cause. Economic and industrial failure, followed by mass emigration and population decline were the ingredients which induced anxiety and a sense of panic, and had since the early 1920s been the perfect feeding ground for establishment and even some intellectual rage against immigrants. One historian has commented, charitably: 'The campaign against Irish Catholic immigration in the interwar era, to which the Presbyterian churches contributed with arguments of a racist nature, should be viewed in this context of perceived crisis about the future of the nation and of the values with which Protestants identified.' [54]

Despite continuing Protestant agitation at a local level in a number of Scottish cities and towns until the mid-1930s, the so-called official campaign had run out of steam, thwarted and ignored by political indifference, dismissal and eventually contempt. Thomson, however, by then heavily involved behind the scenes with developments in both the NPS and the newly established SP and the discussions between both to form the SNP, remained ardently anti-Irish, only this time his efforts were confined primarily to the private rather than the public realm. In his correspondence with Gibb it is apparent that Thomson remained fixated on the Irish Catholic population in Scotland, despite the views of senior figures in the NPS, such as Gunn, that they were opposed to suggestions the party should oppose Irish Catholic immigration. He now wanted to concentrate less on the religious issues and more on the Irish as the representative face of the Irish Free State. 'I suggest we keep out of the anti-RC business, letting it grow as it will, but that we press on with our Irish business,' he told Gibb. [55]

In the spring of 1933 Thomson's plan was to instigate a debate within the nationalist movement which would result in a commitment that a Scottish government would give priority to the interests of the Scottish race and culture in social, financial and administration policy. To achieve this Thomson proposed planting questions at public meetings chiefly directed to the NPS secretary, John MacCormick, to ask him if he agreed with the sentiments behind such a pledge. In Thomson's view, MacCormick would have no alternative but to agree. 'Having done this we should then ask other members of the party executive if they agree with MacCormick.'

In Thomson's fanciful, conspiratorial scenario the leaders of the rightwing SP would be able to quote the NPS. 'We could put someone up to say in public that this sort of thing is the accepted view of the nationalist leaders,' he suggested to Gibb. If the plan worked Gibb would publicly repudiate the Anglo-Irish Treaty on behalf of Scottish nationalism. 'You could point out that it was incompatible with the stated intentions of eminent nationalists whom you could name.' [56]

Later in 1933 Thomson produced another idea on the 'Irish business'; to establish a society in Edinburgh or Glasgow with the sole purpose of producing propaganda in the form of pamphlets, letters and press releases to send to MPs, newspapers and other individuals and bodies. 'By doing this we may force the Irish issue to the front and make people see the value in it for them. I believe the time is ripe or that with little effort – directed to the right quarters – we could do a great deal of mischief.'

Thomson emerges once again from these exchanges as a manipulative figure, keen to orchestrate political machinations for specific, if not always possible, outcomes. But on the Irish issues, whether of religious or overtly racist intent, he now always strives to remain hidden, to be the creator of ideas, or in his words to organise 'mischief' from some point in the shadows.

He confides to Gibb: 'Of course our names must not appear anywhere, nor our hands be suspected. I think we can cover up.'[57] This could be construed as cowardice, or a personal admission that his notoriety could only harm any nationalist cause associated with Irish Catholics; or even fears that his professional position with Beaverbrook – well established by 1934 – would be threatened if his name was linked with religious or racist controversy. None of these justifications, however worthy or tame, allow Thomson to escape the charge of being both deceitful and hypocritical.

Throughout 1933 and 1934 he was also in regular contact and correspondence with Gunn, almost exclusively on matters relating to nationalism, and yet, despite their earlier exchanges he now prefers, at least with Gunn, to maintain a low profile on the Irish question. In discussions with Gibb on the issue of separate Catholic Schools he urged him to press on with 'our Irish business', but added, 'cautiously though, otherwise we will alienate Gunn and gain nothing else'.[58] Thomson's nervousness regarding Gunn is in sharp contrast with his earlier exchanges with him in which he stubbornly argued that the NPS should embrace the immigration issue as a political weapon. In the spring of 1934, however, the NPS and the SP had finally reached agreement on merger to form the SNP.

Thomson's fixation with Irish Catholics was a secondary matter.

Ironically when Scotland's Irish Catholic community did eventually become an issue during a nationalist election campaign the instigator was John MacCormick, the normally astute and level-headed party secretary, and the candidate in the Hillhead by-election in Glasgow in 1937. During the campaign MacCormick was supported by both Sir Alexander MacEwen, the former Chairman of the SNP and his successor, Gibb. One of the issues MacCormick chose to attack the National Government was its failure to implement a provision of the 1918 Scottish Education Act, to raise the school leaving age to 15. More surprisingly he played a sectarian card by calling for the abolition of Section 18 of the same Act which allowed for separate Catholic schools, and also demanded that no benefits should be paid to unemployed Irish labourers until they could prove long-term residency. [59]

MacCormick's words were poorly received by the Hillhead electorate who rewarded him with a mere nine per cent of the vote but they were also criticised inside the SNP. An article in the party newspaper, *Scots Independent*, was typical: 'I cannot agree to the tactic of appealing to a popular prejudice against a class who is attracted to Scotland under capitalism, to become our poorest wage slaves.' [60]

Gibb's antipathy towards Irish Catholics was well known inside the party but at this stage in the development of the SNP he was an influential figure over MacCormick. 'There was no one in Scotland with a keener brain and no one for whom I had more admiration and respect,' MacCormick later wrote of Gibb. The Gibb factor apart, however, there was a sense of ambivalence in MacCormick's approach to the Irish issue. He had been surprised and alarmed at the sectarian abuse which followed when Compton Mackenzie, a Catholic, was elected Lord Rector of Glasgow University in 1931. His opponents claimed it was a Catholic and not a nationalist triumph, further alleging that 'Home Rule would be synonymous with Rome Rule'. Soon there were reports from throughout Scotland that the NPS was under Catholic control. 'I had scarcely realised how deep-seated was the fear among a considerable section of the people of Scotland of a Catholic revival.' Thereafter, although he never shared the extreme sentiments of Thomson and Gibb and both the NPS and the SNP did not embrace Thomson's overtures to adopt anti-Irish policies, MacCormick equally did not want to antagonise the vast Protestant electorate. His miscalculation in Hillhead may simply have been no more than the opportunism of an ambitious politician who believed, wrongly, that certain anti-Catholic views would play well in a mainly prosperous, and Protestant, middle-class constituency in the west end of Glasgow.

He later confessed that the fear espoused by Thomson and Gibb was groundless and that the failure of the Irish Catholic community to be fully integrated lay at the door of the Scots themselves. 'When Scotland has developed a sufficiently healthy national life of her own she will find no difficulty in absorbing the strangers in her midst and turning them into good Scottish citizens.' [61]

Despite Thomson's persistent anti-Irish Catholic tirades it remains remarkable that contemporary evaluations paid scant attention to his sectarianism and concentrated on his attacks on Scottish institutions, perhaps in itself an indication of the understated bigotry which ran through the Scottish Protestant establishment. He wrote at a time when churchmen, politicians, and even academics talked openly of concerns about a growing Catholic population. Like Thomson they did so even as the evidence denied their case, but neither the events of the time, nor the embedded values of the Protestant majority, offer justification for Thomson's campaign. The argument that his exaggerations were motivated by the large scale emigration of native Scots and their replacement by Irish immigrants also crumbles against the facts of the actual numbers of Irish Catholics in the Scottish population.

Despite his later protestations in which he attempted to confuse his attacks with nationalist politics, Thomson cannot escape the charge of opportunism that he deliberately intended to sensationalise the Irish question through his books. In the face of all the contemporary evidence he was unable or unwilling to recant his views, his letters to Gunn suggesting that he had nothing to answer. In the mid-1930s when the Church of Scotland's campaign against the Irish has patently failed, he remained unmoved, hypocritically continuing to protest that he was neither anti-Irish nor anti-Catholic, even as he and Gibb planned to promote anti-Irish policies within the nationalist movement. He also displayed unashamed willingness to reinvent and reinterpret himself and his views if that what was required to ingratiate himself with an important audience, in this instance, the nationalist author, Neil Gunn.

Liam Connell has suggested that the reluctance of the mainstream Scottish press to review *Caledonia* reflected their caution of rousing sectarian violence, 'a measure that is to be applauded if the sales of Thomson's book are any indication of the extent of popular anti-Catholicism'. [62] The problem with this interpretation is that Scottish newspapers had for several years devoted columns of coverage to the Church of Scotland's campaign against Catholic immigrants. Thomson's criticisms of the press aligned with his wholesale condemnation of many sections of Scottish society – newspapers such as the *Glasgow Herald* and the *Scotsman* were at the heart of the establishment – are perhaps more likely reasons for their decision to ignore *Caledonia*.

CHAPTER 5

Facing his Critics

THOMSON'S CONTEMPT for almost all branches of Scottish society included his own profession, journalism. He accused Scottish newspapers of both provincialism and a lack of Scottishness, unwilling to put Scotland first or to report and analyse the world from the perspective of the Scottish interest. There had been, he claimed, no intelligent scrutiny and investigation of Scottish problems, readers had been kept in ignorance of the true state of their country, and an illusion had maintained that any difficulties were identical to those in England.

'A Scottish editor's vital cord is the telegraph wire uniting him with his London office,' he said. [1] Only one newspaper was excluded from his general condemnation, referred to but unnamed by him in *Caledonia*, but easily identified as the socialist weekly *Forward*, at the time published and edited by the Labour politician, Tom Johnston. With the possible exception of Johnston's initial post-war enthusiasm for Scottish home rule – a position he later reversed – it is unlikely that Thomson had any sympathies with the newspaper's left wing views. However, Thomson, the self-styled propagandist, admired *Forward's* success – at one point it was selling more than 30,000 copies weekly – and the reputation it had established as an organ of radical propaganda. Thomson praised it as the 'only' paper that made any effort to gather first-hand information and intelligence about the condition of Scotland. He also admired the quality of its journalism. 'Its editorial comments are characterised by a rough wit and pungency,' he wrote. [2]

Thomson's words appeared in *Caledonia* published in October, 1927. A month later he found himself the target of *Forward's* 'rough wit and pungency' in a full page article headed 'A Silly Book About Scotland: A Reply to a Traducer' written by Lachlan MacNeill Weir, the Labour MP for Clackmannan who was Ramsay MacDonald's principal private secretary. In labelling Thomson a 'traducer' Weir accused him of making false and malicious statements and that by writing *Caledonia* he had brought disgrace on Scotland. 'This indictment of the Scots is so grossly unfair and untrue than any real value is destroyed by the bilious myopia of a prejudiced sycophant,' Weir snarled. He accused Thomson's publishers of 'sensation mongering' and Thomson of wielding 'a poison pen'.

'It must have been difficult to find a man who would stoop to write a book of this kind, difficult but not impossible. This class of writer has a kind of "seated value" to a needy author and an unscrupulous publisher. It has two enticements to an author, inducements much sought after these days, money and notoriety.' Despite his anger and the strength of his language Weir, remarkably, accepted that much of Thomson's indictment was accurate: it was true that Scotland was losing population; it was true that the slums were the worst in the world; it was true that large numbers of Irishmen had arrived because they were cheap; it was true that there was a growing exodus of business from Scotland. It was also significant that the burden of Weir's castigation of Thomson centred on his views of the native – predominantly Protestant – Scots and that he displayed less concern about his Irish Catholic comments, although one third of *Caledonia* was devoted to this issue.

It was not true, Weir wrote, that the working classes were 'lazy, shiftless and physically degenerate' or that Scotland was a land of 'second-hand thoughts and second-rate minds'. Thomson's criticism of Scottish universities was valueless, based on ignorance and stupidity, 'they still furnish leaders of thought to the universities of the world,' said Weir. Convinced that Thomson had written *Caledonia* for profit and notoriety he added with sarcasm, 'let us hope that the author's remuneration for his muck-raking has been adequate.' [3]

One intellectual and literary figure who reacted immediately to *Caledonia* was MacDiarmid. Before the end of 1927, writing under his real name of C.M. Grieve, he had produced what has been accepted in historic terms as his riposte to Thomson, the book *Albyn or Scotland and the Future*. The reality was that Grieve was not spurred into literary or journalistic action by a crusade to counter *Caledonia*. He was not motivated by a sense of anger or disgust at Thomson's accusations and language. He was galvanised by the most basic of human responses, one as common in literary and publishing circles as in any other profession – envy. He was also angry at himself, a state of mind clearly evident from his claim in January 1928 that the book called *Caledonia or the Future of Scots* had been his idea. In a letter to George Ogilvie, his old schoolmaster at Broughton Academy in Edinburgh, and presenting it as 'a curious story', Grieve said he had suggested such a book with such a title to Kegan, Paul, Trench, Trubner, the London publishers who had launched the *Today and Tomorrow* series, a range of books aimed at stimulating modern thinking on the present and future. 'They agreed – and then I found I wasn't in the mood,' Grieve said. 'I was too much in amongst the stuff and simply couldn't write a statement in short compass. They wrote me for the manuscript several times: but I kept putting them off.'

Several months later when he learned that Kegan Paul were publishing *Caledonia,* Grieve wrote in protest to be told that that despite Thomson's book they would still accept a book from him, 'written from a different angle, and would he send on the manuscript at once.' Grieve, still fuming that his idea had been stolen and also doubtful that he could trust Kegan Paul, assembled *Albyn* using material he had already written and syndicated as a freelance writer to newspapers throughout Scotland. 'I hastily furbished up into semi-connected form some of the stuff I'd sent out through the special bureau I formed for the purpose of sending out special articles on Scottish issues and interests of all kinds at the rate of 5 columns per week,' Grieve wrote. *Albyn*, he claimed modestly, was 'just a rough slapping-together of stuff written in a slip-shod and hurried fashion.' [4]

Despite such misgivings – he told Ogilvie that he was 'not proud of it' – Kegan Paul accepted the book and within weeks were marketing it alongside a second edition of *Caledonia*. Thomson's book, said the publishers, was the most compact and mordant indictment of Scottish policy that has yet been written. It revealed the Scottish people as a leaderless mob in whom national pride had been strangled. 'They regard, unmoved, the spectacle of their monstrous slum-evil, the decay of their industries, the devastation of their countryside.' Grieve's book, in comparison, was an 'explicit and implicit' rejoinder to *Caledonia*. It traced the movements of a real Scottish revival in music, art, literature, and politics, concluding that there was a chance for the regeneration of the Scottish people. [5] In simplistic terms Thomson was presented as a gloomy pessimist while Grieve was an enthusiastic optimist, an analytical outcome which pleased Grieve who proceeded to write more than thirty reviews of *Caledonia* in newspapers, magazines and journals throughout Britain and Ireland. 'Thomson's book gave me a chance for a journalistic grand slam. Quite a little feat,' he boasted.[6]

If Grieve, in his role as contributor to numerous weekly newspaper columns, found penning reviews of *Caledonia* a source of additional income, unlike Weir he found no reason to be aggrieved by or heavily critical of the substance of Thomson's book. Grieve displayed no outrage, or even comment, at Thomson's inflammatory language, his wholesale condemnation of most of Scottish society, or that one third of *Caledonia* was devoted to attacks on the native Irish Catholic population. In *Albyn* Grieve confirmed his personal support for the influx of Irish immigrants but confined his criticism to Protestant Church leaders, who had, he said, claimed that the 'Irish Invasion' threatened Scottish nationhood. 'This new found zeal for nationalism is, however, obviously dictated by emptying churches,' Grieve said dismissively.

However much Grieve appeared to be relaxed at the prospect of Scotland becoming a Roman Catholic country with a predominantly Irish population, he believed it more likely that progressive Anglicisation and provincialisation would continue until it became part of England. [7] He described Thomson's words as 'cogent but far too pessimistic' and reserved his main criticism to Thomson's failure to recognise the positive opportunities for regeneration arising from nationalist bodies such as the Scottish Home Rule Association, the Scots National League and the Scottish National Convention.

'The weakness of the book is its failure to realise the recent growth and new tendencies in Scottish nationalism,' Grieve wrote. [8] It was this ignorance and omission, he claimed, that had caused Thomson to develop his 'melancholy outlook'. What is clear from Grieve's comments is that he agreed with Thomson's central thesis about the condition of

Scotland. 'I am at one with him in regard to the desperate state of Scottish arts and affairs,' he said. [9]

His main concern about *Caledonia* was that it would fail to have any impact on Scottish society, that it would be ignored by the establishment and the mainstream media, and if it did succeed in stimulating questions, propaganda against it would mean that Thomson and his indictments were dismissed. 'The way in which publicity is organised – and supervised – will probably ensure not only that a very small percentage of the Scottish people ever hear of Mr. Thomson's book but that most of those who do are immediately re-deceived in the most comforting manner,' Grieve wrote. The Scottish people, he believed, preferred the myth that they were peculiarly religious, patriotic, well-educated, thrifty and enterprising. The evidence Thomson had produced challenging this was likely to induce a form of mental dislocation. 'It is repugnant to our natures to allow ourselves to be convinced that the consensus of opinion is utterly wrong.' Thomson, he predicted, would be dismissed as a clever person, 'too clever for most of his countrymen'. [10]

Grieve's prediction in *The New Age Journal*, that *Caledonia* would be either attacked or ignored by the establishment in Scotland was published on 10th November 1927 and Weir's onslaught against the book duly appeared later the same month, on 27th November. Both of Scotland's two quality broadsheet newspapers, the *Glasgow Herald* and the *Scotsman* did not review the book, their boycott arguably confirming Thomson's charge that the Scottish press was hesitant to stimulate a public debate on the true state of the economy.

Despite this *Caledonia* quickly sold out. Jack Brand wrote later that the book made a considerable impact, 'became well known outside nationalist circles and contributed to the recognition of the acute problems.' [11] Grieve underestimated the influence of *Caledonia* which was surprising in the light of his own swift reaction to it in compiling *Albyn*, which itself was a commercial success.

The poet Edwin Muir later suggested that *Albyn* had extended the renaissance from literary into general culture and politics. [12] Although years later Muir praised Thomson's third condition polemic, *Distressed,* in view of Grieve's own admissions about the origins of *Albyn*, the catalyst for the movement of the renaissance writers into social commentaries on the condition of Scotland was Thomson and *Caledonia*. Grieve had been addressing many of these issues in his freelance writings but without *Caledonia* there would have been no *Albyn* to be followed soon afterwards by Thomson's sequel *Re-Discovery*.

Within a period of only one year three important books on the condition of Scotland had appeared, one from the leading light of the post-war literary revival, Grieve (MacDiarmid) and two from an author until then best known in cultural and publishing circles for his part in launching the Porpoise Press. MacDiarmid was already a controversial figure. Thomson's polemics gave him a public profile as a major critic of modern Scotland and, in historical terms, a long-lasting notoriety for his attacks on Irish Catholic immigrants.

Thomson accepted that by producing within a year a second book, *Re-Discovery*, which continued his criticism of both his country and his fellow countrymen he left himself open to the charge that his arguments in *Caledonia* had been unconvincing, that he had 'deplorably missed his adversary at the first onset'. He dismissed the angry responses of politicians such as Weir arguing that what he had written were statements of the ordinary and the obvious and called on his critics to open their minds and their eyes. No one, claimed Thomson, had produced any material to disprove the evidence and arguments in *Caledonia*. Instead he was accused of stubborn exaggeration and deliberate showmanship. 'Many are to be found who consider the whole thing condemned by its mere novelty,' he wrote.

Thomson remained implacable, refusing to revise any of the hard-line opinions and assessments of *Caledonia*. He described Scotland as one of the most ill-governed and most politically ineffective countries in the world, 'it is confronted by gigantic social problems which are being totally neglected or contemptuously trifled with under the sleepy indifference of its people'. [13]

The writer, F. Marian McNeil, said that it had been suggested that Scotland was in need of 'brutal young men' to expose the indifference of the establishment to the realities of the country's condition. 'Happily the brutal young men are emerging,' she wrote, prominent among them Thomson, MacDiarmid and the Glasgow-born author, Donald Carswell. 'At every brickbat they throw there is a burst of righteous indignation. They may discover that some of the missiles that so badly disturbed their complacency are of considerable intrinsic worth.' [14]

As the 1930s unfolded the missiles fired by Scotland's intellectuals remained unrelenting as a decade of slump moved into depression and politicians struggled to find the right words and phrases to describe the despair. Thomson, although increasingly committed to his work with Beaverbrook Newspapers, was determined to answer his critics and to do so by means of a third major polemic on the condition of Scotland, and one that would be substantially based on the evidence of decline.

That Distressed Area

In the early hours of 20th December 1934 Joseph Tinker, Labour MP for Leigh in Lancashire rose in the House of Commons to challenge a move to change the name of the Depressed Areas (Development and Improvement) Bill to the Special Areas (Development and Improvement) Bill. The name change had been hurriedly sent back to the Commons by the House of Lords following a debate during which a number of peers argued that people living in such areas were not depressed but were distressed, with one peer, Lord Gainford, suggesting that 'distressed' should replace 'depressed' in the title and throughout the clauses of the bill. However on the recommendation of the government spokesman, Lord Rochester, who considered the word 'distressed' no more suitable than 'depressed', the Lords agreed an amendment to replace 'depressed' with the word 'special'. A few hours later in the Commons the Under Secretary of State for Scotland, Mr Noel Skelton, moved the deletion of the word 'depressed' and the insertion of the word 'special' throughout the bill.

Tinker accused the government of attempting to send the idea to other parts of the country that things were not as bad as had been reported, stating that the word 'special' indicates something really good, or better. He said that in the chips shops in Lancashire there are chips which are called 'special chips'. When you buy 'special chips', he added, you are supposed to be getting something extra, and contrary to what had been said in the Lords the families in the 'depressed' areas did not want the word changed. Despite the opposition and cynicism of many MPs the bill passed into law as The Special Areas Act and a separate Special Commissioner was appointed for Scotland. [15]

One commentator observed that peers in the Lords could not stomach descriptions of 'depressed' or 'distressed', 'but the common people of the country have continued to speak of the 'special' areas as 'depressed', 'distressed', and 'derelict' areas, which in fact they really are.'[16] The 'common people' were not alone. One Scottish Unionist MP, Charles Black Milne, member for West Fife, declared that things were not well in Scotland and that compared with England all of Scotland was a 'distressed area'. [17]

Milne's words were appropriated by Thomson, engaged, in 1935, on the completion of his final interwar book on the state of Scotland and which he now called *Scotland That Distressed Area*. On the title page below his own name Thomson quoted Milne, 'That distressed area, North Britain'. Thomson would not have approved of the use of the term 'North Britain', which despite some usage as an alternative for 'Scotland' in the eighteenth and nineteenth centuries had not been popular and by the early twentieth century only appeared in the names of bodies such as the North British Railway Company and the North British Hotel in Edinburgh. He was, however, in complete agreement with Milne that Scotland was 'distressed' and his book intended to provide the evidence to show how economic, industrial and social decline had taken it there.[18]

The poet, Helen Cruickshank, who admitted that as an Edinburgh civil servant she worked daily with an 'enforced diet of statistics', relished Thomson's attention to detail and his use and interpretation of official reports and figures, the evidence she believed gave credible force to his arguments. [19] It was a view echoed by the Scottish press, the *Scotsman*, approving of the book, noted that Thomson's conclusion that Scotland's economic position was 'grave in the extreme' was based on 'impressive arrays of statistics'. [20]

In *Distressed*, Thomson concentrated primarily on the deterioration of the economy, taking account of trends from the beginning of the century, but focused his narrative on the events and developments in the 1920s. He accepted that the signs that the economic model was beginning to struggle against international competition became apparent before World War I but was obscured by the military industrial demands of the War itself. The brief post-war boom created a false optimism that was quickly followed by a slump that continued throughout the 1920s. Thomson confirmed his controversial analysis and arguments of *Caledonia* and *Re-Discovery*, there was no revisionism, nothing was retracted, and he offered no amendments.

Indeed, he claimed, 'they are no longer disputed'.

There had been a whole series of causes of national disquiet, 'crystallised in terse and familiar phrases suitable to an age of headlines,' he wrote. They include, 'the slum problem', 'the Irish invasion', 'the churchless million', and 'the southward drift of industry', the latter a phrase 'which brings a terror to the hearts of the Scottish people,' he said. Thomson resisted the temptation to declare, 'I was right!', 'I told you so!'

Distressed was the third of Thomson's major polemics on the condition of Scotland but coming eight years after *Caledonia* and *Re-Discovery*, like Thomson himself, it was more mature and substantial. It benefitted from the passage of time, providing Thomson with the opportunity for detailed research and the opportunity to draw important comparisons between the performance of the Scottish economy, not only with England, but against smaller European countries.

Thomson looked at seven other European nations, comparable in size, and with populations similar to that of Scotland. He used statistics of population increases and decreases noting that in the 1931 census the population of Scotland fell for the first time in recorded history, by 40,000, despite the fact that in the period between 1921 and 1931 the birth-rate in Scotland was greater than that of England and Wales. The population decline reflected the mass emigration to overseas destinations and 63,000 to England. During the same decade England's population had grown by 2,600,000. 'It seems that the underlying causes of the Scottish decline were not operating in the case of England and that indeed factors of a contrary tendency were at work,' Thomson said.

It also, in his view, contradicted the claims of politicians and captains of industry that Scotland and England's close industrial association meant that both were benefitting from the joint enterprise called Great Britain. 'The conception of a partnership from which both countries derive benefit has been displaced by that of a parasitic relationship in which one country is advised, with a greater or less degree of shameless-ness, to content itself with being a beggar,' he said. Thomson investigated the population movements in countries lying on the North Sea or the Baltic. 'Each is a "small country" and is, presumably, struggling against those terrible economic disadvantages from which Scotland is so happily shielded,' he noted, his words dripping with sarcasm. [21]

Table 1 Populations of Small European Countries

Country	1920	1930	Increase or decrease	Total increase
Norway	2,649,775	2,824,294	increase	164,419
Sweden	5,904,489	6,141,591	increase	237,102
Denmark	3,267,000	3,550,656	increase	283,656
Finland	3.364,807	3,667,067	increase	302,260
Holland	6,856,314	7,937,565	increase	1,081,251
Belgium	7,465,782	8.029,004	increase	563,222
Switzerland	3,880,320	4,066,400	increase	186,080
Iceland	95,000	110,000	increase	15,000

Source: Thomson, *Distressed*, pp 22-25

'In every case,' Thomson said, 'there is an increase of population over the decade.' Had the average increase over the total population of 36 million applied in Scotland instead of the actual decrease of 40,000 people there would have been an increase of 429,000. During this period Scotland's loss by emigration was almost equal to the total number of emigrants who left the eight countries in the table; a population of less than 5 million had lost as many as a population of 36 million. [22] Although the worldwide depression in the early 1930s had effectively stopped mass emigration to overseas destinations, if not internal migration to the Midlands and the south of England, the revelation that 700,000 Scots had moved away between 1911 and 1931 was greeted with astonishment and concern in some quarters.

Thomson's associate, Gibb, newly elected Chairman of the fledgling SNP, said no country in the world could stand such a drain of people, describing emigration and immigration on the Scottish scale, 'encouraged or permitted' by Government as a social monstrosity. 'It is seriously endangering the integrity of the very existence of our people. Why, the corresponding figure in England would be 5,600,000. Had that happened there would have been a nice outcry,' Gibb said. [23]

Thomson focused much of his attention on the events of the 1920s. Firstly, he was able to research and accumulate available and important statistical data from the decade which ensured that he had a sound evidence base for his main narrative on the depth of Scotland's economic crisis; and secondly, to emphasise that Scotland as 'the distressed nation' was not a product of the depression. The events of the early 1930s may have added to the difficulties, but the decline of the country's industrial base and economic wealth had its origins in the first decade of the twentieth century, the increases in output and activity during World War I merely a pause in that decline.

To support this view Thomson reached for the national income figures in the returns of the Commissioners of the Inland Revenue. These showed graphically that whereas in 1906-07 Scotland's net Exchequer receipts from all revenue duties were 17 per cent of those of England, by 1914-15 they had fallen to 11 per cent of the English total. In 1922-23 it was 8.8 per cent, roughly speaking a twelfth. Five years later, in 1927-28, after a steady process of decline it was seven per cent. Four years after that, in 1931-32, it was six per cent. Thomson found these figures 'quite remarkable': had the Exchequer drawn from Scotland what might have been due on the basis of her population in 1931-32 the Scottish contribution would have been 12 per cent, not the actual six per cent.

Thomson also measured Scotland's national wealth by looking at the portion of income paid in direct taxation finding more evidence of national economic decline, and again a decline with its origins pre-dating the post war period. At the beginning of the century the tax on national incomes in Scotland produced one-eighth of the total raised in England, but by 1929 this had fallen to only one-twelfth. [24]

Table 2 Net Income Tax Receipts 1900-1929			
Period	England & Wales	Scotland	Scottish receipts as a % of English
1900-01	£23,772	£2,839	11.9%
1914-15	£52,057	£5,797	11%
1919	£278,739	£30,396	10.9%
1924	£251,766	£21,315	8.5%
1929	£218,851	£17,282	7.9%

Source: Thomson, *Distressed*, p 31

Thomson's interpretation of these figures was that at the beginning of the century Scotland was as rich a country as England, but in the year before the depression started Scotland was only two-thirds as rich as England; her national income had fallen by one-third. 'This without any help from the crisis, slump, or sudden depression, but as the result of a long and steady decline of the ratio which, in fact, had begun before the War,' he said.

Thomson's book, brimful with statistical data from several disciplines, illustrated in stark detail Scotland's economic deterioration. It was consistent in the style and language of its assertions and analysis with Thomson's polemical writing of the late 1920s and early 1930s. Scottish industrial production and output was weak and its failure to secure a foot-hold in the new light consumer industries had left her at a disadvantage, again, not only with England, but with other west European countries of similar size. He concluded that if it was true that England goes up and up, 'it is equally true that Scotland goes down and down'. Scotland, he suggested, was suffering from a wasting economic ailment, one peculiar to herself among European industrial countries and that her power to make goods and to support her population had dwindled while that of her neighbours increased. [25]

It was a verdict confirmed within months by the Clydesdale Bank's economic survey which reported that between 1924 and 1929 the slump in Scotland 'was much heavier than that of the United Kingdom'. What was of greater concern to the survey was that the level of business activity in 1935-36 was only marginally above that achieved in 1924. Scottish industrial and business leaders continued to concentrate their efforts on the production of coal, iron, steel, ships, heavy engineering and textiles, products which struggled to find heavy capital investment and to maintain high levels of international trade. What was implicit in the bank's review was that the country's leaders had failed to recognise, respond and invest in new light industries to meet the consumer demands of a new market place. [26]

They had reacted to the difficulties in heavy industries with a series of rationalisations, relocations, integrations and mergers. Thomson attacked them for the 'gloomy eloquence' they had employed to warn the Scottish people that disasters would follow if they followed demands for home rule, arguing that they were in no position to pass judgement and condemn others. 'They are not in a lofty, unassailable position,' he said. 'They are not the accusers but the accused, they have no prerogative of wisdom or common sense, they have a record of failure and decline.' They should, he said, be summoned to give an account of their steward-ship, 'to explain, how and why, under their guidance, the welfare of their country has been so gravely and uniquely damaged'. [27]

The historian William Ferguson later applauded Thomson's words and his choice of targets, men such as the ship-owners Sir James Lithgow and Lord Maclay, describing them as the 'pontificating captains of industry' who had failed to deliver the streamlining the economy required. 'When every allowance is made for the grave difficulties of these years, Scottish entrepreneurs showed remarkably little initiative. Their main concern seems to have been to shuffle the blame onto their grand-fathers.' [28]

The charge against them was rejected by Scottish business leaders who criticised books, articles and speeches all focused negatively on the theme of 'What's Wrong With Scotland?' and which made gloomy forecasts about the country's economic future. On the eve of the 1938 Empire Exhibition in Glasgow – itself an attempt to showcase modern Scottish industry – under the banner of the Scottish Development Council, upon which many of them sat, the businessmen and industrialists produced a 300 page survey which heralded a range of new developments and projects underway across Scotland. [29] The Earl of Elgin, Scotland's leading nobleman and president of the Council, maintained that Scottish business was in good shape, enterprise was not dead, there was significant progress and development, 'a splendid corrective,' he said, 'to despondent and passive pessimism'. [30]

However, in the wake of the Empire Exhibition the Dundee economist, James Bowie, analysed the Development Council's published statistics and concluded that they revealed the extent of Scotland's failure to develop newer industries and a manufacturing rate floundering behind that of Britain as a whole. Bowie's book, *The Future of Scotland* (1939), was a unique and comprehensive analysis of the decline of the Scottish economy between the wars from an economist who had built a reputation for his radical and progressive ideas, supporting a Scottish Development Commission, regional economic planning, state sponsored institutions, new towns, and the relocation of industries to distressed areas. [31]

Table 3 Comparative Figures of Scottish Employment in Consumer Industries

Industry	No. employed England	No. employed Scotland	Scotland as % of England
Motor vehicles	250,000	11,000	4.4%
Cycles, aircraft	130,000	1,000	0.77%
Electrics, cables	108,000	4,500	4.1%
Music, intruments	19,000	150	0.08%
Total	507,000	16,650	3.04%

Source: Economic Series, No. 8. Report of Scottish Development Council Committee on Manufacture in Scotland of Articles of Common Household Use (1933), Quoted in Bowie, Future of Scotland, p. 160

Thomson's criticisms in *Distressed* were corroborated by Bowie who struck a polemic note describing a body of men on top of the social pyramid who were 'apparently too rich to think'. It had become, he said, the social fashion for the younger generation of industrial and business dynasties to turn their backs on economic affairs and retire to the backwoods. 'The class of men whose grandfathers were the entrepreneurs of Scottish industry seem too often to have demitted their function and given up the struggle. They tend to claim the privileges but not to acknowledge the obligations of their position. Yet the wealth they enjoy was made by creating the townships of today, and it is their elementary duty to take a full share in solving the problems created by the ingathering of that wealth,' Bowie said.

However it was not only Bowie's validation of his critical assessment of the performance of industrialists and business leaders that would have caused Thomson a sense of justification. Bowie spared no class or part of the Scottish population for the failures and missed opportunities; he courageously connected his economic assessments directly to the character and spirit of his fellow countrymen, reaching conclusions that not only mirrored many of Thomson's views in *Distressed* but also echoed controversial opinions from a decade earlier which had brought down disrepute on Thomson's reputation. He described it as 'disturbing' that the spectacle of thousands of Scots suffering from unemployment had failed to stir the rest of the community, instead it had adopted a defeatist and complacent attitude to those faced with misery and poverty. 'It has stimulated no crusade. Perhaps this is not so surprising in the light of our deil-tak-the-hindmost tradition'. He recognised that at one end of the social scale unemployed slum dwellers continued to live in grossly overcrowded conditions and were 'too absorbed in the immediate struggle for bread to have any long term interests'. But he also found it disappointing that despite mass unemployment no 'great leader' had emerged from the working class with a comprehensive plan for a new modern Scotland, 'in which they could look forward to a significant place'. This represented, he said, 'the limp attitude of the unemployed themselves' whereas he would have expected that those who suffer most, and profit most from a solution, might have produced some ideas. 'But it may be that I am unfair and that unemployment atrophies the mind even more than it does the body.' [32]

The sense that Scotland's poor and unemployed had accepted their fate with a mixture of defeatism and complacency was also highlighted in an unsympathetic tone by George Blake who suggested that it displayed a lack of character and fortitude. 'The forces often appear to have been too much for them,' Blake said. 'Largely huddled into drab industrial towns, they find it sufficient satisfaction to delight in the loveliness of the country round about them, blind to the economic ugliness that its empty and deliberately uncultivated condition represents.' Blake surmised that the unemployed had taken refuge in popular pastimes such as music and cinema. 'They sit, curiously complacent, amid the ruins of their own civilisation. It has not dawned on them yet that they may shortly be squatting amid the ruins of that industrial civilisation,' was Blake's gloomy conclusion. [33]

Bowie and Blake in their separate observation and analysis had identified in the heart of the poorer sections of Scottish society no recognition that there was a peculiarly Scottish dimension to the economic events and consequences which dominated their lives and with it, their opportunities. If there was a 'consciousness' of their Scottishness it did not relate to economic factors in the present, only to images from the past.

One man who did sense an awareness of Scottishness across Scottish society was the Secretary of State, Walter Elliot, who warned his cabinet colleagues that the problems affecting Scottish economic and social conditions were real and insistent. 'Opinion in all parts of Scotland is becoming more and more concerned at their gravity.' His message in 1937 was that the 'disparity' between English and Scottish conditions had continued to increase, and that the Scots were aware of it. 'It is a consciousness of their existence which is reflected in the dissatisfaction and uneasiness amongst moderate and reasonable people of every view or rank.' What is particularly telling about Elliot's intervention – even allowing for the fact that his pessimism was confined to an internal Scottish Office memorandum – is that he acknowledged that that dissatisfaction he had found after a year's survey of Scottish affairs confirmed the views 'expressed in every book published about Scotland now for several years'. [34]

The condition of Scotland genre created and nurtured by Thomson established his Scottish reputation. A decade after *Caledonia* was published a newspaper article promoting the opening of a Thomson play referred to him, not as a journalist, broadcaster, commentator or even playwright but as the author of the books on the condition of Scotland. [35] It was the condition of Scotland question which emerged in the late 1920s to dominate contemporary economic, political, social and cultural debates about Scotland's future. Thomson has the rare distinction of being vilified twice by history; in his own time for the contempt and scorn he displayed towards his fellow countrymen, and later for his unrelenting attacks on Scotland's Irish Catholic population.

Thomson's initial optimism and enthusiasm for a cultural led national re-awakening in the years following World War I gave way to the bitter disillusionment reflected in *Caledonia*, which remained the dominant theme of his subsequent books, pamphlets and commentaries. In Thomson's view the events of the 1920s, economic and industrial decline, large-scale unemployment, mass emigration and social inequalities, were the defining issues for Scottish society. Wherever he looked he found a country in denial. His personal exposure to the slums reinforced his negative and pessimistic view of his native country. Thomson believed that his fellow Scots had chosen to accept their fate; he saw defeatism and complacency and a nation too easily embracing a culture of dependency. *Caledonia* was Thomson's open letter to a country which he accused of being second rate.

CHAPTER 6

Response to the Condition of Scotland: the intellectuals

> The decade 1930-40 will see criticism crystallising out along definite constructive lines and a heaping up of emotion and conviction on our side. We are winning over the young because we have a young man's honesty and ruthlessness and imagination. Our enemies are all old, a lot of them will die in the next ten years. [1]
>
> George Malcolm Thomson, 1930

THESE ARE THE WORDS reflecting George Malcolm Thomson's optimism in January 1930, welcoming the new decade in a mood of expectancy, anticipating the future with a combination of prediction and certainty. His critical and constructive analysis of the condition of Scotland will soon reap rewards, he believed, as a Scottish 'resurgence' is bound to come, 'these things grow like snowballs'. The decade now past, 1920-30, can be summed as one that saw the emergence of a 'new uneasiness' and 'a new criticism', one that steadily gained momentum and progression. [2]

Sitting at his desk in his Hampstead home Thomson, now aged 30 exuded confidence. Out of the bleak years of decline he foresaw a spiritual and political re-awakening led by young Scots amidst revived feelings of nationhood. In the years that follow, Thomson's pen continued its relentless review of the Scottish condition but increasingly it was directed at a political and cultural response to the difficulties, even as his own professional career as a journalist took off and the slump of the 1920s was followed by the depression of the early 1930s.

In a short period of time in the interwar years Scottish intellectuals, commentators and creative writers were the siren voices of propaganda for both political and cultural nationalism. Whatever their varied political leanings outwith nationalism they were well-meaning, proud and largely angry Scots who wrote and spoke about Scotland as they found it in their own time. They crossed political boundaries. The interaction between commentators was never confined to the nationalist-unionists. It involved left wing or radical forces, poets and authors, intellectuals and activists within the National Party of Scotland. Their writings and activities provide us with an important snapshot of political, social and identity history within the interwar period. The fact of their personal social and political intercourse illustrates the limitations in terms of size of intellectual discourse in Scotland at the time, even when padded out with the contributions of writers based or domiciled in London. Conversely it represents evidence of the concern for Scotland from those who supported the nationalist movement and also those, such as Edwin Muir and Lewis Grassic Gibbon, who wrote about Scotland from a non-nationalist point of view.

At the heart of much of this is the Machiavellian persona of Thomson whose considerable correspondence reveals the extent of the interactions between other writers and intellectuals. He himself developed relationships and friendships with Andrew Dewar Gibb, George Blake, the journalist and author William Power, Neil Gunn, and a key alliance with John MacCormick, the secretary of the NPS and later the SNP. He had professional connections and friendships as a broadcaster with David Cleghorn Thomson, the first Scottish Regional Director of the BBC and his deputy Moray McLaren. He had occasional and inevitably difficult relationships with radical nationalists such as Christopher Grieve (Hugh MacDiarmid) and the author Compton Mackenzie. He was a friend of R.D. Anderson, the editor-in-chief of the *Daily Record* and in the early 1930s Thomson advised and briefed Beaverbrook on Scottish affairs.

On a number of the major social concerns of the day, notably the Irish Catholic issue, Thomson and Gibb, were misguided and wrong, and their reputations have suffered in consequence. In casting nationalism or home rule as the only response to the condition of Scotland they were overly optimistic. Their expectations were never likely to be met. To sections of both the establishment and popular Scotland they appeared as elitist romanticists out of touch with the class politics of the time and naive to believe that emotional appeals to Scottishness could act as a lightning rod and spark a political and social earthquake, and lead to the renewal of the two centuries old union settlement between Scotland and England. They did succeed in helping to ignite a reaction and then a response from the political establishment and they played an important part and were influential in the creation of the modern SNP. But their self-appointed roles as propagandists made little impression on political and cultural identities of the mass of interwar Scots.

William Power sensed and admitted this failure when he described himself as 'rootedly middle-class'. He had never been a labourer, miner, stoker, deck hand or mill operator. He had never lived in a 'Model', an overcrowded house, in a slummy district, or stood in a queue at a Labour Exchange. Of the Scottish working class Power wrote: 'When I notice the *camaraderie* among them. . . I feel awkwardly "out of it", lacking the right to speak for the majority of the Scottish people.' [3]

George Blake was referring to *The Shipbuilders* when in 1956, looking back, he also admitted to little knowledge of working class life and to adopting middle-class attitudes towards industrial conflict and despair.[4] MacDiarmid, at the time, disagreed. Power's confession enraged Mac-Diarmid who saw it as a disability, but one Power shared with the majority of contemporary Scottish writers, presumably a list that included Blake. 'They have left unknown the only thing worth knowing and it completely invalidates their work,' he said. [5]

Even if tinged with a hint of hypocrisy, MacDiarmid, like Power and Blake, recognised the dilemma of intellectuals – of all political complexions – who assume the mantle of speaking for a nation, for its consciousness, its identity, and its condition. Ultimately all intellectuals are self-appointed and, whether welcomed or not, between the wars the writers and commentators articulated a voice of Scottish identity and gave expression and meaning to it. What they had in common was, as Colin Walkinshaw described it, 'unanimity of patriotism', even if they appeared as the not particularly imposing intellectual leaders of 'an apparently dying people'. Walkinshaw believed, optimistically, that such a collection of similar voices should count for something.

'Almost every influence, political and economic, seems to forbid Scotland's survival,' he said. 'There is only one thing, perhaps, which could make it possible. That intense fervour of spirit which thrice in the past has roused Scotsmen to ignore impossibilities is perhaps not dead. Our generation must see either the end of Scotland or a new beginning.'[6]

Intellectuals Campaign for Home Rule

On 1 August 1930 Thomson sat down at his desk in Hampstead and wrote an angry letter and sent it to an address in Musselburgh, the home of the nationalist activist, George Dott. The letter was Thomson's response to a personal rebuke from Dott at his refusal to join the National Party of Scotland and for criticising it despite publicly professing nationalist sympathies.

'When are you going to do something?' Dott had demanded.

Dott, Thomson railed, did not understand his role as a propagandist for home rule, 'as a journalist, critic, publicist, and idea merchant.' The advantage of this approach was that 'the propaganda is concealed', and that he, an independent outsider without a party stigma attached to him, 'can insinuate propaganda where party men cannot.' In his books, pamphlets, articles and broadcasts Thomson maintained his relentless onslaughts on the failures of the Scottish economy, the shortcomings of the native Scots, and the threat to their racial purity from Irish Catholic immigrants. His private strategy to deal with the condition of Scotland and to promote home rule was as a propagandist, a self-appointed role he argued and justified in his correspondence with Dott. He was, he insisted, unsuited to be a popular leader, an orator, or an organiser, but eminently skilled to run a propaganda campaign for home rule. [7]

Thomson was convinced of the power of propaganda to change attitudes and beliefs, a conviction he shared with Beaverbrook, who within a few years would become the most influential person on

Thomson's professional life and career path. Beaverbrook later admitted to a Royal Commission on the press that he ran his newspapers 'purely for propaganda and with no other purpose'.[8] In Thomson's writings Beaverbrook recognised a writer and commentator of ability but also, crucially, someone with an understanding and intent to use strong, controversial, emotional and convincing language for propaganda purposes. Towards the end of World War I the Prime Minister, David Lloyd George, had put Beaverbrook in charge of propaganda as Britain's first Minister of Information. He was told that Beaverbrook was 'bitten with it, knows it'. [9]

Thomson in the late 1920s, aware of the impact and achievements of propaganda during the war, would have noted how following the war it was increasingly used by the burgeoning advertising and marketing industries, and more particularly, from his personal perspective and objective, for political purposes.

In his embracing of propaganda Thomson subscribed to the theory of the contemporary American political scientist Harold D. Lasswell who claimed that while the spread of accepted attitudes and skills was education, 'the spread of controversial attitudes was propaganda'. [10] In Lasswell's view propaganda was about persuasion and the use of modern communications to engineer public opinion and consent; it was the task of the propagandist to determine how he might 'put over' his solution to alter attitudes. Lasswell believed that the strategy of propaganda was to present the objective in such a manner that attitudes will be swayed toward it. 'The problem of the propagandist,' he said, 'is to intensify the attitudes favourable to his purpose, to reverse the attitudes hostile to it, and to attract the indifferent, or, at the worst, to prevent them from assuming a hostile bent.' [11] Thomson's intellectual justification for his propagandist approach also mirrored that of another American, the journalist Walter Lippmann who had an elitist concept that in any society only a small select group in the intellectual community could really understand the common interests that 'elude public opinion entirely'. The new techniques of propaganda, Lippmann maintained, should be used to 'manufacture consent' but managed by a 'specialised class of responsible men who are smart enough to figure things out.' [12]

Thomson believed he was smart enough but also that there were others who were not and who failed to understand propaganda or the opportunities it presented. He was contemptuous and dismissive of the failure of nationalist groups and parties in Scotland to develop and devise propaganda strategies and programmes to carry their message to the Scottish people. Thomson regarded the NPS and its leaders as amateurs who had neither the knowledge nor the skills to utilise modern political propaganda techniques.

Thomson's two major polemics, *Caledonia* and *Re-Discovery*, were deliberately and unashamedly written to be controversial, to incite feelings of anger and outrage and to stimulate debate. He believed that the extent of the difficulties was not the subject of serious public discourse, that the truth was submerged by the political and business establishment. Thomson, the journalist, also believed that a gap of understanding had been created by the failure of the mainstream Scottish press to report the harsh realities and consequences of economic decline and to present and put them before the Scottish people. He regarded *Caledonia* and *Re-Discovery* as the beginning of serious criticism and contemporary polemical writing in Scotland, 'no one else having found the time to do so'. And his *Short History* was, he stated modestly, 'the first nationalist history of Scotland'. He claimed that his personal research library of Scottish cuttings was unique, without it his propaganda would be as ineffectual as that of the NPS.

'I have written more propaganda articles for Scotland than any other living soul. Many of them have the advantage that their propaganda is concealed. Each of them reaches an audience ranging from 10,000 to 100,000. What nationalist figure speaks to crowds of that size?' Thomson asked. [13]

However, Thomson's admonishment of Dott and his boastfulness of the impact of his propaganda on behalf of nationalism hid the contra-dictions, inconsistencies and the hypocrisies associated with his commitment to, and involvement with, the nationalist movement in the late 1920s, and in the early months of 1930. The established historical view is that Thomson was in favour of home rule and was opposed to separation, favouring a legislature for domestic Scottish affairs in Edinburgh, constructed within a new union arrangement with England. Thomson, alongside Gibb, worked assiduously behind the scenes in the early 1930s to advance a unionist case for home rule and to curtail the demands of radical nationalism. However Thomson's earlier writings, speeches and letters demonstrate that his support for home rule was not long-standing and that even as he voiced sympathies for nationalism he retained misgivings, initially harbouring doubts about the value of home rule itself.

In *Re-Discovery*, published in 1928, the same year that the NPS was founded, Thomson shows no great personal enthusiasm for nationalism or home rule. He displays a typical unionist middle-class cynical disregard and contempt for the movement even as he appears to acknowledge that the *status quo* is unacceptable and that some form of change is necessary. He mocks the 'simple faith' of home rulers who, he believes, correctly diagnose that something is wrong 'somewhere' but are vague in explaining what the solution might be. 'The bewildered observer [. . .] finds it somewhat difficult to imitate their exuberant bounds from premise to conclusion,' Thomson says.

At this point in the evolution of interwar nationalism Thomson has not cast himself inside the home rule camp, the narrative of his polemical writing mirroring similar doubts expressed in his private letters. He appears a classic case of a commentator or potential politician sitting on the fence. On one hand a demand for self-government might be a symptom of returning political honesty in Scotland, on the other it would be wrong to indulge in fancy speculation about home rule: 'The bombardment of castles in the air with toy balloons is a form of mimic warfare which should not be allowed to stray from the nursery into the arena,' he writes.

What appears to be drawing Thomson, slowly, towards political nationalism, or at least to home rule, is a more hard-nosed analysis that Scotland would be forced to stand on her own feet or fall by her exertions, and that if she had no one to blame and had to accept responsibility for her own decisions, these would be positive consequences of home rule.

'It would make life a serious and stormy affair for several generations of Scotsmen, it would wipe the self-complacent grin from their faces, but it would do their souls good. And it may be argued that even if they failed in the huge task that confronted them, as they might well do, death on the operating table is preferable to the prolonged pangs of a criminal self-neglect.' [14]

Thomson's sympathies are laden with negative feelings about political nationalism, of a confused and gloomy mindset confirmed as late as March 1930 when – as he did in his letters to Dott – he attempted to explain and justify to Neil Gunn the reasons behind his 'failure to become a nationalist'. He told Gunn that he had a temperamental dislike of politics, 'a belief that they invariably and inevitably distort and over-simplify and vulgarise. A hatred for the sort of man they bring to the top.' He maintained that the Scots needed something different than political treatment for the country's problems. The Scots needed to rediscover the soul of the nation, something Thomson regarded as lost. 'You can't buy souls in the political market place.'

'A parliament, as things are, would perpetuate our provincialism, or at best would not advance things one jot,' he said. He worried that self-government might be premature but recognised the paradox of doing nothing. 'No body without a soul, but, also, no soul without a body. Which came first: the hen or the egg?' he asked. Again on the one hand Thomson thought a Parliament might help, 'a little'; on the other 'it might have grave disadvantages'. Thomson brooded whether it was possible for Scotland to be a nation with its own national culture without being a separate sovereign state, revealing not only his continuing disquiet about Anglicisation but his personal conflict between loyalty to the union and his passion for cultural and identity renewal, the constant dilemma at the heart of his nationalism.

Economic and social decline and political nationalism may have interrupted Thomson's cultural nationalism but it remains one of his intellectual priorities. Despite his anger and pessimistic prophecies about the future Thomson maintains a lingering hope that a cultural and intellectual renaissance might renew the nation's spirit, that artists and scholars could do more for Scotland by doing their job well than by making their art consciously serve propaganda or a programme. 'Art,' he wrote, 'should have for its creed the soul of the artist, anything else is prostitution.'

Here Thomson serves up another inconsistency. To Dott, the activist, he boasts about his contribution to the nationalist cause through employing his skills as a propagandist; but to Gunn, the writer and intellectual, he suggests that intellectuals who use their 'art' for propaganda purposes are prostituting themselves. Thomson is employing double standards, an apparent dictum that the creative writers of the renaissance should stick to prose and poetry and stay away from political involvement, whereas he, journalist and polemicist, was free to propagandise at will.

The intellectual in Thomson's sight was Grieve (Hugh MacDiarmid) who he praised for the 'immense' service he had done Scotland by writing his 'splendid' poems, far more effective, Thomson believed, than his political campaigning for the NPS. 'He has done more than anyone else to put Scotland on the map and to re-create a healthy life of the Scottish spirit by being such a fastidious and honourable poet. It would have had the same effect if his poems hadn't breathed word of nationalism.'

Thomson does not lack courage. He is effectively suggesting to Gunn, one of the leading intellectuals in the NPS, that the writers and poets of the literary revival should carry their message through their work and not by direct association with the nationalist movement. What Thomson does not state at this point, but which becomes evident later, that MacDiarmid and other writers resolved to take the NPS in the radical direction of separation, is at the heart of Thomson's opposition to them. But, despite his distrust of the MacDiarmid faction, the country, he insists, needs the NPS. 'Yet damn it, there ought to be a national party. Our grandchildren may need it,' he assures Gunn. [15]

Here again another conundrum of Thomson's nationalism; his recognition, if reluctantly, that there must be some form of home rule with a defined political structure; but desperate to believe that Scotland's salvation might still be achieved through the pens of Grieve and others.

Significantly when Thomson was asked to deliver the opening broadcast of a ground-breaking Scottish radio series on the Condition of Scotland he rejected the obvious economic and social issues and chose as his theme the cultural and intellectual deficit of Scottish life.

The series, *What's Wrong with Scotland?* developed by David Cleghorn Thomson, the BBC Scottish Regional Director introduced a new dimension to the discussion of potentially controversial issues on air. It was an initiative not without risk. In what were still the formative years of broadcasting there were ongoing difficulties surrounding the broadcasting of political speeches and Cleghorn Thomson included six politicians among those who would give talks. Malcolm Thomson's critical commentaries on the condition of Scotland had particularly outraged parts of business and political Scotland but despite or perhaps because of it, Cleghorn Thomson (no relation) bravely invited his namesake to launch the *What's Wrong with Scotland* series with the first talk broadcast live from Edinburgh on the Saturday evening prime slot at 7pm in October 1929.

At the time approximately 240,000 wireless licences had been issued in Scotland providing Thomson with an audience whose profile primarily represented the upper and middle class profile of elite, civic, and professional Scotland. [16] However if the listeners had anticipated that Thomson would use this platform as an opportunity to reprise the economic and social invective of his books they were either pleased or disappointed when he chose to focus on cultural, intellectual and spiritual Scotland. Thomson, with a mixture of mischievousness and propagandist skills, provocatively titled his talk 'If I Were Dictator of Scotland', a role from which he intended to reform Scottish society and recreate Edinburgh, once again, as a great capital, a centre of enlightenment in the arts, literature and thinking. [17]

It is in this twenty minute broadcast that we find the essence of Thomson's sense of Scottishness, the cultural and spiritual basis and bias of his nationalism, the vision, almost, of an intellectual dreamer who aspires to put his native country on a plateau high above the lower place where, he believed, it currently resided. Scottish civic life, he said, was second-rate and second-hand, there was a lack of thinking, debate and initiative; thoughts and ideas percolated into Scotland from elsewhere. 'This seems to me the very gravest hiatus in our national existence,' he said. 'What ground have we for calling ourselves a nation if we do not possess a national life of the intellect, if our so-called capital is only a kind of faded legal centre, a pettifoggers' capital?'

Scotland, he suggested, needed more than a mere legislative body based in Edinburgh: 'What this country of ours lacks is a social centre, the nucleus of a society, a set of people whose chief function would be to guard its standards of value, to measure its cultural productivity and, in short, to keep it up to spiritual scratch. These people would not merely read more books and read them with a nicer judgement than the rest of us, they would also do a good deal of our thinking and discussing and initiating. At present we have no such nucleus in Scotland.'

Thomson's solution to this intellectual deficit, 'a first step towards the revival of the national spirit', was the appointment of a Viceroy who would be the permanent and recognised leader of Scotland's social life. His model for a Viceroy was, perhaps surprisingly, Ireland, which he reminded his listeners had a Viceroy long before it had a parliament, 'and, as a result Dublin never ceased to be a capital in the truest sense of the word.'

Thomson's Viceroy would give legitimacy to the nation's cultural activities, be an official cachet to cultural manifestations in Scotland, opening art exhibitions, attending first nights of new plays. 'It would have considerable publicity value, anybody can see that. But it would also bridge that deplorable gap which exists at present between Scottish government and Scottish life.'

And Thomson's *pièce de résistance*, the crowning act of his new cultural policy would be the institution of a great national festival of the arts in Edinburgh, 'attended by delegates not only from all parts of Scotland, but also from societies all over the world.' Such a festival would make Edinburgh not only the capital of Scotland but of the Scots 'in the fullest, highest sense'. Thomson's intellectual and cultural ambition envisaged a substantial prize for the most important work of literature published by a Scotsman, a week of performances of Scottish plays, exhibitions of pictures by modern Scottish artists, 'of a wider and more daring scope than the annual Royal Academies'. There would be concerts at which internationally renowned Scottish artists would perform with awards for original compositions. In the second half of the century Thomson would have been entitled to an amused smile about his words and vision of 1929 as he made occasional visits north from his London home to attend the Edinburgh International Arts Festival.

Thomson's fixation on Edinburgh and his plea for its prime role at the heart of his cultural and intellectual model – his dream of its rebirth as the city he imagined it was in the late eighteenth century enlighten-ment years – was hardly surprising. But as with so many other issues in Thomson's thinking it came bundled with contradiction. Although his birthplace, Leith, had always regarded itself as a separate entity and had cherished its status as an independent burgh until 1920, Thomson throughout his life, even when he spent most of it as an adopted Londoner, continued to refer to Edinburgh as his native city. But in the 1920s and 1930s it was always a strained relationship.

Thomson developed a sense of almost hopeless frustration about the city accusing it at one point of lacking the ambition to be a real capital city, unable to adopt any form of metropolitan ethos. Instead, he said, it preferred to hide beneath a veneer of superior respectability, choosing to be more like Bath and Cheltenham than London, 'a place for maiden aunts to live in'. He likened it to a crownless mummy set among a throne of hills, [. . .] eyes glazed, cheek bones projecting sharply through brown, dead skin, and on her head, the hair long gone, sat a wig. Edinburgh faced the doubting world with chilly arrogance. [. . .] 'Meanwhile, round her feet, there frolics awkwardly the slightly shame-faced, slightly vulgar, rather pathetic creature that is the real Edinburgh.' Society, such as it was, operated like the parlour of a decayed boarding house while posturing as a fashionable drawing room. [. . .] 'It is a city of pretensions but no pride; of crowded tea-shops and empty art galleries; [. . .] a city where an epigram is feared like a civil commotion and a work of art would be regarded with the suspicion due to a novel and unclassified crime; it is not a city of lost causes, for it is itself a lost cause,' was Thomson's damning verdict. [18] His interwar demolition of Edinburgh and its ingrained conservatism and mediocrity did not, however, prevent him from defending its honour when the occasion arose, particularly if the critical voices emanated from the west of Scotland.

In a BBC broadcast debate *Edinburgh versus Glasgow* Thomson, oblivious to any apparent contradictions with his previous pronouncements about the city, maintained that every nation got the capital it deserved and in having Edinburgh Scotland was getting a little more than it deserved. George Blake, defending Glasgow, contrasted the atmosphere of Edinburgh with the heartiness of Glasgow; a city he claimed was the real capital of Scotland not only in business but in arts and politics. And, in words which undoubtedly should have resonated with Thomson, Blake complained of the chilliness and conservatism of Edinburgh, of the fractured structure of the city's society. But, apparently, it was one thing for a native to say such things. The difference between the cities, Thomson declared, was that Glasgow stood or fell as a commercial city; once its commerce went, Glasgow was done for. It had no school of literature or drama, and if there had been one it would have been provincial. The debate chairman, Dr. J.M. Bulloch, observed that Glasgow and Edinburgh appeared to be complementary, 'though certainly they were not very complimentary to each other'. [19]

However, Thomson's personal confusion regarding the worthiness of Edinburgh as a capital city persisted. When, along with his fellow nationalist Gibb, he campaigned to bring the 1932 World Disarmament Conference to the city he conceded that some might have the 'bad taste' to suggest that Edinburgh was not a capital city. Thomson's response was that Edinburgh, at least, was a 'has been' capital and in any case conferences had been arranged in other 'provincial' cities such as Locarno, Genoa, and Geneva. [20]

Whether he is praising or damning it Edinburgh is pivotal to Thomson's home rule ambitions. Having dispelled previous doubts about the value of a parliament in Edinburgh he sees it not merely as a legislator for domestic affairs but more importantly from his personal ambition as the stimulus for Edinburgh to emerge as the beating heart spreading a renewed cultural and intellectual spirit across the nation, the dream embodied in his *What's Wrong with Scotland?* broadcast. Yet with the dream there was also a practical calculation that although unionist Scotland, at least then, had little sympathy for nationalism in any guise, it did care about the separateness of Scotland's national identity and culture. Thomson was convinced that beneath the surface unionist Scotland shared his fears and concerns. He finally committed himself to the home rule movement with the clear objective of targeting the conservative unionists in Scotland's elite, professional and middle classes.

The Secret League of Intellectuals

Thomson's home rule strategy had two main objectives, the first to persuade unionist Scotland that there was a good case for home rule, one that could be achieved within the union and the empire; the second to infiltrate the NPS and dilute its stated aim of Scottish independence and replace it with a policy of measured home rule. Thomson gave his cause a name, 'nationalism for Tories – that's our gospel – a synthesis of Toryism (real Toryism) and nationalism'. [21]

Thomson used both 'Tory' and 'unionist' as terms to link with 'nationalist' – he refers to Gibb as a 'Unionist-Nat' – although he would have known that in Scotland the Tories had effectively banned the official use of both 'Tory' and 'Conservative', preferring to be known as the Scottish 'Unionist' Party. Following their defeat in the 1929 General Election the Scottish unionists declared that the use of the word 'Conservative' was 'injurious to the interests of the Party', whereas the term 'Unionist' better expressed their passionate beliefs. The annual conference agreed to ban the use of 'Conservative' in speeches and writings, 'the term "Unionist", which is the correct and official designation in Scotland, be always used'. [22]

The unionism that the Scottish 'unionists' were 'passionate' about in relation to the historical 'union' between Scotland and England, was no more than a flag of convenience. Its political significance was more recent, referring to unionists who ensured that Ulster remained part of the United Kingdom and separate from the Irish Free State. Following the signing of the final agreement of the Northern Ireland boundary in 1925 the party in England took the view that the name 'unionist' was outdated and returned to the official use of 'Conservative'. Conservative Scotland would remain unionist for another thirty years, and with the exception of the 1945 General Election, it was a home grown policy that delivered political success, not least because of the unofficial association between unionism and Protestantism.

For Thomson the terms were interchangeable and consistent. Toryism and unionism represented the post-World War I consensus between traditional, moderate but progressive Conservatism and the best elements of Liberal Unionism, but also, crucially in Thomson's view, the party of the Empire and the Anglo-Scottish Union. The Glasgow academics Rait and Pryde argued that conservatism made Scottish unionism stronger, better able to resist the radicalism of both socialist and separatist movements, and was 'striving for security and stability, especially in the financial sphere'. Thomson was by background and instinct unionist and imperialist but now believed that in Scotland moderate progressive unionism required an injection of moderate home rule nationalism. [23]

To achieve his objective, for the propaganda to be effective, Thomson decided to recruit a group of like-minded unionist home-rulers, all of whom, like him, could act as propagandists. He confided to Dott that this work was already underway. 'The secret league of intellectuals is in being and grows more coherent every week,' he declared.[24] Another description he gave his group was the 'secret league of the friends of Scotland', the use of the word 'secret' signifying that it should not advertise its existence. 'It should consist of opinion formers, men who as journalists, teachers, writers, lecturers and so forth can shape the national view, and that it should have some common body of doctrine.' Those who became part of the group should be people in positions of influence, power or authority, from where they could find additional converts. His belief was that sooner or later the idea or the message would have an effect and people would begin to talk about it, 'it enters subtly into the mental make-up of the time; and in the end someone acts'. [25]

He remained ambitious in his recruitment policies, spreading his net from Scotland to London. He advised Gibb, Dott and Gunn that he had successfully converted the renowned English travel writer H.V. Morton to the nationalist cause. 'In my humble way I do what I can,' he said to Gunn. 'I go for what I call "key men" – journalists, authors and the like. My bag is one a week.'[26] He told Dott that he sometimes had the opportunity to make a conversion to nationalism, 'My last victim was H.V. Morton of the *Express.*'

Thomson had approached Morton, a columnist on the *London Daily Express*, following the publication of Morton's classic travel and guide book, *In Search of Scotland* (1929) in which he had written movingly about his passion for Scotland and particularly the Scottish National War Memorial at Edinburgh Castle. 'There is nothing like it in the world: it is the soul of Scotland,' Morton wrote. He contrasted it favourably against the Cenotaph in London: 'One Saxon and inarticulate; the other Celtic and articulate. Grief locks the English heart, but it opens the Scottish. Scotland's Shrine is a requiem and a hymn of praise with more pride and less regret than any other war memorial. Scotland has built the greatest war memorial in the world.' [27]

However while Morton was apparently happy to restate his love of Scotland and lend his personal support to the home rule cause it remained a silent bond between friends. 'Did I tell you I converted H.V. Morton to the new faith?' he wrote to Gibb. 'Alas, he was unable to commit to a public confession.' [28]

Thomson was keen to find a dozen men who would make gestures of support for home rule, 'names the public has at least vaguely heard of,' one of whom was the Duke of Montrose, son of the Marquis of Bute. 'He is said to be shivering on the brink,' he wrote. He also claimed that the highly respected biologist, sociologist and philanthropist, Patrick Geddes, had asked to meet with him. 'He will, I hope, fall a willing victim.' Geddes, he told Dott, was representative of men who were able to make converts of their own. [29]

He asked Neil Gunn if he would care 'in a friendly, casual way' to sound out the well-known Scottish playwright James Bridie about his general attitude to nationalism. 'I should be interested if you were able to divulge to me in private the result of such an approach.' [30] In addition to their mutual interest in publishing and nationalism Gunn came with other attractions for Thomson. As a leading figure in the Scottish Renaissance his views attracted the attention of important people across cultural Scotland and as a well-known native Highlander he was influential in nationalist circles across the country and, additionally, in left-wing politics in the north of Scotland. In Thomson's view, a positive dialogue with Gunn was crucial to the plan to persuade the NPS to adopt moderate home rule positions. On one occasion Thomson asked Gibb to visit Gunn at his home near Inverness: 'He is the real directing intelligence of the NPS. I know he will welcome a visit from you.' [31]

Another section of Scottish society which Thomson was eager to woo, one with which he – having prophesied the end of the pure, Protestant Scottish race – would have found it personally uncomfortable to engage with. Hypocrite or not, Thomson understood that Scottish Catholicism was not confined to poor, working class, Irish immigrants. There was a burgeoning and increasingly politically influential Catholic middle-class, much of it with Scottish ancestry dating back several centuries and with historical connections to the Jacobite cause. He confided to Gunn that the man assigned to the task was Moray McLaren, a Catholic. Thomson found it impossible not to add some subterfuge to this revelation. 'He is mine, quiet about this just now.' [32] McLaren, educated in Edinburgh, had left his position as Assistant Editor of *The Listener* in London to take up a senior post with the BBC Scottish Region, announcing his return and his Catholicism in literary style with the publication of the book, *Return to Scotland: an Egoist's Journey* (1930). He was conscious of the Catholic tensions in some parts of Scottish society recalling an encounter with an Edinburgh landlady. 'I asked her to call me early so that I could go to the early Mass. It occurred to me to tell her that I was Irish, just to test those stories one hears about the panic the Scots are in about the Irish coming to work in Scotland. She did not show the slightest displeasure, and even went so far as to say that she preferred the Irish to the English.'[33]

Although Thomson was aware of the potential difficulties McLaren could face because of his BBC position, he urged Gibb to use him for 'Jesuit' work, as a missionary to carry the message. Thomson later acknowledged that McLaren had successfully worked the Roman Catholic channels; 'he understands Jesuit tactics which are, of course, the line we must take.' [34]

Thomson's machinations over McLaren illustrate the conspiratorial nature of his pursuit of converts to his cause and equally his manipulative approach towards colleagues and friends. His correspondence reveals him as optimistic and passionate but also mischievous. He was argumentative and opinionated; he offered praise but could equally be patronising, rude, and domineering. There is also a sense that he constructed his letters as vehicles of persuasion, specifically targeted at the recipient. The views he expressed to Gibb about the NPS and the tactics of their 'secret' group were invariably different from those he made to Dott and Gunn. He assured Dott that the group he was assembling to campaign for home rule was not a rival to the NPS, 'but a necessary auxiliary'. A week later he suggested to Gibb that when the time is ripe the group should make 'a spectacular embracement of the NPS which will probably be profoundly embarrassed.' But any decision that a member of the group should join the NPS was in his view a question of timing. Thomson's consistent reference to 'the group' suggests that although there is no formal structure – it remains a loose assembly of individuals with shared political leanings and aspirations – he, at least, regards them as one body of home rule persuaders or advocates. [35]

Thomson had consistently tried to find a way of tapping into Scotland's universities: 'I always urge action in the universities and why I mean to practise action there myself on every possible occasion. We must make them our four power stations.' Thomson was certain that the home rule cause would win over Scotland's young people: 'We have a young man's honesty, ruthlessness and imagination.' As ever from Thomson, the journalist with an eye for a label, he created a phrase for the task. The universities, and the schools, were to be 'Re-Scottiaged', to stop treating English universities and their models as superior. The universities, training schools with no prestige, must raise their standards and, in the face of administrative and academic obstruction and denial, the route to change was through the students. He urged Gibb to find some way to 'get at and put some ideas into the heads' of the members of the student association at Edinburgh University. Although Edinburgh was Thomson's alma mater his motives were purely mercenary suggesting that the association might change its name to avoid accusations of being Glasgow copycats. In return, Thomson and Gibb could provide funding for their propaganda. Thomson's view of the students was patronising and arrogant, reflected in a final comment to Gibb: 'You will probably find them naive, innocent creatures but we only want them as tools after all.' [36]

The same disdain was also shown when he made references to those he regarded as extremists within the NPS, writers such as Compton Mackenzie, Christopher Grieve (Hugh MacDiarmid) and Lewis Spence, all part of the radical left wing of the party. He suggested to Gunn that Mackenzie 'should shut up about compulsory Gaelic', and that Grieve 'should cease to proffer bouquets to Roman Catholics', arguing that it would be in the party's interest if they curbed their opinions. Thomson told Dott that he had met with MacDiarmid and liked him, although: 'I detest his dishonest, irresponsible and intriguing policies.' When Gibb suggested that they should approach Mackenzie to join their group, he warned him off: 'he has no grasp of Scottish realities and is definitely opposed to our point of view.' He suspected that Mackenzie, MacDiarmid and a few others had a 'curious personal antipathy' towards Gibb and himself, although, he added, 'perhaps it is only to me'. [37]

Thomson evinces surprise over why this should be, conveniently forgetting or ignoring that if his goal of moderating the NPS policies was to succeed, it would inevitably require a clear-out of radical figures like MacDiarmid. Thomson, however, had good reason to be wary of Mackenzie. The successful author regarded him and his group as 'arrivist politicians' attempting to use the NPS as a 'vaulting horse' but who had done little of practical value for nationalism. Mackenzie told Thomson when they met in London that he was 'profoundly unimpressed' by his efforts to exert influence on the party, a view he also shared with his fellow Catholic Moray McLaren and the nationalist activist Tom Gibson. 'I said that I thought a party which was good enough for me to join was good enough for anybody else to join. There is only one thing for Thomson, and the rest of them to do, and that is to fork out their half-crowns and get enrolled on the list of membership. And then, if they have the guts to get elected members of the council, they can make their influence felt within the party.' He threatened to resign if Thomson and others were allowed to interfere: 'the real difficulty would begin when the NPS began to go ahead and interested outsiders wanted to capture it. This is precisely the position we are in.' [38]

Mackenzie's suspicions concerning Thomson would have been reinforced had he been aware of the comments Thomson made to Gunn about Gaelic language and culture. Thomson was convinced that one of the weaknesses of the nationalist appeal in Lowland Scotland was the importance many in the party attached to the protection and expansion of Scotland's Gaelic identity. He dismissed this as part of the fascination with the past and a waste of time and energy since Gaelic was the language of only a small minority of the population. 'The mass of Scots are divorced from Gaelic by centuries,' he told Gunn and 'it would be a frightful, spiritual shock to bring them back to it, even if it were possible.' He dismissed the special pleadings against the use of English made frequently by MacDiarmid and others, insisting that English was one of the world's great languages: 'it is as vigorous as ever, the vehicle of as much good literature as any other two languages. We Scots may not be such great shakes as a literary race but we have done as well in English as we have in Gaelic,' he said.

Conscious of Gunn's 'Highlandism', and in an attempt to assure him that he did not possess a 'bad anti-Gaelic' streak, Thomson claimed that he was both pro-Gael and anti-Gael in the same manner as he was both 'a nationalist and not a nationalist'. However he patronised his argument by linking his support for the survival of Gaelic culture with Highland dress. 'I think the kilt a most handsome garb and have never failed to say so. I couldn't say fairer than that, could I?' he wrote. Thomson found it impossible to hide his irritation with the NPS's focus on Gaelic language and culture, divorced from the important issues facing Scotland. 'I am a

Scot, not a Celt or a Norseman or an Anglo or a Pict or a Strathclyde Welshman,' he said. [39]

What is evident from Thomson's correspondence is that while he had a high regard for Gunn, for his brilliance as an author and for the intellectual force he brought to the nationalist movement, he does not reveal to him the depth of his contempt for what he sees as a lack of organisation and leadership within the NPS.

His solution to the problem is to continue to persuade others that it is 'their duty to join the NPS' but specifically to convince Gibb that at some point he might have to take on the mantle of leadership. 'When we do get the length of joining that disastrous body ourselves I am afraid you will be our sole political brain actually on the spot. Obviously we will have to work through you.' Thomson increasingly believes that support for home rule will continue to grow and as it does so too will the need for a real leader, one who can prove to the Scottish public that the movement contains sane people. 'The material is there, the potential following is growing every month, but it will never get much broader until there is sound leadership,' he tells Gibb, assuring him that it is a job for him. 'I don't believe you'll begin to realise yourself as a human being until you go into the thing openly and up to the hilt.' [40]

Thomson's words were written in 1931. Five years later Gibb was elected Chairman of the SNP.

CHAPTER 7

Response: A Right-Wing Nationalist Party and a Unionist Breakaway

Gibb, Power and Thomson's 'New Nationalism'

In the early 1930s Thomson's key partner and main point of contact in Scotland for his 'unionist-nationalism' strategy was Andrew Dewar Gibb whose conversion to home rule had also been gradual. He shared Thomson's view that Westminster had failed to protect Scottish interests during the slump years of the 1920s, but remained a committed supporter of the union with an enduring belief in Scotland's partnership role in the empire.

For most of the 1920s Gibb was the quintessential face of Scottish unionism. He had served as adjutant to Winston Churchill during World War I, was an advocate and barrister at law, and had lectured at Cambridge, Edinburgh and Glasgow universities. He was twice unsuccessful in attempts to enter Westminster as a unionist MP. Gibb's intention had been to campaign for reform of Westminster policy towards Scotland from inside Conservative and unionist channels. Official unionism stood firmly opposed to the idea that the Conservative government in the late 1920s should develop a separate Scottish policy, dismissing Gibb's pleas that it would be a 'fatal mistake' not to do so. When Gibb sent in a resolution for a conference advocating a policy change it was rejected on the grounds that there already existed Scottish departments for education, health, housing, agriculture and fisheries plus the separate judicial system. He was rebuked by the Scottish Unionist Whip's Office which told him that Scotland and England were economically interdependent and that separate commercial and industrial legislation would be 'disastrous'. He was mocked for his suggestion that Scotland was suffering from 'provincialisation, I do not know what this means', the political secretary at the Whips Office wrote. 'I cannot help feeling that those who talk of Scotland suffering from injustices, and so forth, are suffering from an inferiority complex which is quite unjustified by the facts.' [1]

Official snubs and setbacks such as this did not deter Gibb, and despite his growing rebelliousness he continued to garner support from powerful political sources, at least in his attempts to become a Unionist MP. When he was selected as the Unionist candidate for Greenock at the 1929 General Election Winston Churchill sent him a personal letter of support. The Prime Minister, Stanley Baldwin, also personally endorsed him: 'I express the hope that every elector who believes in conservative principles and the justice of our cause will give you his or her unqualified support.' [2]

In the event Gibb failed to win the seat against the popular sitting Liberal member, Sir Godfrey Collins. Again, undeterred, Gibb resolved that he would continue to seek a parliamentary seat but next time he would stand as a unionist-nationalist. Thomson raised doubts as to whether any Unionist Association would find this an attractive proposition but was impressed by Gibb's determination to label himself a unionist-nationalist. 'I see no reason why you should not use Tory funds to fight a nationalist election,' he said. In September 1930, as he and Gibb planned tactics to widen their home rule appeal to Scottish unionists, Thomson was convinced that Gibb's election strategy was right and gave him encouragement: 'It is very important that you should stand as a Tory-Nat at the next election, so do try and fix things with the local party.' However in October after reading an advance copy of Gibb's book, *Scotland in Eclipse,* Thomson changed his view and told him that he could give up his hopes of a Conservative candidature.[3]

Gibb's book, which described itself on publication in 1930 as a damaging study of the condition of modern Scotland, represented a fitting extension of Thomson's gloomy analysis in *Caledonia* and *Re-Discovery.* Gibb ranged across the themes of the urban slums and deserted Highland glens; the mass emigration of native Scots; the inward migration of Irish Catholics; the decline of the economy and English ownership of Scots industries; the crisis in literature and the arts; the state of the union and the need for a new political association between Scotland and England. Gibb believed that the Scottish Renaissance represented more than a call for a cultural revival, regarding the 'propaganda' writings of himself, Thomson and others like MacDiarmid and Gunn as an extension of the movement. If the pure art form of the novels, poems and plays were a protest against Scotland's false literary tradition, Gibb wrote, the words of the propagandists went further and criticised the failings of the Scots themselves, 'showing the Scotsman what a contemptible fellow he really is'. And if some Scots found this 'irritating beyond words' . . . it remained 'compellingly true'.

Gibb saw Scotsmen like himself wrestling with the problems of cultural and political rescue and rehabilitation, difficulties which he believed were smothering the country, and the reward for their efforts was to be exposed to 'ridicule and dislike'. But important as the cultural awakening might be, Gibb's disillusion with official unionism convinced him that the greater prize was to regain some form of parliamentary independence. Gibb had lost patience and faith in the leaders of the Unionist Party in Scotland, accusing them of being 'a caste with tastes and associations more truly English than Scottish'. They were opposed to any form of change and were not prepared to debate the condition of Scotland. 'The ruling Junta simply draws a pen through it, refusing to allow it,' Gibb said.

Such public criticism and his assertion that there was nothing incompatible in a blending of nationalism and conservatism deepened Gibb's rift with the unionist establishment. And although he described the NPS as poor and 'more than a little suspect on account of a socialist and pro-Irish bias' – handicaps which both he and Thomson agreed the NPS had to lose if it was to have any success – he regarded it important that the party had been formed. For the first time there was a party 'utterly hostile to the other three and pledged to a policy of [. . .] independence.' He claimed that a majority of Scots were 'formally if tepidly' in favour of 'home rule' and that a minority favoured independence.

In the absence of robust surveys or polls, it is doubtful if he possessed any hard evidence to support such beliefs. Gibb's evidence is more likely to have been his own optimism that the spirit of independence was stronger than it had been in previous generations. He could point to a tendency towards nationalism in literary, economic and political lines, 'in every direction the train is set, and one day the spark may fall which is to set fire at last to the imagination of Scotsmen,' he declared. [4]

Gibb's positive public acceptance of the NPS was mirrored soon afterwards by Thomson when he wrote the pamphlet, *The Kingdom of Scotland Restored* (1931), his proposal for an alternative constitutional arrangement between Scotland and England, one that confirmed Scotland's status as a partner in the Empire but also restored its legacy as one of Europe's historic kingdoms. He conceded that the NPS had brought some needed focus to the question of Scotland's political future, but shared Gibb's misgivings that it had failed to provoke serious public debate or that it had produced any original thinking about the Scottish problem.

Thomson, mischievously and as it turned out inaccurately, styled himself as both 'an independent observer' and 'not a nationalist in the accepted sense', and accused the NPS of failing to display 'constructive genius'. It had failed to give an answer to the question 'What to you intend Scotland to become?' and instead had offered a vague mist of pretty, empty words, like 'independence', 'self-government', 'a reversal of 1707'. To Thomson such phrases were meaningless and bankrupt of original thinking. Surprisingly, given his own obsession with a cultural awakening, he condemned those who saw Scottish nationalism as no more than the extension of the cultural movement, dismissing this as 'the drawing room twitterings of pseudo intellectuals, snobs and hangers on'. The concept of nationalism was shared between intellectuals and the man in the street, even the illiterate, all were part of the nation state, which 'exists to contain and serve the national culture'.

Thomson's model of nationalism or home rule within a reconstituted empire came branded as 'new nationalism'; it dispensed with the sentimental version of old nationalism, one steeped in the past, fighting old battlegrounds. 'It would be one that would be intensely critical, above all self-critical,' he said, and would make no attempt to shirk responsibility. In the 'new nationalism' a hatred of England would not exist. He wanted the Scots to look in the mirror, at themselves, to accept that if the country was in a bad way, the fault lay with the Scots: 'the duty of re-building and re-vitalising is theirs alone.' The task of regaining control of the nation's destiny had to be grasped by them; if it was called nationalism it had to be creative. 'It exists, independent of artificial stimuli such as alien oppression, grievances, and so on, as an expression of the innermost compulsions of a people who must perfect themselves in a perfect art-form, the nation.'

In Thomson's vision the establishment of a parliament in Edinburgh was only the beginning and not the end of the struggle to renew Scotland politically and culturally. In structural and constitutional terms he was insistent that home rule could be achieved within a rearrangement of the current union legislation, one that maintained Scotland's role as a 'mother nation' of the Empire: 'Scotland has not the slightest intention of purchasing national self-control at the price of relinquishing her imperial interests. If she did that she would be profoundly false to her own nature,' he said. And as he constantly signalled, nationalism, unionism and imperialism walked together; all were part of the Scottish tradition. 'Three hundred years of association with England cannot be overlooked; it is woven into the fabric of the nation's spiritual complex, and cannot be lightly discarded.'

Sitting on top of this new constitutional arrangement Thomson wanted a dual monarchy, one which would administer the joint concerns of defence, foreign affairs, the crown colonies and the other imperial dependencies, a structure that could be the stepping stone towards a federal integration of the empire and towards a federal commonwealth. Scotland would be the first of the British nations to assert a right to self-government without relinquishing her claim to the common tasks and responsibilities of the Empire. [5]

Blake, Power, McLaren and Gibb gave Thomson their seal of approval by jointly authoring the introduction to the pamphlet, a move initiated by Blake.

'I sent my essay to Blake who approved heartily and suggested that "we" ought to sign a sort of vague manifesto to form an introduction to it. Power approved and is willing to lend his name,' Thomson recalled. The public endorsement by four well-known writers gave Thomson's pamphlet added legitimacy but did not indicate that his group of propagandists had acquired a formal status, or had transformed into an official league, secret or otherwise. It remained two dimensional; on one level the imagined concept from the creative but focused mind of Thomson, and on another something real as a growing group of like minded people corresponded and talked together, intent on using whatever powers or influences they had to argue the case for home rule and, separately, to influence the NPS.

Thomson claimed that Blake and McLaren were prepared to join the NPS, and that at some point 'they' would need to take editorial control of the party newspaper, the *Scots Independent*, with William Power earmarked as the potential editor. In characteristic Thomson duplicitous style he decided not to tell Power. 'Power was down last week. I thought it more tactful not to mention our *Scots Independent* intrigue,' he cautioned Gibb. [6] All of the scheming proved to be neither fanciful nor wishful thinking on Thomson's part. In March, 1931, John McCormick, the secretary of the NPS, told Gunn that Blake had become a member and that he had also had a 'long talk' with Power: 'I think that very soon he will follow the same course.' [7]

Thomson had both a friendly and professional relationship with Blake while his association with Power was never close. Despite his endorsement of the home rule pamphlet and their common goal of self-government, Power unlike Thomson and Gibb was neither a 'Tory-Nat' nor a 'unionist-nationalist'. Power's humbler origins in the Woodside district of Glasgow from where he left school at the age of 14 to work in a bank, contrasted sharply with the other four nationalist signatures on the home rule pamphlet. Thomson, Gibb and McLaren all had privileged backgrounds and educations while Blake, the son of a successful Greenock businessman, trained as a solicitor before serving in World War I. Power, largely self-taught, eventually landed a position as commentator and leader writer on the *Glasgow Herald*, from where his journey to Scottish nationalism had begun, shaped by the opinions he formed writing on Scottish affairs. He admitted later that in his youth he had been a committed 'Tory Imperialist', opposed to home rule, Scottish or Irish, to extending the right to vote, to trade unions, 'and everything that menaced the privileges of rank and property.' He had believed in the power of landlords to put people off the land and to employers to cut down wages. His sense of his Scottish identity emerged when as a member of a civilian army corps, the 1st Lanark Volunteers, he found it had no native traditions, no Scottish cultural base. Power recalled that there were no Scottish songs, books, or anything about Scottish history. 'The spiritual home of our officers was Aldershot, and an English adjutant spoke of "the people in these parts", as if we had been Hottentots. I slipped my political cables and drifted into the open sea.' [8]

In 1926 Power left the *Glasgow Herald* to become editor of the *Scots Observer*, a new weekly journal of 'religious and national interest', in reality the unofficial organ of the Church of Scotland. Power had no doubts, at least at the outset, that the growth of the national movement was a major factor for the journal's existence. 'That movement was mainly cultural, and therefore in essence spiritual. Scotland was a spiritual entity, of which the Church, as representing the basic spiritual impulse, ought to be the centre.'

In his enthusiasm, Power believed that the church was at the heart of the 'new Scotland' and his task was to synthesise through the journal the national, spiritual, intellectual and social elements of the nation. He quickly found that he had the support of cultural Scotland as contributions were received from writers and artists, alongside those from parish ministers. However, the Presbyterian Church establishment was less impressed. 'I was backed loyally by most of the ministers and by all the Scottish writers, artists and musicians. Significantly enough, it was certain of the Church leaders who were most critical both of the over-intellectual character of the paper and of my "nationalist" tendencies.' Power wrote an account of a meeting of the NPS in Glasgow only to have the article censured by one his directors who accused him of preaching Scots nationalism, 'which, indeed, I had been doing ever since I began journalism,' Power conceded. He increasingly found that although the response to the journal from ordinary church members was positive, 'the church leaders were not in favour of it. I was not sorry when my term of office expired.' [9]

Power's treatment from leading figures in the Church establishment did not surprise Thomson. He believed that the Church was actively against the re-emergence of the Scottish national spirit, and to any form of nationalism 'in its widest, most comprehensive aspect'. Thomson recognised that one reason why the church opposed nationalism was that, in the absence of a Scottish state, the Church, primarily through its General Assembly, had remained unchallenged as the vehicle for the nation's aspirations. What he found puzzling was the Church's 'obvious suspicion and dislike of every attempt to restore a real national spirit operating in thought and the arts'. The opposition towards Power's inclusion of intellectuals and renaissance writers in the columns of the *Scots Observer* was an indication that they equated cultural ambitions as a form of nationalism. [10]

Power's experience confirmed the leadership of the church was in the hands of ministers opposed to nationalism, political or cultural; their commitment was to God and the union. The Rev. John White, the predominant influence in the Church throughout this period was a 'wholehearted unionist' and a member of the Scottish Conservative Club, 'an elite Tory institution'. [11] Power's shared passion with Thomson was their enthusiasm for national culture embodied in the literary revival. 'The whole of Scottish literature today, indeed, including the majority of books by Scots about Scotland, represents mainly the discovery of Scotland by the Scots,' Power said. McCulloch said Power was 'no narrow nationalist' seeing nationalism and internationalism as being essentially complementary. However, if the passion of Power's nationalism was inspired by its spiritual and cultural possibilities, his association with Thomson, Gibb, Blake and McLaren and his formal links with both the NPS and subsequently the SNP confirm his determination to play his part in the campaign for political nationalism. He was also another prominent Scottish writer wooed by Thomson and Blake for the Porpoise Press and in 1934 it published his book, *My Scotland*, in which he said the real inspiration for the modern literary movement and of every other national movement in Scotland was Scottish literature itself: 'entertained by cultured and active-minded young Scots, who see in it the organic principle of our nation from which they draw their inspiration. It is from Scottish literature that they derive their "Freedom of Scotland".' [12]

As Power had done, and despite his earlier pleas to Dott that he had greater value as a propagandist outside of official party labels, Thomson had also joined the NPS, something he deliberately chose to keep hidden, particularly from Beaverbrook. MacCormick later revealed that 'unknown to his chief,' Thomson 'was, and had been, a keen member of the NPS and the author of much of our literature.' MacCormick's revelation refers to a meeting he had with Beaverbrook in autumn 1932 when Thomson was also in attendance.

'Beaverbrook had gravely introduced him to me as a distinguished Scottish historian, little knowing that I had spent many a happy evening with him and his lovely Norwegian wife in their home in Hampstead,' MacCormick recalled. This suggests dangerous duplicity on Thomson's part. He is a working journalist and private advisor to Beaverbrook, who also regards him as a 'distinguished Scottish historian', but to MacCormick he is both a member and is active behind the scenes in the NPS while at the same time he is engaged, along with Gibb, in attempts to convert unionists to support some measure of home rule.

Ironically, at the East Fife parliamentary by-election, held early in 1933, Beaverbrook sponsored an Empire unionist candidate promoting empire free trade, while the nationalist candidate was the novelist, Eric Linklater. Beaverbrook took a personal interest establishing an entourage at Rusack's Hotel beside St. Andrews Old Course, among them Thomson as his personal advisor. MacCormick described Thomson's quiet and cynical humour as he contemplated his situation, 'in the van of the Agricultural Unionist and Empire crusade or crossed swords with Linklater in mock duel.' [13]

During the campaign, while serving Beaverbrook, Thomson continued to send advice to Gibb about their ongoing talks with the NPS and update him on the nationalist campaign. 'There is tremendous nationalist sympathy here, it is most impressive, but I doubt if it will be worked up into voting power. Still what has been done has in view of the lack of organisation and amateurish tactics been remarkable,' he wrote.[14] MacCormick was the secretary of the NPS with a responsibility for membership, but despite his confirmation in 1955 that Thomson was a fully-fledged member of the NPS, certainly from 1932, historians have continued to insist, without source reference, that he was never officially attached to any nationalist party. [15]

Thomson's nervousness that his nationalist activities should remain hidden from Beaverbrook did not curb his continuing efforts to influence the NPS through regular meetings, discussions and correspondence with Gunn and MacCormick. He met MacCormick on several occasions at his Hampstead home while Gibb was a regular visitor to MacCormick's office in West Regent Street, Glasgow. Both Gunn and MacCormick had accepted the premise that if the nationalist cause was to earn greater public legitimacy the NPS had to lose its image as a party of extremists and it had to gain the support of unionist elements inside mainstream Scottish society. Such a breakthrough seemed impossible, but in the early summer of 1932 a dissident faction emerged in an unlikely setting, in a previously secure unionist stronghold on the south side of Glasgow.

A Public Face for Unionist-Nationalism

Thomson's unionist-nationalism or 'nationalism for Tories' was given a very public face by a group of staunch Tory unionists who demanded home rule and with it a new role for Scotland within the Empire. This group was not led by an intellectual, commentator or a leading political figure, but by a Glasgow solicitor, John Kevan McDowall. At the time his father, also named John, was better known in Scotland as the former secretary of the Scottish Football Association, a post he held for almost fifty years. McDowall himself had been secretary of the Cathcart Unionist Association since 1921 and the parliamentary agent for the constituency since 1922. His efforts had transformed the Cathcart Branch into one of the strongest in Scotland. Like Gibb he was a typical conservative product of the Glasgow professional middle-classes, committed to the union and the empire.

But if McDowall was a 'dyed in the wool Tory' he also celebrated his Scottishness. He was an authority on Robert Burns, secretary of the Scottish Burns Club, a member of the Glasgow Haggis Club, and also ran the Harry Lauder Cronies Circle. Westminster's indifference to Scotland, he believed, was echoed across the official Scottish Unionist Party and among unionist MPs. In June 1932 McDowall and almost fifty followers inside the Cathcart Association formed the Imperial Committee of the Cathcart Unionists, producing a manifesto with key objectives. [16]

1. To replace the British Parliament with an Imperial Parliament;

2. To create dominion governments and parliaments for England, Scotland and Wales;

3. To enshrine the rights of Scotsmen to manage their own affairs providing England and other members of the British Empire had similar facilities.

They also indicated their willingness to co-operate with other parties with similar aims. This very public display of disagreement with the official unionist line was clearly planned in advance as within days thousands of copies of the manifesto were distributed, not only across Scotland, but also to Scottish organisations across the world. McDowall had also had private talks with Gibb and MacCormick. Thomson could barely control his excitement about these developments teasing Gibb that he was 'one of the Cathcart rebels' and urging him to do more than merely join their forces. 'I hope you will sail in and become one of the arch conspirators. What Fun!' [17]

Within weeks McDowall and his supporters met with MacCormick and other leaders of the NPS issuing a joint statement in which the two groups agreed on the need for home rule, and to hold further discussions. This caused uproar in the unionist establishment, an anger intensified when a defiant McDowall compared his Committee's actions with that of the Conservative Party's agreements with the Liberals and Socialists to form a National Coalition Government supporting Ramsay MacDonald, 'for the good of Britain'. 'The Imperial Committee,' declared McDowall, 'can equally claim the right to meet and negotiate with any party to ascertain any points of agreement, for the good of Scotland.'

James Paterson, chairman of the Glasgow Unionist Association described the aims of the dissidents as 'preposterous, arrogant, unauthorised, inflated, anonymous, presumptuous and disloyal.'

McDowall in response accused the Unionist Party of complacency in the face of the problems facing Scotland. 'Unemployment may be more than doubly acute in Glasgow than elsewhere; Scottish trade may be racing to the south, but the chairman of the Unionist Party is not ashamed to acknowledge that he has "not the time or inclination" to discuss the constructive and remedial proposals submitted by the Imperial Committee.' [18]

The absence of formal meetings and discussions meant that the arguments were carried out in the columns and letters page of Scotland's major unionist newspaper, the *Glasgow Herald*, and the coverage extended to the other daily Scottish newspapers. McDowall understood that the actions of the Cathcart unionists had come at an opportune time and that only a few years earlier had he been advocating self-government he would likely have been a 'lone voice crying in the wilderness of derision'. But now there was a great concert of voices, commentators, intellectuals and activists, 'a choir fearlessly singing the praises of Scotland and proclaiming the right of Scotsmen to govern better, and alone, their own internal and domestic affairs,' McDowall said. [19]

The *Daily Record*, edited by another associate of Thomson, Donald Anderson, and self-styled as 'Scotland's National Newspaper', welcomed the widening support for home rule within the Unionist Party, and pledged its support to the Cathcart rebels referring to them as 'our new unionist devolutionists'. It criticised the leading Tory politician, Sir John Gilmour who had dismissed them as 'narrow nationalists', describing him as being out of touch with what was happening.

'He may take it that there is a profound concern for Scotland's social, cultural and industrial future, manifest in a hundred and one ways, and that that concern is an indisputable reality.' However the *Record* attacked the NPS for its calls for independence and for its anti-Englishness arguing that love of Scotland did not equate to antagonism towards England. The blame, it said, lay with an overloaded Parliamentary system, one which the Scots themselves had encouraged. 'It is only now, under the terrible pressure of circumstances, that our real Scottish loyalty and sentiment are properly manifesting themselves.' It called for the formation of a new Scottish party but urged that it should not call itself 'nationalist'. The *Record* quickly turned the Cathcart development into a campaign for home rule within the union; a scheme which it claimed in July, 1932 had the support of the Prime Minister, Ramsay MacDonald. Across its front page the *Record* headline reflected the newspaper's boast that this was an important development: 'A Great Day for Scots People, Premier Adopts Our Plan, Home Rule when World Affairs are Settled, Devolution to fit Modern Economic Conditions, Momentous Interview'.[20]

The basis for this was a brief interview with MacDonald when he visited his home town of Lossiemouth during which, the *Record* claimed, he had indicated sympathy for home rule and given a commitment that the National Government would 'not only give the matter consideration, but would pursue it'.

Not to be outdone by its main rival, the *Express*, now printed in Glasgow and with a new masthead proclaiming itself the '*Scottish*' *Daily Express* to affirm its Scottish credentials, carried a front page statement from Lord Beaverbrook stating that he was in favour of Scottish self-government. 'It should be the ultimate intention to capture the Unionist Party for the home rule project,' the paper said. The *Express* followed this up with a second article from Beaverbrook headed 'Remove the Deadwood' in which the press baron condemned the Glasgow Unionist Association and expressed his admiration for Kevan McDowall. Although both newspapers took care to emphasise that their backing for nationalism was limited to a form of home rule within the union, nationalism had never previously secured such a degree of popular editorial coverage and support. [21]

Some scholars have suggested that Thomson played no part in Beaverbrook's personal intervention in support of home rule, the Cathcart dissidents and the Scottish Party in 1932.[22] This scenario I reject since the available evidence demonstrates that Beaverbrook did seek Thomson's advice on Scottish matters, certainly between 1931 and 1933, the period when Beaverbrook took an interest in nationalism and tested his Empire free trade crusade at Scottish elections. MacCormick confirmed that Thomson was part of Beaverbrook's team during the East Fife by-election in February 1933. And in two remarkable letters to Dott,

Thomson not only boasted that he was able to influence Beaverbrook but in typically Thomson Machiavellian style asked Dott to assist him with his 'devious diplomacy'. It was, Thomson said, 'a secret, a real secret – to be divulged to only a chosen few, very discreet people.'

The subject of Thomson's conspiratorial intrigue was his claim that he had persuaded Beaverbrook to support the Rev.T.T. Alexander, the nationalist candidate for the East Edinburgh constituency at the General Election in November 1931. In return for his pledge to campaign for Empire free trade Alexander received a financial contribution from Beaverbrook and the editorial support of the *Scottish Daily Express*. 'Beaverbrook is sick of the Scottish Tories yet can't support the socialists,' Thomson wrote, urging Dott to ensure that the offer was treated with the greatest respect and that the local nationalists supported Beaverbrook's policy. 'They can easily say that Empire free trade is a natural sequel to the Scottish Dominion and Imperial Federation we aim at. If they do it may lead to very big things,' Thomson wrote.

When Dott objected to Alexander's acceptance of Beaverbrook's money, Thomson claimed he had anticipated this but had concluded that the intervention was worth the obvious risks. Beaverbrook, he argued, was genuinely interested and sympathetic to Scottish nationalism; 'his father was a Scot from Bathgate and he knows as much Scots as I do.' Thomson, however, was nervous, pleading with Dott to keep his name out of any discussions about Beaverbrook's initiative within nationalist circles. 'Beaverbrook, of course, does not know that I am a nationalist,' he wrote. 'It would be very awkward for me if it got back to Beaverbrook through his agent or his paper in Scotland that I was claiming to have influenced him. Please see that everything possible is done to avoid any appearance of discourtesy to Lord Beaverbrook. That would be a terrible mistake.' [23]

None of this intrigue or Beaverbrook's support benefited the Rev. Alexander, who lost his deposit, the worse performance of the five nationalist candidates fielded during the election.

Apart from Thomson's unease and fear that his job could be at risk if Beaverbrook was aware of his 'devious diplomacy' this episode is also significant for the insight it reveals of Thomson's rapid rise within the Beaverbrook group. He was recruited to work on the *London Evening Standard* and the *Sunday Express* only months before the 1931 General Election, demonstrating that he had already been identified by the press baron as a useful political advisor, particularly on Scottish affairs. And while the outcome of the exercise was one of failure, it demonstrates that Thomson was prepared to use Beaverbrook's influence, and money, to support the nationalist cause.

It is inconceivable that Thomson was not an influential background figure in the newspaper circulation war between the Scottish *Daily Express* and the *Daily Record* in 1932, a battle that enabled the dissident breakaway in Cathcart and the infant SP to gain maximum public exposure. Thomson had no doubt that Cathcart had changed the establishment's view of nationalism. 'The present gang of Scottish MPs seems to be scared about nationalism,' he wrote to Gibb. 'We shall get them on the run yet!' [24]

The Cathcart dissidents added to this mix the anxieties and frustrations of sections of the middle classes, primarily Protestant, and normally dependable supporters of the Unionist party. Finlay has written that in the early 1930s there was a widely held expectation that Scottish nationalism would 'take off', a view held by 'many different shades of opinion'.[25] In the event 'take off' would prove an prediction too far, but nationalist commentators and intellectuals, inside or outside the NPS and the SP, in the summer and autumn of 1932 were entitled to enjoy the spectacle of an establishment displaying signs of unease, and if it is arguable that the catalyst for this was the unionist dissidents, the nationalist commentators and activists could claim, with some justification, that it was their writings and propaganda which kept the condition of Scotland firmly in the public arena.

CHAPTER **8**
The Establishment Strikes Back

'Ragman's Roll' and John Buchan's Anti-Nationalism

In public the unionist establishment poured scorn on the dissidents and their supporters among commentators and popular newspapers. But in private there was growing alarm. The angry debate over Scottish home rule spread from the Scottish press to the London newspapers with *The Times* leading the broadsides warning that 'the malcontents' were sufficiently numerous and important to carry weight with impressionable Scotsmen, and that the SP 'cannot easily be dismissed'. Similar concerns were expressed by large sections of the Scottish business community with many issuing warnings that a separate parliament would inflict serious and lasting injury to the interests of both the employed and the employer. 'The trading and industrial interests of Scotland and England cannot be treated as separate,' the Scottish Branch of the Federation of British Industries, declared, 'all proposals should be strenuously opposed.' [1]

In November 1932 the Scottish unionist establishment organised a unique 'invitation only' meeting in Glasgow, its objective the defence of the union and the *status quo* and to reject any form of home rule. The chairman, Lord Maclay, the Scottish shipbuilding tycoon, said Scotland had benefited most from the union and that any form of severance from England would be a disaster. The meeting agreed a statement that there should be no interference with the present constitutional arrangements, and they would oppose any proposal for a Scottish parliament. The statement was signed by 456 notable Scots. They included: six dukes, three marquises, nine earls, three viscounts, ten lords, fifty seven knights, two highland chiefs, four senior clergymen, seventy six justices of the peace, eleven professors, thirty nine senior military figures, scores of Scottish industrialists, bankers and businessmen. There were also two ladies. [2]

The nationalists immediately dubbed the statement 'The Ragman's Roll' – a direct reference to the petition signed by 2000 Scottish nobles and clergy in 1296 when they pledged their loyalty to Edward I and opposed Robert the Bruce.

The speeches and final statement from the meeting moved even the normally loyal unionist supporting *Scotsman* newspaper to describe it as 'deplorable' and full of 'violent negations'. In a leading article it said: 'The speeches by their complacent acceptance of the present state of affairs and their unimaginative outlook do the worst possible service to Scotland.' [3] The Glasgow meeting was quickly followed by another unique occasion when the Government decided that during the course of the King's Speech to mark the new session of Parliament one full day should be allocated as a Scotland Debate.

Inevitably the spectre of nationalism dominated the debate. George Buchanan, the Labour MP for Glasgow Gorbals, told the Commons that the surge in nationalist sentiment was now coming from the professional and middle classes although it still lacked strength among the working classes. 'I meet lawyers and sheriffs, and nearly every one of them is in sympathy with the movement. I met a distinguished sheriff of the city only the other day and he was a keen nationalist. It is the same with the doctors and the higher paid civil servants,' Buchanan said. He warned parliament not to dismiss the demands for reforms with cheap sneers. 'There is genuineness behind this demand,' Buchanan argued, even if his own view was that it would not matter if there was a parliament in London or Edinburgh if it did not address economic want, misery and needless poverty. [4]

The debate is best remembered for the contribution from the novelist, John Buchan, the Unionist member for the Combined Scottish Universities who berated his Unionist Party colleagues for regarding home rule as a trivial matter.

'Something must be done and done soon if Scotland is not to lose her historic individuality,' he said. 'The source of the nationalist surge is a passionate feeling that Scotland should not lose her personality.' Many people now believed, he added, there was a danger that Scotland could sink to a position where it was a mere northern province of England. Coupland in a charitable interpretation of Buchan's speech contended that Buchan had used the occasion to demonstrate 'how far his cultural nationalism was also political'. But in truth, as Buchan's biographer Janet Adam Smith admitted: 'it was a good rhetorical performance; the Scottish nationalists almost thought they had gained a convert, and members half-expected him to come out in favour of the full Home Rule programme for an independent legislature.' The anti-climax came when Buchan revealed that his intrusions into political nationalism did not extend beyond a call for greater executive and administrative devolution to Scotland, and a 'dignified' building in Edinburgh, an appeal eventually met when the Scottish Office moved in 1939 from Whitehall to Edinburgh. A parliament in Scotland would not cure the country's problems, he maintained. 'It would create artificial differences, hinder co-operation, and engender friction if we attempted to split up services which Scotland has had in common with England for 200 years.' [5]

Despite what the historian Christopher Harvie has called a 'moving plea for recognition of Scottish nationality', the speech reflects the contradictions inherent in Buchan's traditional conservatism and unionism and his devotion to Britishness and Empire, neither of which would allow notions of his Scottishness, no matter how passionately expressed, to entertain any form of home rule nationalism. He paraded his nationality by asserting that 'every Scotsmen should be a Scottish nationalist'. But he was worried about the 'evils of a too narrow nationalism' and questioned if Scottish nationalism was a 'sane nationalism'; finally concluding 'that an artificial nationalism, which manifests itself in a barren separatism and in the manufacture of artificial differences, makes for neither peace nor prosperity.' [6]

Kate MacDonald in considering the depth of Scottishness in Buchan's writing says that despite being creatively active at the same time as the writers of the Scottish Renaissance 'his politics remained old school conservative'. Buchan, of course, attained fame and success far in excess of other Scottish writers of the time, and as he did so he dropped the Scottish dialogue, settings and themes of his early fiction. 'He developed a separate, less Scottish, strand of his writing,' Macdonald states, but he still had an inescapably dual identity: 'he was a Scottish poet, a Scottish critic, and was also a public Scot.' [7]

In 1927 in correspondence with Gibb, Buchan had indicated that he was involved in political discussions about the economic and social state of Scotland. 'There is a strong growing movement among Scots conservatives to tackle the grave condition of Scotland, and it has the support of the wiser people in the Labour Party', Buchan wrote. 'Something has got to be done, and done soon,' he said, the same phrase he would use five years later during the Scotland Debate. 'I am glad to know that I can count on you for your help, and you may be quite sure I am going to ask for it.' Buchan may have been genuine and confident of his words at the time, yet no such conservative or unionist moment or movement emerged until the Cathcart breakaway in 1932. [8]

While Gibb, frustrated by his failure to persuade the Scottish Unionist Party to take action, eventually became a whole-hearted advocate for home rule, Buchan, elected to parliament in 1927, increasingly emerged as a figure of the political establishment. He was close to both Ramsay Macdonald and Stanley Baldwin and as a moderate conservative he 'was often called on to put the Liberal Tory view in the house'. When he addressed unionist students at Edinburgh University, Buchan described the doctrine of his political beliefs, firmly based on a combination of Unionism, Conservatism, and Toryism. He said: 'First we are unionists, we believe the Union makes strength, that co-operation is the seed of success. Secondly we are Tories, with a critical and questioning attitude of mind which refuses to take things on hearsay. Lastly, we are Conservatives; we wish to preserve the continuity of history, we are the creators of the past, and if we are to build anything enduring it must be erected on the foundation laid by those who have gone before us.' [9]

Nationalism for Buchan was a matter of identity, geography and culture; his political nationalism was non-existent. It was a political position Buchan had adopted in the years before World War I when he was strongly opposed to Irish nationalism including moderate proposals for home rule. His commitment to the Union was total, believing that the principle it invoked was the same as that Abraham Lincoln had stood for during the American Civil War. Addressing a Unionist rally at Innerleithen in Peebleshire in 1912 he had laid out his views on unionism and nationalism. 'We are standing for a principle which is a universal truth in politics, the principle that union is strength, that the rights and duties of the whole cannot be sacrificed to the selfishness and vanity of the part. It is a principle that cannot die.' [10]

William Power recalled that as editor of the *Scots Observer* Buchan had sent him an article about Scottish nationalism, 'I gladly printed it. It was enthusiastically Scottish, but – none of that nonsense about self government'. Adam Smith is clear that Buchan was firmly against the creation of any new government based on nationalism. 'His Scottishness marked his thinking. For him there could be a strong national sentiment and a sense of national identity without any desire for political separation. [. . .] His own Scottish sentiment demanded no political expression.' [11]

On such a basis Buchan could sympathise and appreciate the force of Ulster sentiment, 'since it was directed towards *maintaining* union.'

In assessing the impact of writers with nationalist sympathies, Brand remarked ruefully that had Buchan supported nationalism 'an entirely different situation would have been created'. [12] Despite a genuineness for the preservation of Scottish national identity that he projected in large measure during his contribution to the home rule debate in November 1932, the reality is that politically Buchan exemplified the wait and see, *laissez-faire* approach adopted by the unionist establishment to the condition of Scotland issue. They resisted what they regarded as the ill-informed despondency and pessimism of commentators from the right such as Thomson and Gibb, until forced to respond by their fear of an apparent surge of public interest and support for home rule from within their own ranks.

The establishment's aversion to nationalism, whatever its guise and from whatever source, remained unmoved. It was also prepared to move ruthlessly to remove any nationalist sympathisers it found in its midst, even in an arm's length body like the British Broadcasting Corporation.

BBC Sacks Scottish Regional Director with 'nationalist sympathies'
In 1926 David Cleghorn Thomson, 26, had been hand-picked from the staff of the *Radio Times* by John Reith, Director General of the BBC, and

sent to Scotland as Northern Area Director, a post re-titled Scottish Regional Director in 1928. He fitted Reith's ideal profile of a BBC executive, particularly one to lead the Scottish operation. Cleghorn Thomson was a classical product of upper middle-class Edinburgh: the son of a doctor, he had attended Edinburgh Academy and gone on to Edinburgh University and then Baliol College, Oxford. He had trained as a lawyer but had opted for a career in journalism and twice stood, unsuccessfully, as a Liberal candidate, all before he was 24 years old. [13]

Cleghorn Thomson had a high regard of his own abilities as a playwright, poet, composer, and intellectual; qualities which he pursued in Scotland both personally through various theatre, musical and arts organisations, and professionally by opening up the airwaves to cultural broadcasts. The journalist in him also responded to the economic, social and cultural issues with innovative current affairs programmes such as *What's Wrong with Scotland?* in which he gave George Malcolm Thomson a prominent role. By any measure Cleghorn Thomson was a key figure in the formative years of broadcasting in Scotland.

Yet histories of the BBC make few mentions of him. In McDowell's officially approved history of BBC Scotland, Cleghorn Thomson rates one reference, his appointment as Regional Director. Cleghorn Thomson, if arguably sidelined in the BBC memory, has been noted by some historians, particularly for his angry opposition to London's much-heralded regional policies and also for the concerns he raised about BBC centralisation which he regarded as contrary to Scottish interests. He believed the BBC was London-centric, a policy deliberately encouraged by Reith. It was a strategy supported by Reith's senior executives who were wholly convinced of their metropolitan superiority and who resisted any attempts to pander to regional variations in taste, 'which, in any case, they considered to be merely capricious. The BBC gazed out of its metropolitan base on to an audience which it regarded vaguely or sometimes with indifference,' said one historian. [14]

In June 1932 at its regular monthly meeting in London the BBC Board of Governors decided to dispense with the services of Cleghorn Thomson. One member, Lord Gainford, described him as very capable but unsuited to his position because of personal faults, 'such as conceit, egotism, tactlessness and so forth'. Another member, Lady Snowden, said that from what she had heard from 'outsiders', broadcasting in Scotland would never prosper so long as Cleghorn Thomson was Regional Director. The Board instructed Reith to see him and explain that he was 'considered unsatisfactory, request his resignation, one year's notice being given'. [15]

However one issue regarding Cleghorn Thomson is not mentioned in the brief minute of the board meeting, one which becomes evident in subsequent BBC internal documents. It was the view of some members, particularly Snowden, that Cleghorn Thomson supported Scottish nationalism. It was an issue of concern to a Board filled with hand-picked establishment figures, many of them, like Gainford and Snowden, political appointments. Gainford, a Liberal, and former Postmaster General, had been the first chairman of the British Broadcasting Company. Snowden, the wife of the Labour politician and former Chancellor of the Exchequer, Philip Snowden, was the main force within the Governors to remove Cleghorn Thomson. Snowden's antagonism towards him and his alleged links to Scottish nationalism surfaced – in private correspondence – four years later, when Cleghorn Thomson had left and Snowden was no longer a governor.

In December 1936, a note on Cleghorn Thomson's departure marked 'Staff Private' sent to the Postmaster General, George Tryon, said he had been asked to resign or accept dismissal because he had exhibited 'certain defects' as the public representative of the BBC in Scotland. These included 'violent quarrels with certain public men'; and a 'general feeling of untrustworthiness and inability to handle staff'. Lady Snowden had become aware of the situation in Scotland 'and the prejudice to broadcasting which was resulting from Mr Cleghorn Thomson's bad public contacts and from his enthusiasm for Scottish nationalism.' [16]

In addition to the note to Tyron there is other substantial internal BBC documentation to confirm that it was Scottish and London establishment fears about Scottish nationalism and his alleged nationalist sympathies which finally convinced the Governors to sack him. However when he eventually left in April 1933, the brief BBC announcement said he had resigned. Cleghorn Thomson, in a separate statement, claimed his resignation was due to disagreements over matters of policy in Scotland, 'and a consequent unreadiness on my part to continue to work in the face of obstacles which have proved insuperable.' Both statements were agreed in advance. [17]

The BBC, anxious to control what he might say in public, agreed to give him an ex-gratia sum of £1,000, in addition to all severance, redundancy, holiday, pension and expenses payments. In return Cleghorn Thomson promised his departure would be professional, and that, whatever his personal feelings he would not display any unpleasantness or bitterness in public. Val H. Goldsmith, the Director of Business Relations, was given the task of finalising the financial arrangements and controlling the public and press aspects of his departure. Cleghorn Thomson told him: 'you can rely on me absolutely to honour my word regarding my actions at this juncture with regard to a dignified bearing.'

Cleghorn Thomson and Goldsmith had also agreed that in making any public statements he would refer to 'policy differences'. The phrase 'policy differences' was suggested by Goldsmith and when Cleghorn Thomson wrote asking what these might be Goldsmith replied, 'for example you had backed the nationalist policy strongly'. Thomson, in response, said he was grateful to Goldsmith for letting him know that the Governors 'disagreed' with his nationalist policy. 'It is to me privately a matter of great importance to have found out at last part of what the Board considered a substantial reason for their decision.' [18]

Goldsmith's reaction to this was to attempt to separate his own words from the Governors. 'I do not know that the Governors have ever mentioned your nationalist policy,' he wrote. He had mentioned that Thomson had backed the nationalist policy strongly because 'it is very definitely an issue between two sections of the Scottish press'. Thomson wrote again to Goldsmith reminding him that he had repeated his remark about backing the nationalist policy. 'Every intelligent person in Scotland knows that I have often repeated in public that I am opposed to the nationalist policy, and no careful follower of the programmes in the past seven years could accuse me of backing the nationalist policy.' Thomson sent this letter to Goldsmith one day after he had officially resigned. [19]

Only at the end did Thomson discover that no matter his protest-ations of innocence, the BBC Board of Governors had decided they did not want someone in charge of the Scottish Region who they believed was sympathetic to the Scottish nationalist movement.

In his final letter to Goldsmith, Thomson conceded that he had 'seized with eagerness' the first evidence he had seen of the 'substantial reason' for the Board's action, but that in view of Goldsmith's words 'such a reason might be mistaken'. Had Thomson been aware of other BBC documents that confirmed the Board's concerns regarding his 'nation-alism' he would have been less inclined to accept Goldsmith's protests that he was unaware of the Board's position on the nationalist factor.

Cleghorn Thomson's departure was treated as an important news story by the Scottish media, yet in the coverage there are no references to 'violent quarrels with certain public men', 'bad public contacts', or 'enthusiasm for Scottish nationalism'. The *Scotsman*, unionist supporting and the official voice of the Edinburgh establishment, praised his leadership of the Scottish Region and his involvement with cultural and educational organisations. 'He showed himself an ardent advocate of Scottish interests, of the employment of Scottish talent, and of the formation of a national sentiment.' [20]

The view that Cleghorn Thomson was sacked primarily because of personal and managerial failures is perpetuated in a recent 'insider's look' which claims that among staff 'dislike for Thomson was growing' and 'the Scottish director's lifestyle and pyrotechnic displays of management had wearied London colleagues in general and Reith in particular. It was his short fuse in dealing with colleagues that caused the greatest concern.' [21]

There is no dispute that Thomson frequently clashed with executives in London, and that he was arrogant, often acting without tact or diplomacy, and regularly complained to Reith about London's interference or control over the Scottish Region. However this version or interpretation takes no account of BBC internal documents which challenge the issue of staff morale, their loyalty to Thomson, and which also open up further the issue of nationalist sympathies within the BBC

Scottish Region. Reports on Cleghorn Thomson and the Scottish Region, written separately in the months before he left by two London executives, provide an alternative and positive view of him and the Scottish operation.

Lindsay Wellington, the Regional Co-ordinator, charged with investigating alleged shortcomings in programme building and business controls, reported that he found the Scottish station 'in a more lively condition and potentially a source of better programmes than any other region I have visited.' Wellington recommended a structural reorganisation to deal with the business issues but praised Thomson's external relations work: 'he is essentially a man of public affairs, which seems to be what Edinburgh wants at the moment. He is a figure in Edinburgh, which is all to the advantage of the Corporation.'

J.M. Rose-Trump, Director of Talks, wrote that his general impression of the station and the staff was extremely favourable. 'I was struck by the enthusiasm of everyone I spoke to and by a sense of loyalty both to the BBC and to the Scottish Regional Director. The output of energy and ideas is remarkable.' Rose-Trump told Reith that he found the station a great deal more favourable than he had anticipated: 'Cleghorn Thomson deserves credit for having got together a staff with such abilities as I have not found in any other regional station.'

This memorandum written only two weeks before Cleghorn Thomson's resignation was announced also reveals that Rose-Trump was under instruction to investigate the strength of nationalist feelings among the staff. His report said he found the nationalist sentiment was 'clearly very strong among some members of staff' describing it in a later reference as 'overstrong'. However he believed the nationalist sentiment was 'a healthy manifestation and quite easily capable of reasonable control.' [22]

It is likely that the author of each report, particularly Rose-Trump, was aware of Cleghorn Thomson's impending departure yet both produced papers praising the Scottish Region, the spirit of the staff, the quality of the programmes, and Thomson's leadership, even his public profile in Edinburgh. With the exception of a question mark over his business skills, both reports, written by senior executives from London, appear to dispute the personal views of Cleghorn Thomson expressed by two governors. And Rose-Trump's questioning of the staff about their nationalist leanings provides further evidence that Reith and the governors were concerned about connections between the BBC Scottish Region and Scottish nationalism. All of these internal events, discussions and reports within the BBC were occurring at the time when the surge of support and the media coverage of nationalism was at its strongest.

Through the summer months of 1933 the BBC sought to assure influential Scottish political and business opinion that the Corporation was not supportive or sympathetic towards Scottish nationalism. In October the BBC Programme Board received a report from the Director of Programmes which said that the nationalism issue had been successfully defused. 'Responsible opinion in Scotland was unanimous, that the disassociation of the Corporation with the Scottish nationalist movement was welcomed,' the report stated. [23]

The response of the BBC in London to the surge of support and unprecedented media interest in Scottish nationalism in the early 1930s was no more than a reflection of the fear and antagonism which engulfed the political and business establishment in Scotland and Westminster at the time. Reith and the Board of Governors may well have been legally and editorially at arm's length from the political position towards nationalism taken by the National Government, and the Scottish Unionist party, but in such matters the BBC hierarchy could be depended upon to ensure that broadcasting protected the interests of the government.

The BBC's unspoken and unofficial position was one of hostility towards Scottish political nationalism – when the SNP was eventually formed in 1934 the BBC would not allow it political broadcasts before general elections – but 'it did permit expressions of cultural nationalism, and debate of political issues'. Reith's dictum that 'broadcasting should be established under the auspices of the state, but certainly not conducted by the State' did not mean that on occasion broadcasting policy decision-making could not be conducted in the interests of the state, whatever the interests of the government of the day. [24]

The name on the door was the 'British' Broadcasting Corporation, and Reith ensured, with the support of the Governors, that listeners in London, Cardiff, Belfast and Glasgow had 'gentle but frequent reminders of their nationality, their membership in the *British* nation'. The BBC strived to develop a unitary and consensual version of Britishness, 'to make *Britain* a community of listeners'. Christopher Harvie's view is that Reith had taken it upon himself to tell the masses what they ought to hear, a prescription that did not include letting the Scottish Renaissance anywhere near a microphone, 'as Moray McLaren and David Cleghorn Thomson found out to their cost at BBC Scotland'. [25]

David Cleghorn Thomson: A Cultural Nationalist

Cleghorn Thomson, belatedly, realised that he had been undone, not just by the BBC Governors and Reith, but by influential individuals and groups within the Scottish establishment who were opposed to what they saw as his cultural nationalism. He described them in the *Scottish Daily Express* as the 'silent forces of conservatism'; the 'fortresses of buddiedom', the 'dead fencing the hearts of men', and the unenlightened mediocrity and middle-aged respectability entrenched and fighting against all change'. In his view the change they resisted and which he had, apparently, come to personify, was the cultural revivalism enshrined in the renaissance movement, the arts revival he had embraced with excitement when he returned to Scotland in the mid-1920s, and which, he freely admitted, he had tried to influence through his position for the benefit of Scots composers, artists and writers. [26]

'Such was the feeling of a new stirring on the air on every hand,' he said. 'There was hope and encouragement then for such causes as the Scottish National Theatre, the Edinburgh Little Theatre, and the National Orchestra.'

William Power, like Malcolm Thomson also a friend of Cleghorn Thomson, observed that although he was successful in creating space for modern Scottish arts in Scottish broadcasting, 'he was in too great a hurry to remould the cultural scheme of things to his heart's desire.' Power presented a picture of Cleghorn Thomson as the leader of the

BBC contingent at the Scottish Arts Club in Edinburgh – 'the spirit of resurgent youth in Scotland' – appearing in full Highland dress on Gala nights as a latter day *Pheobus Apollo*, the Greek God of poetry, music and prophecy. In Power's view, and to continue the Greek analogies, Cleghorn Thomson treated older, established figures as part of a citadel of backward *Boeotians* holding back the advance of the modernists of Athens.' [27]

Cleghorn Thomson believed that part of his mission was to broadcast aspects of modern Scottish music and literature and by doing so to promote cultural Scotland as a representation of national identity. It was the theme he pursued in what was the high point of his reign as BBC Scottish Regional Director when, on 29th November 1930, the eve of St Andrew's Day, he welcomed the Secretary of State for Scotland, the Lord Provost of Edinburgh and a host of establishment figures to the grand opening of Scottish Broadcasting House in Queen Street, Edinburgh. He had persuaded Reith that the Scottish headquarters of the BBC should be switched from Glasgow to Edinburgh, a decision which Reith later regretted. Reith was also present, as was his main critic, Lady Snowden, representing the Board of Governors.

Cleghorn Thomson had successfully lobbied the National Programme in London to broadcast across all UK stations his St Andrew's Eve programme 'A Celebration of Scotland in Poetry and Song', aimed at projecting the cultural spirit of the Scottish race as expressed in one hour of broadcasting.

The Listener noted that the programme had been greeted critically by English newspapers that complained of its sadness and asked 'what had become of the Harry Lauder element which the English have come to look for in all Scottish ntertainment.' The review neatly captured the typical stereotype of the Scot and Scottish culture as viewed, even in 1930, in metropolitan London.

However, his commitment to Scottish arts and culture did not go entirely unrecognised, even in unlikely places. In 1940 an editorial in *The Gramophone* journal praised the quality of the performance of the Scottish Orchestra, 'a repertory which no other orchestra can touch'. The reviewer added, 'much of the credit for that BBC Scottish Orchestra belongs to David Cleghorn Thomson, who, like other prophets, got short shrift from his own country and even shorter from the BBC.' [28]

A year before he left the BBC Cleghorn Thomson edited *Scotland in Quest of Her Youth* (1932), described as a 'scrutiny' of Scottish consciousness and cultural identity, and which included contributions from a virtual hall of fame of contemporary Scots literary figures; names like Gunn, Linklater, Mackenzie, Blake, Bridie, McLaren, Scott Moncrieff, Catherine Carswell and Naomi Mitchison. While in his introduction Cleghorn Thomson acknowledged the growing interest in the nationalist party, 'a significant force in politics', it is clear that his interest is the role of culture in the development of Scottish broadcasting. 'Broadcasting,' he wrote, 'has provided an increasingly valuable platform for the views of those who, whether nationalist in politics or not, are vitally interested in the future of Scotland as a cultural entity.' [29]

In BBC folklore Cleghorn Thomson's fate was deserved, self-inflicted and inevitable. There may have been other corporate reasons to remove him – his boorish behaviour and poor business management skills – but although, as a broadcaster and journalist he was interested and excited by the surge of nationalism, no evidence exists that he had any personal involvement with political nationalism. Three months before his departure he admitted to a BBC executive in London that he had enjoyed a unique experience of working in Scotland 'my own country' during the emergence of the political national movement, before adding, 'a movement with which, incidentally, I am wholly out of sympathy'. This was written before Goldsmith's revelation that his 'sympathies for nationalism' was one of the policy difficulties between him and the Corporation.[30]

His deputy, Moray McLaren presents as a stronger suspect in terms of personal connections and sympathies with the home rule cause in the early 1930s. Malcolm Thomson's references to McLaren in correspondence identify him as one of his 'secret' group of unionist-nationalists, and McLaren, quite publicly, supported Malcolm Thomson's home rule pamphlet *The Kingdom of Scotland Restored*. McLaren, however, survived Cleghorn Thomson's departure before being transferred two years later to the Talks Department in London.

Cleghorn Thomson had an inflated idea of his own importance and influence, and while he freely admitted to revelling in the profile and trappings of his position, his flamboyance and personal arrogance made him many enemies. His interests and passions were focused on the arts – music, dance, poetry and literature – and he shared the aspirations of other intellectuals like Malcolm Thomson and the renaissance writers for a new, modern Scottish culture.

His political commitment and journey took him from the conservatism of Edinburgh and Oxford, and post-war Liberalism to the Labour Party of the depression years. His conversion to socialism is likely to have occurred after he left the BBC and spent six months with the Rev. George MacLeod – later the founder of the Iona Community – at the Pearce Institute in Glasgow's Govan district working with the poor and unemployed in the slums. MacLeod, who had accepted the call to Govan Old Parish Church in 1930, was outraged by the hopelessness and misery he encountered, an experience that transformed him into an outspoken Christian Socialist.

The contrast with the genteel and privileged streets of Edinburgh's New Town made a marked impression on Cleghorn Thomson, who returned to Edinburgh and joined the Labour Party. In 1936 as the Labour candidate he found himself facing the former Prime Minister Ramsay MacDonald representing the National Party, and Gibb for the SNP at a by-election for the Scottish Universities seat. MacDonald, with the reluctant force of the Scottish Unionist Party behind him, won with 56 per cent of the vote, Cleghorn Thomson trailed in third place with 12.5 percent. One Labour MP described him as a 'lad o' pairts' of great ability and outstanding achievement. 'He had a brilliant career and was as keenly enthusiastic for Scotland as the nationalist candidate but he believed that Scotland's economic and political betterment could be won by the policy of the Labour Party.' [31]

The BBC's first Scottish Regional Director, officially labelled by it in internal papers as an enthusiast and sympathiser of Scottish nationalism, had provided Malcolm Thomson with a public platform for his vision of a new cultural and intellectual enlightenment in Scottish life. But he did not agree with Malcolm Thomson's home rule nationalism. He turned to the left and found shared ground with intellectuals like Edwin Muir and Lewis Grassic Gibbon who argued that the solution to the condition of Scotland was to be found in socialism.

The story of Thomson and his fate holds a mirror to the response of parts of the Scottish and British establishments to the surge of interest and enthusiasm for Scottish nationalism, particularly a fear that it was gaining attention from the unionist middle-class. Cleghorn Thomson was to all intents and purposes an establishment figure. Yet his passion for all things Scottish and his closeness to many of the leading comment-ators, many of them, like Malcolm Thomson and Compton Mackenzie, known nationalists, caused concerns in some circles in Edinburgh and, fatefully, also at BBC executive and boardroom level in London.

A recent historian of the BBC suggests that between the wars the BBC played a pivotal role in sustaining and reinforcing 'a complex sense of national identity in Scotland,' that it existed to reflect the politics, society – the culture – of Scotland. The evidence for this analysis is that 'special days' such as St. Andrew's Day or Burns Night *allowed* for the expression of Scottish patriotism, and that, despite its admitted hostility to political nationalism 'it did *permit* expressions of cultural nationalism, and debate of political issues.' [32]

In the early 1930s the BBC Governors and its Director General's dispensation on what was 'allowed' or 'permitted' did not extend to accepting that its Scottish Regional Director might have political views with which they disagreed, and if he did, finding the evidence to support the charge. The BBC's fear of nationalism even extended to issuing instructions to a London executive to investigate feelings of nationalism among the staff; and in the wake of the sacking of Cleghorn Thomson to carry out soundings across the Scottish establishment to confirm that they were now assured that the BBC and its executives in Scotland were not sympathetic to Scottish nationalism. Expressions of Scottish patriotism had limits.

CHAPTER 9

Malcolm Thomson, Gibb and Nationalism before World War II

The Scottish Party and the SNP

By the summer of 1932 George Malcolm Thomson and Andrew Dewar Gibb could claim with some justification that their two main objectives – to develop greater unionist support for home rule and to dilute the radical separatist policy of the National Party of Scotland – were beginning to show some practical progress. Members of their so-called 'secret group' had a foothold inside the NPS, they had regular contact with NPS figures like MacCormick and Gunn, and the breakaway Cathcart unionists were creating confusion and concern across official Scottish unionism.

Gibb played a prominent role alongside the leader of the dissidents, Kevan McDowall, in attracting the Duke of Montrose and Sir Alexander MacEwen to support the Cathcart plan. Montrose had been involved in nationalist politics throughout the 1920s but although a public supporter of the NPS since 1928 he was uncomfortable with its separatist policies and continued to take the Unionist whip in the House of Lords. His mixed loyalties were in evidence when he refused to back the nationalist candidate in a Glasgow University Rectorial election because the other candidate was the Tory prime minister, Stanley Baldwin. Aware of Montrose's uncertainties, Thomson and Gibb deliberately appealed to both his Scottishness and unionism and flattered his abilities as a leader suggesting that those who were seriously interested in nationalism needed direction. Gibb in a letter to Montrose wrote: 'A true national movement is one which affects the whole outlook of the people both spiritually and materially. The ranks and file require guiding, instructing and shepherding towards the proper course.' [1]

MacEwen was an Inverness solicitor prominent in local government and business circles in the Highlands. A Liberal nationalist he had added his voice to the home rule debate through his book *The Thistle and the Rose: Scotland's Problem Today* (1932) in which he rejected separatism, dismissed the anti-Englishness of some sections of the NPS and called for self-government within a British Federal system. A pragmatist, he was convinced that the case for home rule had to be justified on economic grounds: 'there is not the remotest chance of any form of self-government or devolution unless the people are satisfied that the change is going to contribute to their material as well as to their spiritual advantage.' [2]

The separation of the economic and political forces on one side from the cultural and spiritual forces on the other was fundamental to MacEwen's nationalism and he had no doubt that the latter had to follow the former. To him nationalism implied freedom for both the nation and the individual: 'we seek political freedom so that we may develop the spiritual and cultural heritage of the nation.' His high profile presence brought to the new movement a commentator of some intellectual strength but also someone who could claim to represent the private, public and cultural constituencies of the Highlands. [3]

John MacCormick recognised that MacEwen would be regarded as the voice of moderate nationalism – 'many who would otherwise have been apathetic would take a new and livelier interest in the national movement'. MacCormick also gave public backing to Kevan McDowall's manifesto. In the *Scots Independent* he claimed that the NPS had always favoured national status for Scotland within the British Commonwealth or Empire, 'we agree with the Cathcart Unionists in demanding for Scotland a full voice,' he said. Despite overtures for prior talks from MacCormick, Gibb, Montrose, MacEwen and McDowall held the first public meeting of their self-government group, took the name the Scottish Party (SP), and announced their support for a parliament in Edinburgh with control over Scottish domestic affairs. An Edinburgh conference appointed Montrose as President, MacEwen as Chairman, McDowall as Secretary, and Gibb was given charge of strategy and propaganda. Montrose told an enthusiastic audience they had forced the NPS to declare itself against separation and had put the issue of self-government into the public sphere: 'the question has grown from a stream into a roaring cataract and is being discussed in every home.' MacEwen reinforced the message that the party was against separation, but wanted 'a richer and more enduring partnership' with England. [4]

Throughout 1933, Thomson and Gibb were involved in the merger discussions between the SP and the NPS, with Thomson, again, staying in the background while Gibb had a more high-profile role, inevitable given his senior position within the SP. This took on greater significance when he was selected as the SP's candidate at the Kilmarnock by-election, a move which surprised and angered the NPS. Gunn who was in regular correspondence with Gibb about a merger between the parties warned Gibb that he would oppose him: 'I shall do my utmost in every possible way to support the NPS candidate.' Gunn saw it as an act of betrayal at a time when efforts to find common ground had led to internal accusations that the NPS had watered down policies and 'stultified its essential being' in order to make overtures to the SP. He accused the SP of attempting to take advantage of the spadework done by the NPS, 'a deliberate and provocative challenge which could end hopes for fusion between the parties.' [5]

The reaction of Gunn and other NPS leaders forced the SP to retreat and a defensive Gibb claimed that he had only been adopted because they believed that the NPS would not be fielding a candidate. [6] The two parties met and agreed to field MacEwen as a compromise joint home rule candidate. Gibb, the conservative unionist, worked hard to heal the wounds, praising the NPS and its leaders for their positive pronouncements on home rule. MacEwen told him that his actions and words had helped to smooth the path towards the merger: 'I think immediately the by-election is over we should try to bring fusion about as soon as possible'. [7] In retrospect the dispute acted as a catalyst for better understanding in the discussions between the two parties; they worked together at Kilmarnock and MacEwen polled over 6,000 votes, almost 17 per cent of the turnout, the best nationalist result recorded to date in a parliamentary election. The turnaround was reflected in a more emollient dialogue between Gibb and Gunn who argued that the behaviour of the NPS at Kilmarnock should have removed any remaining doubts about it within the SP.

In the months leading to the final merger, the man who emerged as the determined and dominant voice and who provided crucial strength and direction to MacCormick was Gunn. He abandoned his writing, telling his fellow nationalist and friend Eric Linklater that he had neither read nor written for almost a year. 'I have dropped out of the business altogether – into nationalism, I admit. But there, that can't be helped. At the moment things are extraordinarily critical.' Gunn, who had always taken a detached view of politics – 'I don't give a damn about politics' – said that there had been many previous political shows in Scotland. 'I have been doing my utmost to see if, at last, we cannot pull off one show. Is it the biggest, a hopeless sort of pantomime? No doubt, but we'll see.'[8]

He opposed the siren voices opposed to change within the NPS who continued to argue that it should stay independent: 'I am dead against this and shall use all of my influence to counter,' he said. It was, he believed, impossible to run two organisations without loss of drive, internal disharmony and mutual recriminations, 'which human nature cannot avoid'. Speeches which tried to explain both parties were a trifling waste of time while nothing was being done about economic failure, the fishing fleet, unemployment, and the transfer of industries from Scotland. Gunn was concerned that the whole nationalist movement could lose the prestige it had gained in recent years and while he did not intend to take a high profile personal role he was anxious to see a result for Scotland from the vast amount of anonymous work of himself and others. He told Gibb: 'It is absolutely clear to me that if we came out into the open as a single party with a more progressive programme we would induce the country to take notice.'

Thomson was also urging Gibb to ensure that nothing prevented the merger taking place. 'We must not rest until the fusion or union is complete,' he wrote. 'We shall get our rewards in heaven if not in history.'[9]

In January 1934 the NPS and the SP reached agreement to merge and formal approval followed from both parties within two months. When the Scottish National Party was formed in April 1934 the agreed principles on which the merger took place enshrined the values of nationalism, unionism and imperialism. Thomson and Gibb had good reason to feel satisfied with the outcome. The language of the new party echoed the aspirations of their stated 'unionist-nationalism': home rule for all Scottish affairs including finance and taxation; shared responsibilities with England as 'mother nations' of the Empire; and joint machinery to deal with customs, foreign affairs and defence.

Many members of the NPS refused to join a party they believed to be under the control of conservative right-wing elements. MacCormick, the man who had ultimately made merger possible, was unapologetic. 'We felt that we had taken a real step forward in the fight for a new Scotland and our mood was one both of gaiety and of an underlying realisation of the opportunities which now opened before us.'

The credit for the creation of the SNP has mainly been directed at MacCormick, who, it is claimed, transformed the NPS by his purge of the radicals and made it fit for merger with the right wing and elitist SP. MacIver argues that the two parties were brought together because of MacCormick's desire 'to harness the prestige and supposed political competence of the SP.' [10]

MacCormick had concluded that nationalism would not succeed politically until the Scottish establishment was converted to the home rule cause, and that could only be achieved by adopting a more moderate form of nationalism. He justified his expulsion of MacDiarmid by describing him as one of the greatest handicaps to have burdened any national movement. His love of bitter controversy, anti-Englishness and woolly thinking were 'sufficient excuse to condemn the whole case for home rule out of hand'. MacDiarmid's biographer, Alan Bold, wrote, 'Party policy was to present a moderate front to the Scottish people by getting rid of men like MacDiarmid.' MacDiarmid never forgave MacCormick. [11]

Several years after MacCormick's death in 1961 he remained bitter. 'I could never be bothered wi' MacCormick,' he said, accusing him of sacrificing Scotland's culture on the altar of practical politics. 'Art and culture mean everything to Scotland. Practical politics, as everybody knows, are rubbish.' Although their personal political persuasions were totally divergent – the left leaning instincts of MacCormick and Gunn, as opposed to the unionist-nationalism of Thomson, Gibb and others –

they were able to blend their varieties of nationalism under one label. It was not a brand without problems and external weaknesses and failures and internal battles and divisions would dominate its existence for the next twenty years. [12]

The SNP that emerged, flawed and disunited in 1934, was the product of the efforts of intellectuals, authors, poets, journalists, students and activists from both the political left and right. Thomson's group of propagandists, his so-called 'secret league of intellectuals', can be see today as little more than a right wing pressure group of unionists serving up a cocktail of genuine passion and concern for the future of their country mixed with an agenda which aimed at ensuring that if the Scots were attracted by nationalism it would be a watered down home rule dish; one that would pose no threat to the union between England and Scotland.

With the exception of MacCormick as the secretary, the chief office holders, Montrose, the first President and MacEwen, the first Chairman, were drawn from the SP. 'The policies of the party were a public guarantee that the SNP had broken with its past.' Brand observed that it was 'more and more in the terms of home rule' that the policy of the party was couched, while Kidd, more recently, noted that the provisions of the merger alienated some of the more extreme nationalists, provoking departures. 'In the short run the loss of these hardliners helped to ease the amalgamation of the conservative SP with the moderate core of the NPS.' This consensus has been challenged by Finlay who maintains that following the formation of the SNP many of the radicals returned to the party 'and accepted the SNP as the legitimate bearer of the nationalist standard.' There was no drop in membership and the majority of the branches, previously NPS, remained in healthy condition. [13]

Thomson was unimpressed with MacEwen as Chairman, telling Gibb, as he previously urged him to do in the SP, to push himself forward into the limelight. 'MacEwen is not harsh enough in his mind or his utterance,' he said. 'You have the real leadership in your pocket if you like to make the effort. You must make yourself the wise.' [14]

Both had less than two years to wait before Gibb was appointed

Chairman, although his ascent reflected more on MacEwen's lack of leadership qualities than Gibb's wisdom. Gibb's elevation was remarkable when set against four factors: the radical origins of the NPS in 1928; his continued unionist-minded focus on Scotland's place within the British Empire; the racism and sectarianism implicit in his views of Scotland's Irish Catholic community; and his refusal to consider separation or dominion status as an option for Scotland. He had, however, gained support from a strong performance at a by-election. At the 1935 General Election Gibb won 14 per cent of the vote for the Scottish Universities seat and when a by-election was held in the same seat in January, 1936 he achieved the SNP's best electoral performance to date when he won over 31 per cent of the vote.

In *Scottish Empire* in 1937, Gibb argued that the weakness of Scottish national identity had its origins in the Empire itself and Scotland's junior role in the relationship with England. He retained the Imperial hue of the Victorian and Edwardian Scots: that Scotland was a mother nation of the Empire; that since the union she had pooled all of her resources with those of England; and that she had been a partner in the development of the Empire. Gibb believed implicitly that the Empire had been the most important factor in the relationship between the two countries since the eighteenth century. He compared it with the child who unites parents who may be irked by the ties of marriage, 'so have the imperial brood formed a common interest for the two ill-assorted partners in the Union.' But in Gibb's eyes this was a conditional and unhappy marriage in which the identity of one partner, Scotland, had been sacrificed to the interests of the other, England. Scottish resources and skills had been used by the bigger partner, said Gibb, 'as a means towards the attainment of her own greatness.' Gibb claimed that England would have considered any other national sentiment, other than her own, 'a menace to her imperial destiny'. Scotland, her poorer neighbour, had been 'englobed and assimilated', and even if she was richer and more powerful than before, she was 'essentially England'. In Gibb's thesis Scotland helped to make and run the Empire and in doing so she contributed to the greatness of England. Gibb, already emotionally burdened by his conviction that there had been no shared Empire identity – the British Empire was in reality the English Empire – now saw Scottish identity further threatened by the contention of mainstream unionism that 'Scotland cannot live without England'.

Gibb continued to reject this argument in public debate, speeches and broadcasts, accusing the Westminster parliament of both encouraging and permitting almost 700,000 Scots to emigrate between 1911 and 1931. 'No country in the world can stand up to that sort of drain. Emigration and immigration on a Scottish scale is a social monstrosity which is seriously endangering the integrity of the very existence of our people.' [15]

Despite the SNP's lack of popular support and electoral failures, Gibb maintained that the events of the last two decades and the pressures brought about by the nationalists had led to a series of government policy u-turns. He cited as evidence reports on the Highlands and Scottish light industries and economic planning strategies published by the Scottish Economic Committee. 'Ten or fifteen years ago no body of conservatives would ever have dreamed of issuing any of these reports,' Gibb said. Scots were now convinced that Scotland had specific problems that could only be solved by actions taken within Scotland. [16]

It was a view echoed by Rait and Pryde who said nationalist activities had produced and continued to produce 'useful results'. Nationalism, they argued, had succeeded in forcing the government to pay attention to Scottish grievances, 'in securing special treatment for Scottish problems and in inducing governments to undertake needed reforms'.[17] Historians since, however, have mainly judged the performance of the SNP in the years before World War II as one of failure and disappointment. Such analysis has been consistent: 'No great results ensued, it was faction-ridden and failed to make any real electoral progress,' was Ferguson's view in 1968.[18] The party had 'negligible political impact,' was 'small, isolated, devoid of any realistic approach to politics.'[19] A more recent assessment concluded that electoral impotence was an important characteristic. [20]

Such judgements are not only based on the party's poor record in parliamentary elections but also on the evidence of internal divisions and rebellions, much of these often played out in the full gaze of public scrutiny. The marriage of the NPS and the SP was unhappy from the outset with individuals mistrustful of the motives and objectives of others. McDowall was rebellious, suspicious that many of his colleagues were anti-imperial and had no real commitment to the Empire, issues which he regarded as more important than home rule itself. Within two years in a blaze of anger and recrimination, McDowall was gone, the dreams of the Cathcart rebellion of 1932 an unfulfilled memory. But in the years that followed he remained defiant, describing himself as a 'Scottish Home Ruler and British Imperialist'.[21]

McDowall's legacy, probably not one he would have wished, was the contribution he made to the formation of the modern SNP, perhaps the key legacy from a group of interwar Scottish intellectual and middle-class unionists who were instrumental in redefining the relationship between identity, nationalism and unionism. Gibb, made of sterner stuff, continued to argue the cause of unionist-nationalism from his position inside the SNP although as chairman he was never trusted by radical elements suspicious of his conservative and unionist roots, regarding his so-called nationalism as little more than tepid devolution. Before World War II the SNP remained fractured by internal feuds and disputes between factions of the right and left. Gibb considered resigning as Chairman in 1939 because of the party's 'rapid leftward lurch' but held on before he eventually quit a year later when anti-war forces persuaded others that the party should contest by-elections in defiance of a wartime electoral truce. It was anti-war, anti-unionist and anti-conservative, 'too much for Gibb to stomach'. [22]

Malcolm Thomson, Beaverbrook and the BBC

Despite Beaverbrook's flirtation with Scottish home rule between 1931 and 1933 Thomson took great care to keep his nationalist activities away from the gaze of his employer. However, his low public profile position was fractured by the publication of *Distressed* in 1935.

The book was well received in Scotland but it marked a fundamental change in Thomson's working relationship with Beaverbrook who took the view that as the chief commentator of the *London Daily Express*, a position which it was generally accepted made Thomson the press baron's public mouthpiece, he should not be associated with political parties or causes. Thomson signed a contract which effectively banned him from writing books on politics and current affairs while he wrote for the *London Daily Express* and other Beaverbrook newspapers and was his personal advisor.

Thomson's son, Peter, confirmed this arrangement. 'There was certainly an understanding that while he was engaged with Beaverbrook and the *Express* he would not write books, any books. He mentioned this to me to explain why he didn't write books while he was in Beaverbrook's employment.' [23]

The impact of Beaverbrook's ban was felt within months when Thomson was asked to take part in a BBC series on nationalism to be broadcast on the National Programme. Ironically, the BBC executive who asked Thomson to speak on the economic case for nationalism was Moray McLaren, relocated by the BBC from Scotland to its Talks Department in London. Thomson, although keen on the idea for the series, told McLaren he could not take part. McLaren advised the BBC Scottish Regional Director, Melville Dinwiddie, and the Scottish Programme Director, Andrew Stewart that Thomson 'was not allowed to talk by his lord and master, Beaverbrook. This is, of course, confidential; please don't pass it on.'

Stewart in a response wrote that he was sorry to hear about Thomson, 'but it is a little difficult to appreciate Beaverbrook's attitude when he allowed him to publish *Scotland That Distressed Area*.' Stewart's remarks indicate that while the book was widely regarded as the best of Thomson's 'condition' trilogy there were parts of professional Scotland – even in the late 1930s – either still in denial about the economic and social state of the country or opposed to books and articles critical of the establishment.

Thomson suggested to McLaren that Gibb should undertake the broadcast on the economic case and recommended that the speaker for the proposed second talk on the historical, identity and cultural case for nationalism should be another friend and 'group' colleague from the early 1930s, George Blake. McLaren passed this on to Stewart: 'the more I think of it, the more I think that Blake would do an extremely good talk. He has the case for the cultural and historical point of view absolutely pat.'

At the time Blake contributed a regular 'The Week in Scotland' broadcast for the BBC Scottish Region and although Stewart did not veto him – he would have preferred Eric Linklater – he had doubts about Blake's impartiality. 'This is probably rather straining at gnats, as the tone of Blake's writings – particularly *The Heart of Scotland* and *The Ship-builders* – show all too clearly where his sympathies lie.' [24]

Again Stewart's reaction is negative, revealing not only his personal misgivings about the nationalist views of Thomson and Blake, but of the concerns within the BBC Scottish Region management about how Scottish nationalism would be presented on the National Programme and how it would be received in other parts of Britain, particularly in London.

The series had been requested by Reith, the Director General following correspondence he had had with Gibb. Reith gave Gibb an undertaking that the BBC would 'take cognisance' of Scottish nationalism in a series of talks: 'I am in fact making a suggestion to our programme people that they should consider a series in which you might participate'. Reith's programme executives treated the series as a sensitive project from the outset and were determined that it should not become a propaganda vehicle for Scottish nationalism. The editorial guidelines, laid out in an internal memo circulated by the Director of Talks, J.M. Rose-Trump, insisted that there should be no emotional appeals, 'no references to the distant past with its alleged injustices. One gets out of the realm of purely propagandist talks by the nationalist in Scotland, intended to attract more Scottish people to their side.'

BBC London programme makers wanted a series focused on practical matters, particularly those which highlighted the problems faced by nationalism. These included issues such as the administrative and constitutional difficulties of producing a workable scheme for devolution and the 'inconsistencies of the nationalist case'. However the series could state, 'that no one denies that Scotland has its own separate culture'. [25]

Despite the best efforts of BBC executives to exclude emotional appeals to nationalism Gibb, in discussing the modern economic and social condition of Scotland, also focused on the wider issue of the decline of Scotland as a nation. He said Scotland had been permanently absorbed into the civilisation and the political and economic fabric of England. 'Her very name has disappeared from world affairs and been replaced by that of England.' He attacked the Scottish elite and professional classes for their Anglicisation and lack of sympathy towards their fellow Scots. To them, Gibb said, Scotland was no more than a romantic background; 'London, Oxford, the Services and Empire was their home. This contemptible transfer of loyalty they called "displaying the larger patriotism".'[26] Their case against nationalism and the message they had for the Scottish people was that Scotland could not live without England. [27]

At this time, Thomson continued to correspond with Gibb in private, and occasionally he would meet him in London for dinner, discussing ideas for the SNP election leaflet for the next general election which Thomson insisted, wrongly, would be in the spring of 1939. In March 1939, with the prospect of war with Germany looking more certain by the day, Thomson continued to believe that there would be a general election, and recommended to Gibb that the SNP should seek a pact with the Liberal Party on home rule, claiming that he had already initiated discussions with two prominent Liberals, Arthur Irvine and Joe Grimond. He also suggested that nationalist speakers at the general election should support the foreign policy of the Prime Minister, Neville Chamberlain. [28]

By this time Thomson's political antennae was largely switched to the views of Beaverbrook who had thrown his newspaper's support behind the embattled Prime Minister. The previous year, Thomson penned a remarkable article published at Beaverbrook's insistence in both the *London Evening Standard* and the *London Daily Express*, in which he predicted that there would be no war in Europe, 'now, nor for a long time to come'; that the German armies invading Austria were poorly equipped, had inferior tanks and obsolete airplanes; that the Sudeten Germans would make settlement with the Czechs; that the Japanese in the Far East would pursue a more conciliatory policy towards Britain; and the menace of the bomber to London was exaggerated. 'London cannot be destroyed by attack from the air.'

Having exhausted his raft of predictions and prophecies Thomson told *Express* readers to be of good cheer and dwell not dismally on the past. 'Look with confidence into the future, and equip yourself with machinery to enable you to share in the harvest of commerce and industry that is to come.'

Unlike his more serious prediction from a decade earlier that the pure Scottish race would be overrun by Irish Catholics hordes, Thomson could claim, as he subsequently did, that he often wrote things for Beaverbrook he didn't agree with. [29]

CHAPTER 10

Lewis Grassic Gibbon
and the Socialist Commentators

He who set the flame of his native genius
Under the cumbering whin of the untilled field
Lit a fire in the Mearns that illumines Scotland
Clearing her sullen soil for a richer yield.

                    Helen B. Cruikshank, 'Spring in the Mearns' [1]

THE POET, Helen B. Cruikshank wrote her *In Memoriam* poem as a tribute to the novelist Lewis Grassic Gibbon on the evening of 23rd February, 1935, the day his ashes were buried at Arbuthnott Churchyard in the Mearns, south of Aberdeen. Cruickshank, like most contemporary Scottish authors and poets, had known Gibbon for only three years, since 1932 when he arrived on the literary scene with *Sunset Song*, the first book of his trilogy, *A Scots Quair*, regarded as one of the outstanding achievements of twentieth-century Scottish literature.

Thomson had reviewed *Sunset Song* for a London newspaper. He wrote to Cruickshank recommending she should get a copy: 'it seems to me the pioneer of something new and very interesting in Scottish letters, perhaps the first really Scottish novel.' But like Cruickshank, prior to *Sunset Song* Thomson had never heard of Lewis Grassic Gibbon, 'whoever he or she may be,' he wrote. Cruickshank contacted her Edinburgh bookseller who, also, knew nothing of Gibbon but located the book and sent it to her. [2]

'My excitement mounted as I read, and the conviction grew that this was a major work of fiction by a new author,' Cruickshank recalled, a view not shared, at the time, by critics in the Scottish press – 'sour reviews began to appear, accusing the author of unnecessary coarseness.' There was no recognition among Scottish reviewers that *Sunset Song* was a book of major significance or that, in Gibbon, Scotland had found an emerging literary figure. The *Scotsman* relegated the book to the tail end of a column on 'New Fiction', the reviewer, while finding many of the characters highly convincing, less impressed that Gibbon had found it necessary to 'unduly emphasise the unpleasant aspects of the lives he seeks to portray.' The harsh realities of rural life in the Mearns country-side in the years before the Great War were, apparently, too rich in detail for the soft Edinburgh stomach. Scottish literary and social history would suggest that Thomson and Cruickshank, who shared with many other intellectuals of the time a determination and passion that modern Scotland, warts and all, should be projected through literature, had a better and truer realisation of the value and importance of Gibbon's novel than the staid, establishment minded reviewers of mainstream Scottish newspapers. [3]

Both Thomson and Cruickshank contacted Gibbon, establishing friendships which lasted for the remainder of his short life. Thomson wrote personally to Gibbon expressing his view that in *Sunset Song* he had attempted an experiment, 'and it seems to me you have made a triumphant success of it'. Thomson, who had previously written about the paucity of outstanding modern Scottish literature, told Gibbon that he may well have written the most important Scottish novel since George Douglas's *The House with the Green Shutters.* 'This is the real Scotland at last. The book is a triumph; its closing passages moved me very much,' Thomson wrote.

He was equally enthused by *Cloud Howe*, again sending a personal message to Gibbon: 'It is magnificent. The humour, irony, realism and poetry are simply overwhelming.' When he read *Grey Granite*, the final book of the trilogy, Thomson told Gibbon that the work as a whole was the biggest thing ever written by a modern Scotsman. Thomson, who, unsurprisingly, regarded himself as one of the country's leading literary reviewers – he was already reviewing books for Beaverbrook Newspapers and after World War II would become the Chief Book Reviewer of the *London Evening Standard* – was convinced that Gibbon had developed a new idiom in fiction writing, a medium and fertile novel technique that was 'beautiful and moving. It has poetry, sweep, life and humour.' [4]

Gibbon followed up his dedication of *Cloud Howe* to Thomson by agreeing with MacDiarmid in 1934 to dedicate *Scottish Scene* to Cruickshank. Such interactions and dedications were common among intellectuals of the Scottish Renaissance who frequently met, talked, argued and gossiped together at informal social occasions. Cruickshank was renowned for the gatherings she assembled at her home, Dinnieduff, in the then village of Corstorphine, near Edinburgh, events occasionally attended by leading literary figures such as Muir and MacDiarmid. Gibbon accepted an invitation from her to stay at Dinnieduff and meet other Scottish authors and poets.

'We were all agog to meet this new author, and so began my friendship with this brilliant young man, who alas was to burn himself out within three years,' Cruickshank later recalled. Gibbon visited Cruickshank on three further occasions before his death, their friendship strengthened beyond the literary connection to their shared interest in the Doric language of the north east and the broad, native Scots which Cruickshank used in many of her poems. Unlike Gibbon, Cruickshank was a committed Scottish nationalist, but as a civil servant she was unable to translate her support into serious activity until she retired in 1945. [5]

Gibbon's association and friendship with Thomson is more difficult to comprehend since, with the exception of a mutual interest in publishing and Scottish affairs, they did not appear to share many political or cultural beliefs or interests. He was neither comfortable with nor an advocate for Thomson's home rule nationalism nor his vision and aspirations for a renewed civic and cultural society, particularly one that came adorned with a Viceroy.

Gibbon, whose real name was John Leslie Mitchell, had been raised in the farming communities of the Howe of Mearns. He represented a face of Scottish identity different in background, outlook and values from that of the well-heeled upper middle-classes of the central belt epitomised by intellectuals like Thomson, Gibb, McLaren and Cleghorn Thomson. In *Sunset Song* Gibbon retraced much of his own early experiences, choosing to do so through the character of a woman, Chris Guthrie – in Thomson's view 'the greatest woman character in Scottish fiction, intensely drawn and yet universal' – the central theme focusing on the disappearing old life and identity of rural Scotland as mechanisation takes over and society itself changes in the years before and during World War I. [6]

Gibbon's journey from the rural north-east was harsh and his experiences, first in Aberdeen, and then Clydeside fomented his youthful radicalism and idealism, attracting him to socialism and communism. The poverty and degradation he found in Glasgow stirred his anger against industrialism and capitalism: 'There are over 150,000 human beings living in such conditions as the most bitterly pressed primitive in Tierra del Fuego never visioned. They live five or six to a single room,' he wrote. He cast a cynical eye in the direction of contemporary nationalist writers, some of them new friends and associates from the literary revival, and he mocked with imaginary scenes what he regarded as some of the absurdities he envisaged as representative of contemporary expressions of nationalism. He risked 'dying of laughter' at the idea of a Scots Expeditionary Force trying to reclaim the Scone Stone of Destiny; or Compton Mackenzie as Prime Minister in a Scots Catholic kingdom; the country's intellectuals sent to re-colonise St. Kilda 'for the good of their souls and the nation'; and George Blake, 'that ephor of the people' reviving and setting in order the ancient Scots aristocracy. But the chiding had a purpose, to remind Gibbon of the priorities as he saw it, the stark realities of urban life.

'I cannot play with those fantasies when I think of the 150,000 in Glasgow,' he said. In Gibbon's world there was nothing in culture or art worth the life and happiness of one of the thousands rotting in the slums, and if creeping Anglicisation or even a 'Chinese army of occupation' could cleanse the slums and provide food and elementary human rights to all he would welcome it. While Thomson had written in similar harsh terms about the slums, he did not share Gibbon's cynical dismissal of nationalism and cultural and intellectual renewal remained central to his vision of a modern Scotland. [7]

Despite his misgivings when approached by Neil Gunn, Gibbon agreed to write an article for the nationalist newspaper, *The Scots Independent* but was unable to resist the opportunity for further mocking of nationalist figures, even MacDiarmid, now, also, a close friend who had moved to the Shetland Islands: 'Why do Scots nationalists all go and live on islands and moon romantically? Why not live in the Gorbals of Glasgow or the rot-gut stinks of Dundee and really get close to the soul of the people?' he asked.

Despite these and other irritations, Gibbon claimed that he was not 'really anti-nationalist', but he loathed fascism and all the 'dirty things' that hid under its name, adding: 'I doubt if you can ever have nationalism without communism,' although he himself was not an official communist. 'They refuse to allow me into the party.' [8]

One scholar has translated this into a version suggesting that Gibbon could equally not contemplate a socialist answer to society's ills which did not include nationalism. The evidence suggests otherwise, that while Gibbon was close to many nationalist figures on the left he himself remained firmly in the radical camp railing against the economic and social injustices of both urban and rural Scotland but resisting, as he saw it, the parochial messages of Scottish nationalism. He was a socialist, a communist, but never a nationalist. It has also been suggested that the best label to give him is that he was an 'anarchist' since there was never any doubt in his mind about the kind of free and egalitarian society to which he aspired; 'what was less certain was the process by which to get there.' [9]

Gibbon's social and political intellect and soul was left wing and even if, as he claimed, he was not anti-nationalist he believed that socialism, whether of a Scottish or international variety, could provide a solution to the economic and social problems. Such political views were unlikely to endear him to Thomson and yet the dedication exists as evidence of a growing respect and friendship between them: 'since the publication of *Sunset Song* Thomson had become a close acquaintance of the Mitchell family'.

One possible explanation is Gibbon's admiration for *Caledonia*. He found much of his own, personal anger and frustrations about rural and urban poverty reflected in its pages. Tange has argued that Gibbon's intention in dedicating *Cloud Howe* to Thomson was to stress the connection between Thomson's non-fiction and the fictional narrative in his work. *Cloud Howe* moves the story of Chris Guthrie from World War I to the 1920s into a time of hardship and injustice and the urban politics of socialism, nationalism and fascism. The theme is continued in the third book of the trilogy, *Grey Granite*, a book Gibbon dedicated to MacDiarmid. The possibilities of socialism and communism are presented as strong and positive in contrast to negative and dismissive views on nationalism. [10]

At one point in *Grey Granite* Chris recalls earlier feelings about nationalism: 'Chris minded back to her days in Segget and said that nationalism was just another plan to do down the common folk. Only this time 'twas to be done in kilts and hose, with bagpipes playing and a blether about Wallace, the English to be chased across the border and the Scots to live on brose and baps.' [11] However, the friendship between Thomson and Gibbon transcended any differences they had about socialism and nationalism. Following Gibbon's premature death Thomson was one of many Scottish literary figures who provided assistance to his widow Ray and their children who were still living in Welwyn Garden City. The support reflected all shades of Scottish literary opinion and also included Blake, MacDiarmid, Linklater, Muir, Mackenzie, Gunn, Cruickshank, James Bridie and James Barke. Cruickshank inevitably played a central role, 'we raised over £200 in one Plea Fund, and Ray wants it invested, £100 for each child, as a fund to help their education later on.' [12]

The support and generosity provided to Gibbon's family was evidence of the esteem with which he was held by his peers in literary Scotland. The praise for Gibbon's work expressed by Thomson and Cruikshank became common currency among intellectuals across the political and cultural classes. The nationalist novelist, Compton Mackenzie, described *Sunset Song* as 'the richest novel about Scottish life written for many years'. [13] Gibbon's work gave little solace to the nationalists of the right and perhaps, inevitably, the narrative in a trilogy which exposed the difficulties experienced by many in the early decades of the twentieth century, was claimed by anti-nationalist commentators and writers on the left of political and social life.

Prominent among these was James Barke, the Glasgow based socialist and staunchly anti-nationalist author who found it impossible to conceal his contempt for right-wing commentators such as Thomson, his disdain magnified by the fact that so many of these contemporaries had claimed a stake in Scottish nationalism. Barke dismissed Thomson, Gibb and others as no more than 'minor poets and petty scribblers'. However, like Thomson and others, Barke regarded Gibbon's *Sunset Song* as the major novel of the times. 'A masterpiece,' Barke wrote, 'the greatest Scottish book in the English language,' and his ultimate accolade was to tell Gibbon that the book had given him 'a greater, richer, fuller and deeper enjoyment than anything he could remember reading, with the possible exception of the Communist Manifesto.' Gibbon's reply would hardly have met with Thomson's approval. 'Glad there is at least one soul in Scotland unspotted by this dreary rash of nationalism,' he wrote. [14]

Barke, the son of a Borders dairyman and dairymaid, had held down a middle-class job as the manager of a Glasgow brickworks while he was developing his writing career. He was convinced that only socialism could cure Scotland's social problems. His 1936 novel, *Major Operation*, is a personal view of working class life in Glasgow during the slump and depression years. Despite their rhetoric he believed that the nationalist intellectuals and writers had closed their eyes to the plight of the Scottish working classes, they were isolated, divorced from the workers, and had lost perspective on where and how they fitted in as part of wider Scottish society. Their response to the condition of Scotland question was a cocktail of home rule and nationhood, anti-Englishness, and 'a great chatter about the Scottish Renaissance, nationalist ballyhooing, to which the average Scot remained cruelly indifferent.'

Barke sensed a massive gulf between the nationalism of the so-called Scottish 'intelligentsia' – drawn mainly from the middle and professional classes and the universities – and the 'overwhelming' majority of the Scottish people. 'They do not feel they are suffering from the oppression of a conquering nation. Nationalism – political, economic or cultural – is not a deep and fundamental issue,' said Barke. This did not mean that the Scots did not retain their sense of national pride and nationhood. Despite the aura of decline and dependency the Scots maintained an attitude of infinite mental, moral, physical and cultural superiority to the English, but none of these feelings manifested into popular support for nationalism. The problem as far as Barke was concerned was clear, it was capitalism. [15]

'When,' Barke asked, 'will Scottish intellectuals and writers open their eyes to the class nature of society and the realities of history?' Barke's fellow Scottish communist colleague, the writer Robert McLennan, described attempts by nationalism to appeal to national sentiment as 'fascist', fostered by capitalist elements, and against the interests of wider British working class solidarity. Like Barke he claimed there was no national question in Scotland, and dismissed the efforts of right wing nationalists to create one as 'reactionary'. McLennan conceded, as Barke did, that there did exist in Scotland a distinct character and culture but argued that Scottish songs, poetry, music and dancing did not embrace the mass of workers, who – unfortunately, at least in McLennan's view – preferred the capitalist cultures of jazz songs, music, dancing, and Edgar Wallace books to the homespun legacies of Sir Walter Scott and Robert Burns. 'The good in the old folk songs, dances, and poetry won't get popularised among the workers,' McLennan predicted, 'until we have swept away capitalism and its decadent jazz culture.' [16]

Barke and McLennan were among a coterie of Scottish socialists and communists in the 1930s that rejected the strategy proposed by some that left wing groups and parties should consider nationalist arguments more carefully, and that the Communist Party should clarify its policy towards Scottish home rule. One of the strongest advocates for this was Helen Crawfurd, the Gorbals-born former suffragette and radical activist who emerged as a leading figure in the British Communist Party. Crawfurd disagreed with McLennan's view that nationalism in Scotland was little more than an arm of fascism, an assessment she claimed ignored the evidence of nationalism's advance, particularly in districts where the middle class and small shop-keeping class 'are being crushed while the big industrialists are attempting to stabilise British economic life in their own interest'. They were victims of industrial rationalisation schemes, increased taxation and an economic axe imposed by the National Government upon state employees such as teachers. Crawfurd believed that Scottish nationalism was no longer an academic discussion among a handful of people; it had been transformed into an active militant movement, had forced the political establishment to take notice, and was receiving widespread coverage in the press. It had branches throughout Scotland, district committees, groups in the universities, a youth movement and was attempting to widen its appeal to women by establishing the Scottish National Women's League.

'To treat this movement as of purely romantic character and origin is to fail to see the economic reasons for its rise and development,' Crawfurd warned. Her concerns about Scottish middle-class teachers and shopkeepers did not impress the editor of the *Communist Review* who claimed she had completely overlooked the relationship between 'the Scottish peasantry and the Scottish proletariat' to both the communist and the national movements, and therefore, 'its analysis of the class forces in Scotland is inadequate'. To make certain that *Communist Review* readers understood this deficiency the editor published his comments at the head of Crawfurd's essay. [17]

Despite this very public put down Crawfurd's warnings about middle-class discontent was echoed by another communist commentator, Oliver Bell, who reported that Scottish nationalism was making 'rapid strides' across the Highlands and Islands, south-west Scotland and rural districts in the central lowlands. [18] Where Crawfurd had identified middle-class anger in the urban areas Bell wrote that the Communist Party had paid too little attention to the links between agriculture and nationalism: 'The farmer's views are essentially those of the middle class – the petit bourgeoisie – there are great possibilities for the nationalist movement in Scotland. We shall have to make our position clear in the very near future,' Bell said.

The reality was that both Crawfurd and Bell misread and exaggerated the political impact of nationalism on the middle class, whether located in the cities or the countryside. They reacted to the surge of interest in nationalism from their vantage point and what it might mean to the interests of the Communist Party. Yet what seems striking is that their focus is not on the working class but large sections of the professional middle-class. It was the same fear of middle-class agitation – if for different reasons – which produced alarm and reaction across the unionist political and business class in Scotland and Westminster. Throughout the 1930s the Communist Party remained confused about nationalism even if the official policy was to oppose it.

The Marxist historian, James D. Young has described a party with a troubled conscience about the Scottish national question: 'the Scottish leftwing intelligentsia's uneasy endorsement of unflinching opposition to even a mild form of devolution inhibited the development of serious analysis.' Neil Gunn reacted angrily to attempts by Barke and other left wing commentators to link nationalism to international fascism, accusing them of a deliberate failure to recognise that nationalism represented no more than a fundamental aim to construct a nation in which a people could develop its own destiny. 'But they fly from it and cover their desertion by calling the Scot who would like to attempt the job a Fascist.'

Scotland, Gunn argued, was historically more radical and progressive than England, 'with a social consciousness that can be traced in all distinctively Scottish institutions to this day.' In Gunn's view Scottish nationalism was a natural home for intellectuals and others of the proletarian persuasion. But such arguments and invitations continued to fall mainly, if not exclusively, on stony ground. When in 1938 the Communist Party in London agreed to adopt a policy of home rule for Scotland and to talk with the SNP, Scottish communists remained stubbornly reluctant to embrace any form of political nationalism. [19]

Nationalism Fails to Ignite a Spirit of Scottishness

Edwin Muir, it has been suggested, had an ambivalent attitude towards Scottish nationalism, but came down firmly in favour of home rule having been persuaded by the economic evidence and arguments presented by Thomson in *Distressed*. In his review of the book Muir does accept that Thomson is justified in calling for self-government on the basis of the comparisons he makes between the economic fate of Scotland and other small European countries such as Norway and Denmark. 'Home rule should in any case be freely granted by England now, both for her own sake and for the sake of Scotland; otherwise she may find that a still important part of her kingdom will have sunk past hope and past recovery,' Muir wrote. However, despite his enthusiasm and praise for the book and the persuasiveness he found in Thomson's evidence-based arguments, Muir was doing no more than stating that Thomson had presented solid facts to support his own advocacy; but the diluted, moderate model it proposed for home rule was one Muir rejected. [20]

When he had completed his *Scottish Journey* Muir did not conclude that what the country needed was some form of home rule or nationalism. He had tried, he claimed, to approach the nationalist movement as sympathetically as possible; he believed that it was an admirable objective; and what he had seen provided the justification for it. But it was not enough. His experiences and observations convinced him that whether Scotland was governed from London or Edinburgh was irrelevant, only socialism would produce meaningful solutions and changes. Muir was not inspired by the prospect of a parliament in Edinburgh made up of Scottish members currently sitting in Westminster. He believed that in any age it was rare to find movements with the knowledge, commitment, passion and understanding of life and the means to prevail and create change and history itself. 'I think that in a socialist Britain Scotland would be given the liberty to govern itself. A hundred years of socialism would do more to restore Scotland to health and weld it into a real nation than a thousand years of nationalist government such as that to which the National Party of Scotland looks forward.' Muir agreed with the nationalist view that Scotland needed o reawaken, 'to become a nation', but the more pressing task was 'to become a Socialist community.' Muir added, 'I could not see it becoming one without the other.'

He accused nationalists of boasting that they would put an end to unemployment and poverty without providing evidence of how it would be achieved. Another weakness he identified was that by attempting to attract all shades of political support – Conservative, Liberal, Labour and Socialist – they could not make any statements with real opinions, in case it scared away prospective members. 'This has put them in the absurd position of being unable to make any pronouncements on the one question which most concerns everybody today, not only in Scotland, but in the whole civilised world – the economic question,' Muir said. [21]

The English playwright and feminist activist, Cicely Hamilton, who studied the impact of Scottish nationalism in 1937, concluded that Muir had little faith that it was a remedy for Scotland's problems. 'To Muir,' Hamilton wrote, 'capitalism appears to be the prime enemy.' She sensed that any merit Muir found in nationalism was limited to its possible value in helping to maintain Scottish identity against 'modern forces that make for a cosmopolitan sameness of character.' [22]

These comments are less a ringing endorsement for home rule for reasons of nationalism and more a view based on Muir's conviction that if there was genuine social and economic change in Britain brought about by socialism, England and Scotland could maintain separate cultures and identities, a position wholly consistent with Muir's indifference to political nationalism. In *Scott and Scotland: The Predicament of the Scottish Writer* (1936) Muir wrote that he did not believe in the programme of the Scottish nationalists: 'It goes against my reading of history and seems a trivial response to a serious problem.' And, again, he stressed that he could only conceive a free and independent Scotland following as the result of a general economic change in society, adding, 'there would be no reason for England to exert compulsion on Scotland, and both nations could live in peace side by side.' [23]

Muir's socialist views of the 1930s largely reflected his angry reactions to the poverty experienced by the working classes in the urban slums and rural communities. Such socialist views had been a part of his life since he was in his teens and had witnessed the hardship of life in the south side of Glasgow after his family moved to the city from Orkney. Following the move south, Muir's father, mother and two brothers all died within a four-year period from 1902-1906. Muir later recalled that his conversion to socialism at the age of twenty-one had been a recapitulation of his first conversion when he was fourteen. 'I read books on socialism because they delighted me and were an escape from the world I had known with such painful precision,' he said. [24]

George Blake did not share Muir's socialist vision for Scotland, and since he had joined the NPS in 1930, had been a close associate of Thomson and a signatory to Thomson's home rule pamphlet *The Kingdom of Scotland Restored*. He might have been expected to be a committed nationalist. However in *The Heart of Scotland* in 1935 Blake revealed himself a disillusioned nationalist, a state of mind he blamed, almost entirely, on the Scottish people who, he claimed, had been slow to embrace it. 'Scottish nationalism, in the political sense, is but the last-ditch expression of the will that the country should not lose its cultural identity. It is a worthy sentiment, but it has to be feared sometimes that the will is not shared by the Scottish people as a whole,' was Blake's lament. [25]

Muir, reviewing Blake's book, shared his pessimism and despair, finding common ground with his judgement that while Scottish nationalists were correct in their diagnosis about the decline of Scotland, it was unlikely that nationalism could provide a solution. 'The problem is too vast. If an independent authority were to take over Scotland today it would take over a bankrupt concern. It may be that the problem is too vast for nationalism to solve.' [26]

The air of pessimism articulated by Blake is a common theme among writers and intellectuals on both the right and the left. Hamilton, again viewing this trait from the vantage point of an English onlooker, regretted the cheerlessness of Scottish literature even if it was the natural product of post-war disillusion 'and the long, lean years of industrial depression'. Her gaze fell on Gibbon's *Granite City*, 'a relentless piece of work if ever there was one,' and extended to the fictional chronicle of life among Glasgow gangs, *No Mean City*, the book which would tarnish the city's image for half-a-century. She found the same pessimism in *Scottish Journey* and *The Heart of Scotland*, 'the work of men who have surveyed their country, its conditions and prospects, through spectacles anything but rose-coloured.' [27]

The pessimism Hamilton encountered was not restricted to right wing, radical or moderate writers and commentators. The nutritionist, John Orr, had little in common with literary figures such as Thomson, Muir, Gibbon, Blake, Power or Barke. However, like all of them, he did not view his native country through rose-coloured spectacles. He rejected nationalism but understood that a mood of dissatisfaction with London's response to Scottish affairs – not least among sections of the middle classes – had led to the establishment of a modern national movement with demands for home rule and even separation. He was less charitable when he detected nationalist resentment about the greater prosperity of England.

'The bleating of a national party about grievances against England is as futile as the grumblings of a man with a sore head,' Orr warned. He recognised the inequalities and injustices in Scottish society which gave sustenance to both nationalist and socialist voices and feared that the growing importance of London as the capital and headquarters of Scottish business and administration was also a direct threat to Scottish national culture. He warned that Scotland was already beginning to affect an English culture, 'which is ill adapted to our traditions and characters'. Orr, aware of a feeling of uneasiness and discontent with the present state of affairs, believed, however, that this might represent the first step towards a national movement for the re-birth of Scotland. As he had done when he wrote passionately about the scandal of the slums, Orr was again echoing one of Thomson's constant refrains of the links between economic decline and its possible threat to culture and identity. [28]

The Glasgow publisher, Alexander Maclehose claimed the nationalist leaders and intellectuals had misunderstood their own countrymen, and had failed to articulate the meaning and purpose of nationalism. 'It is not so much a new party that we want, or a new set of measures to be passed into law, as new men and a new spirit within us,' Maclehose said.

Thomson was doubtful that nationalism could call such a spirit into being since it might require a revolution in habit and thinking 'which have grown up through many generations.'[29]

Thomson's doubts were shared by others. John Robertson Allan, farmer, novelist and journalist, a contemporary of Gibbon's from north east Scotland, believed that there were Scots in all political parties who, in their hearts, were in favour of some form of home rule or devolution. Despite this, Allan said, the nationalists had failed to inspire the nation. 'Scottish nationalism is not violent, not even in words. It remains very respectable and law-abiding. Many Tories would confess themselves home rulers in everything but name,' he claimed. However they and their political opponents on the left were loyal to their parties, 'the affairs of Scotland must be subordinated.' Like Orr, Allan believed that attempts to make anti-Englishness an emotional driving force for nationalism was doomed to fail since most Scots do not believe it when they were told they were dominated by England. 'And among those who do it does not strike powerful emotions. So they cannot make progress by raising a kind of patriotism that is better dead.' Nationalist attacks on the power of the city of London only served to persuade the working classes to listen to the Labour Party, 'so the national party does not yet stand for or appeal to any powerful body of national feeling.' Allan's negative assessment was that nationalism had not only been politically impotent, it had failed the emotional and identity test. This, more than any electoral setbacks, was a true measure of the ingrained pessimism displayed by the interwar nationalist commentators and of the ineffectiveness of their message to the Scottish people. [30]

Thomson recognised that however much satisfaction he, Gibb and others may have drawn from the establishment of a nationalist party pursuing a moderate home rule programme, political nationalism, whatever the variety, had failed to capture any meaningful popular mandate or support. The achievement of intellectuals and comment-ators between the wars was to prioritise in the public discourse the issue of the condition of Scotland. Had economic, industrial and social decline been left to other agencies, such as the mainstream Scottish newspapers, it would not have received the degree of attention and response from the political, elite and business establishment. Writers, activists and intellectuals of both the right and left were also successful in creating interest and support for nationalism beyond the hard core of nationalist loyalists. In my view it is unlikely that the unionist dissidents would have emerged if commentators, led by Thomson, had not created a climate in which concern and anger raged. Even as late as 1938 on the eve of the Glasgow Empire Exhibition Scottish business leaders were still decrying those who wrote articles under the title, 'What is wrong with Scotland?' almost a decade after Thomson through his books and David Cleghorn Thomson in his BBC broadcast series had first asked the question. [31]

A modern nationalist party was born, even one that Thomson agreed was a minority movement, one seen in popular terms as being the preserve of 'cranks' and 'intellectuals'. The dismissive accusation did not offend Thomson, since these were the classes he expected to react 'most swiftly and sensitively' to any change in the spiritual atmosphere. But recognition that there was a change in the spiritual atmosphere had its limitations. Outside of the intellectual bubble and the hard core of activists, whatever advances the cause of nationalism had made, its arguments had failed to strike any chords with the country's wider sense of nationhood. Thomson said that the task before the nationalists was not to rouse a nation but to make one, that there must be a revolution in the mindset of the Scots, a spiritual awakening. Exposing social and economic evils was pointless unless it was connected to a re-awakened national consciousness.

Despite the best efforts of many intellectuals and commentators to attach nationalism to spirit, identity and consciousness, what success it had was limited to two practical achievements; the formation of the SNP, which, despite internal difficulties and external political failure, would endure; and secondly, and only for a limited period, to force action and change from the elite, political and business establishments in Scotland and London. Nationalism did not become a great cause; it failed to inspire popular enthusiasm for Scottish national identity or to operate as a vehicle for a national reawakening. Nationalism cloaked in home rule colours failed as a political force in the interwar period, not least by its repeated failures at the polls in general elections. It had some limited impact at by-elections but the mainstream unionist parties could justifiably claim that the nationalists did not enjoy any meaningful popular support. Nationalism fluttered, flattered and deceived, light weight and suspicious, the rejected alternative to the class struggles of both the middle and working classes. Unionism, whether from the right or the left, was established as the representative arm of Scotland's newly established dependency culture. If the move of the Scottish Office from London to Edinburgh in 1939 signified a political, structural, administrative and establishment response to Scottish feelings it also affirmed the union.

The Saltire Society and the Cultural Dividend

The Saltire Society was a body conceived following an original idea from George Malcolm Thomson. It is yet another of the ironies of Thomson's contribution to the political and cultural debates of the interwar period that a suggestion he made to Gibb was the inspiration for the creation of a society still dedicated, in the twenty-first century to fostering and enriching the cultural heritage of Scotland. George Bruce, who produced a history of the first fifty years of the Society, observed that there is frequently a chance factor which provokes the first act, 'in such circumstances the Saltire Society came into existence. The stimulus was a conversation between George Malcolm Thomson and Andrew Dewar Gibb.'

Gibb's wife, Margaret, said later that Thomson, living in London, had been amazed to find that the English knew about and appreciated their heritage while the Scots displayed ignorance and were indifferent about preserving it.' Thomson and Gibb had a shared view about what they regarded as Scotland's cultural and intellectual deficit, an issue they pursued throughout the 1930s. On this issue, however, Gibb reacted to Thomson's prompting that 'something should be done to engender in the Scots some appreciation of their cultural inheritance.' [32]

Through the efforts of Gibb, his wife and Alison Bonfield, the first secretary, the society was founded in April 1936, although Gibb withdrew from any active participation to avoid any conflicts with his position within the SNP. Bonfield said later that Gibb 'was the onlie and first begetter of the Society'. Others who were involved from the outset included James Fergusson, a historian, Agnes Mure Mackenzie, Christian

Fordyce, Professor of Humanities at Glasgow, Eric Linklater, who was also Bonfield's brother in law, and William Power. Thomson's original idea that it should be known as the Saltoun Society after the Scottish patriot, Fletcher of Saltoun, was dropped in favour of Saltire, the heraldic name for the St. Andrew's Cross, 'a more instantly recognisable symbol of Scottishness'. [33]

As the literary revival had been, so too the Saltire Society was the creation of intellectuals but from the outset it was non-political. It was primarily a defensive organisation, dedicated to the preservation and protection of Scotland's culture, heritage and history. It was conceived, 'at a low point in the life of Scottish culture'. But it also had ambitions to improve the quality of life in Scotland and restore the country's reputation as a creative force in Europe. [34]

Agnes Mure Mackenzie was reading from Thomson's script when she said that the Society wanted not just a 'mere revival' of the arts but a renewal of the creative spirit that Scotland had experienced in the eighteenth century. The Saltire founders believed that the intellectual, philosophical and literary glories of one era were the basis for a cultural re-awakening in modern Scotland. This, in turn, would inspire the future. 'A nation's prime health is in spirit and in mind,' Mackenzie wrote. 'We need to give life more abundantly to the body, the mind, and the spirit. And the first need for that is broad, abundant vision, abundant in both its content and its use.'

In its first annual report the society conceded that it had a tendency to look back to the past; but only, it argued, to enable it to look forward. As late as the eighteenth century Edinburgh was, it said, the centre of intellectual life famed throughout Europe. It envisaged a new Scotland with a vigorous intellectual life, 'drawing on the past for inspiration to new advances in art, learning and the graces in life.' Thomson could hardly have put it better! [35]

The narrative of the society mirrored his relentless calls for a restored intellectual vigour in Scottish life, one approved by Gibb and others like Mackenzie, Linklater, and Power, and one intent on moving the rhetoric about the uniqueness of Scottish culture from books and speeches into an organisation specifically dedicated to the renewal, not just of culture, but the wider reaches of Scottish society.

The lofty ideals and ambitions of the Saltire Society were not confined to narrow definitions based around the arts. It sought to promote and encourage artists and writers in drama, music, painting and sculpture, but also in fields such as architecture, and it argued for the revitalisation and broadening of education and within it greater study and understanding of Scottish history.

'Self-knowledge was a thing that Scotland needed very badly. This was a task for the teacher, historian and, above all, the artist. The artist was the teacher of the teacher. He not only recorded but created the country's values,' Mackenzie said. The economist, James Bowie, suggested that the creation of the Society was one of the signs that Rip Van Winkle was about to wake. 'There is a faint stirring of the dry bones. Micawber, tired of waiting for something to turn up, may be about to turn up something.' [36]

Other organisations that had 'turned up' with cultural aspirations as part of their remit included the National Trust for Scotland, which Thomson's friend, the nationalist architect, Robert Hurd welcomed alongside the Saltire Society as a necessary antidote to widespread apathy. 'Much has been irretrievably lost,' he said, 'without even the provocation of indignant protest, let alone constructive effort to safeguard the future.' Hurd detected the 'hesitant beginnings' of a national revival in arts and culture 'infusing new life into modern Scotland.' Despite occasionally bearing the mantle of being referred to as cranks the cultural revivalists were 'forging new experiments in architecture, music, literature, politics, fine arts and industrial arts,' he wrote. [37]

If Hurd's optimism remained guarded at the tail-end of the 1930s Thomson, a decade later, was confident enough to declare that the cultural revival had been pivotal in creating a more resolute and certain society. Addressing the Scottish Centre of the International PEN Club in Edinburgh in 1950 he suggested that the renaissance had been in part a protest against a prevailing sense in Scottish society that culture and other things in life were of less value than those of business which was given excessive importance, creating in some influential circles 'a mood of rather smug, cosy, comfortable confidence'.

Thomson sensed that post-World War II Scotland was now a more aggressive and happier country and that Scottish life was livelier than at any point in his lifetime, an improvement, he believed, brought about by the renaissance. The cultural revival had produced 'the most extraordinary' proliferation of institutions; the creation of theatres and audiences to fill them; publishing houses and magazines had sprung up; cultural societies of every sort had flourished; and there was a more active field in academic scholarship. Thomson, the one-time youthful and optimistic co-founder of a small Scottish publishing business; the disillusioned, pessimistic and notorious critic of the interwar economic and social condition of Scotland; the manipulative and secretive plotter for home rule nationalism; but throughout the two decades an unashamed champion and campaigner for the protection and nurturing of Scottish culture and national identity, claimed to have found, finally, a Scotland which met with his approval. Thomson's tribute to the positive contribution and impact of the Scottish Renaissance on the post-World War II cultural identity of Scotland was made almost thirty years after he and Roderick Watson Kerr had launched the Porpoise Press into the hopeful early post-World War I years with their calls for a national re-awakening. When he spoke in the Roxburghe Hotel – only two hundred yards away from the original home of the Porpoise Press in Stafford Street – he was not introduced as the interwar commentator on the condition of Scotland. Thomson was now the visitor. His speech was entitled 'A London Scot's View of the Scottish Renaissance'. [38]

CHAPTER 11
Thomson 1940-1996

'He abandoned Scotland'

CHAPMAN PINCHER, the renowned *Daily Express* Defence Correspondent, worked alongside George Malcolm Thonson from the end of World
War II until Thomson's retirement in the late 1960s. 'The only thing
Scottish about him as far as I was aware was his Scottish accent. I knew
nothing about his Scottish background or that he had written books
before the war,' Pincher said. Gerald Isaaman, the former editor of the
Hampstead and Highgate Express, knew Thomson in the 1970s and 1980s,
often meeting him with friends and regulars in the Coach and Horses
pub in Hampstead. 'He never talked about Scotland or his Scottish past,'
Isaaman recalls. 'He was a great raconteur with an acute understanding
of political life, interested in people who had changed history, hence the
subjects of many of the books he wrote.'[1]

Between 1964 and 1985 Thomson wrote eleven books and in only
one of them *A Kind of Justice: Two Studies in Treason* (1970) – which looks
at two famous Scottish murder mysteries from the seventeenth and
eighteenth centuries – is there any reference to books published in the
interwar period. The sleeve notes that Thomson 'is the author of *A Short
History of Scotland* and has written extensively on problems in Scottish
history,' the history background considered relevant to the subject matter
of *A Kind of Justice*. His final book *Kronstadt 21*, a historical thriller set in
the twentieth century, published in 1985 when Thomson was 85 years
old, lists all of his post- World War II books, fiction, biographies and
histories. The Scottish interwar books are ignored, presumably not
relevant to Thomson's post-war authorships.[2]

In the course of my first discussion with him, his son Peter, without
prompting, said, 'My father abandoned Scotland. He became a
Londoner.' Peter and his sister Anne, born respectively in 1934 and 1930,

were infants in the 1930s, but even in adulthood both remained unaware of their father's Scottish interwar reputation, the impact of his writings, his involvement with Scottish nationalism, or that he retained notoriety in the modern era for his controversial views on Irish Catholic immigration. A copy of *Caledonia* still sits on the shelf of a bookcase in the house at Holly Hill in Hampstead which Thomson and his family moved into in the early 1930s. But Peter was ignorant of the book's significance, either at the time, or in the present.

The understanding of both Peter and Anne is that his professional career began and ended with Beaverbrook. 'My father never spoke about Scottish politics, nothing about Scottish nationalism and he never mentioned anything at all, ever, about the Irish, immigrants or anything else,' Peter said. Thomson was, however, conscious of his Scottish family background and aspects of Scottish culture. Photographs of his Scottish family adorned the Hampstead house alongside examples of Thomson's academic achievements and prizes. 'My father was quite a private animal. I cannot remember one instance of him talking about his childhood in Leith, even on occasions when my grandmother came down from Edinburgh and stayed with us.'

He was an enthusiast for the Scottish colourist, Anne Redpath, one of the Edinburgh School of painters Thomson had followed in the early 1920s. 'At one time he had several Anne Redpath paintings,' Peter recalled. 'When he bought paintings they were usually by Scottish artists.' Thomson was himself a keen amateur artist; scenes of Hampstead and self-portraits he painted still hang in Holly Hill. Family holidays were spent in Norway with their mother's family and only occasionally in Scotland.

'We very rarely went up to Edinburgh or anywhere else in Scotland although I remember one occasion when we went to Dornoch and took a car across to Ullapool. Our holidays in the summer months were spent in Norway. You see it in the best light, lovely sun, warm weather, and beautiful people. My mother was a big influence on my father; she was a free spirit but didn't enjoy the damp cold. She found it very miserable. Like my father she did not talk about Scotland. My sister and I knew that we were half Scottish and half Norwegian and I certainly did not regard myself as English. However we were both given essentially middle-class English educations.'[3]

Peter attended prep school in Hampstead before becoming a boarder at Charterhouse School in Surrey while his sister Anne attended Channing's School for Girls in Highgate, North London, before going on to RADA.

The recollections of Thomson's son represent a familiar story of the life of a prosperous London family in pre-war and post-war Britain. In the early 1930s when he was plotting and agitating for Scottish home rule Thomson was already a settled and adopted Londoner, but again, as such, he was not unique. George Blake, his colleague at the Porpoise Press during the Faber and Faber period, who, at that time, lived nearby in Hampstead, also supported Scottish home rule, as did William Bell, author of *Rip Van Scotland* (1932), who lived at Henley-on-Thames, and Archibald G. Macdonell, who wrote *My Scotland* (1937) and who lived in Oxford. Thomson, the Anglo-Scot, made his life and career choices, conscious of whatever contradictions that might suggest when set against the anti-Anglicisation narratives in his books, journalism and broadcasts. If he fell silent in middle and later life about his interwar writings and experiences, in the period itself Thomson appeared unrepentant and stoic even in the face of the wrath of sections of the Scottish establishment.

A Scotsman 'on the make'

> 'The telescopic of Fleet Street and Piccadilly sees it through the dazzle of a million restless nights and it seems dark and dull. But we, who see it in the light of the stars, find it throbbing with vitality. It is not dead. It is not depressed. It is not dishonoured. It has not lost its soul. And Heaven be praised, it has not lost its sense of humour'.
> Rosslyn Mitchell, *What's Wrong With Scotland,* 12 November 1929

Rosslyn Mitchell, the Labour MP for Paisley, defending modern Scotland and decrying the London-based Thomson and his fellow Anglo-Scot and

Hampstead resident Donald Carswell for their 'dreary and inaccurate diatribes' against Scotland and its people. They were, he said, freelance journalists who make a theme of the peculiarities of their motherland 'and hold her up to the ridicule of strangers'. The Glasgow-born Carswell, who had worked on the *Glasgow Herald* and *The Times*, lived a bohemian lifestyle in London with his wife, the writer Catherine Carswell. In his view Scotland was a cultural desert unique in the civilised world in having 'no theatrical or musical tradition and no spirit of live and let live'. He sympathised with Scots who head across the border 'where life is a shade or two merrier'. 'What is there to keep us?' he asked. [4]

The Edinburgh businessman, Will Y. Darling, said some spoke and wrote as if the opportunity of 'staring complacently, contentedly, and economically' at the free electric signs displays of Piccadilly Circus and Trafalgar Square gave them authority to pose as superior persons and dictators of the Scots, a barely disguised criticism of Thomson's *What's Wrong with Scotland?* broadcast. They seemed to suggest, he said, that all the talents and all the merits left their native land with them. 'Scotsmen have been too much encouraged in the belief that the best road in Scotland is the high road to England,' Darling said. 'It is a mistake. It is an illusion.' Darling, who also wrote books and was a freelance writer; he later became Chairman of the Scottish Travel Association and Lord Provost of Edinburgh. He followed up his attacks on the Anglo-Scots by calling for a 'Stay in Scotland' movement to persuade educated and skilled Scots to remain at home. [5]

Thomson was the target of politicians and establishment figures, not only for his ongoing negative comments about modern Scotland, but that he did so from a comfortable perch in north London where he had set up home in 1926. His move to London was neither unusual nor remarkable; he had followed a familiar and well-worn path taken by thousands of Scots for more than two centuries, many of them to find success and fame in journalism and publishing. The Scottish playwright, J.M. Barrie gave the established practice its own legend when he asserted that there are few more impressive sights in the world than a Scotsman on the make.

The English poet and journalist, T.W.H. Crosland, agreed that

Scotsmen were on the make but he parted company with Barrie that it was impressive or worthy. In a relentless tirade of invective resentment against Scots, aimed particularly at Scots who achieved success in Fleet Street, Crosland concluded that the reason for this was that it was a profession 'into which you can crawl without inquiry as to your qualifications'. [6]

Thomson would have rejected any suggestion that he was 'on the make' and he would have insisted, correctly, that he was competent and qualified. What he would have found it more difficult to answer, had he paid any attention – and there is no evidence that he did – were accusations that his views were tainted because he had chosen not to remain in Scotland, had opted for the lure of London, and then attacked the country he had left behind. While Darling accepted that Scotland had a history of exporting her people he believed that modern Scotland needed Scots who would concentrate 'what genius they have' on their native land as previous generations had endowed other countries. The Darling principle was one which Thomson himself had endorsed in *Caledonia* when he was critical of the drain of the 'educated, intelligent, and energetic middle-class youth who would normally become the leaders of the commercial, political and intellectual life of the country.' This tendency, Thomson insisted, though numerically unimportant, 'is as serious and deplorable as the artisan exoduses.'

At no point does Thomson equate his own life and career choices with his general condemnation of the intellectual drift to England and overseas destinations. He did not appear to understand or acknowledge that the profile and reputation he had both sought and gained allied to the vehemence of his criticism placed him in the dock where he stood accused of double standards and hypocrisy. Had Thomson faced such charges at the time he would have reached for his substantive denouncement of his native country, that it was second rate, 'a land of second-hand thoughts and second-rate minds'. And as evidence he would have looked no further than his own profession, journalism, arguing, as he did in *Caledonia*, that it was the deliberate policy of Scottish newspapers to stamp out original thinking which marked out journalists with talent 'from the humdrum routineers'. To show literary skill was suspicious, 'a symptom of the inferiority complex that is hag-riding the nation.' [7]

Thomson, perhaps as his son Peter later suggested, influenced by a combination of his Norwegian wife, Else and the appeal of 'the fleshpots of London' distanced himself from – as he saw it – the second rate and inferior mindset of Scotland. However the fleshpots of temptation in the gaze of Thomson, the disillusioned Presbyterian Scot, were to be found in the so-called 'Street of Shame', Fleet Street, where he was convinced that, unlike Scotland, journalistic and literary skills and original and creative writing was encouraged and rewarded. He was equally attracted by its reputation as a great centre of literature and publishing. His early efforts to raise London interest in the Porpoise Press and his work with Blake in the early 1930s after the imprint was acquired by Faber and Faber, confirming the obstacles and difficulties faced by the Porpoise Press in its Edinburgh origins.

Thomson's harsh and negative views of Scottish society did not cause him to lose his enthusiasm for the renewal of Scottish culture and arts or for political home rule, but inevitably, as he gained success and reputation as a Fleet Street journalist and moved increasingly in media, literary and political circles, Thomson's cultural universe was fixated on London. In the interwar period he and his wife were members of the Norwegian Club in London but Thomson was ambitious to become a member of the Garrick Club, in Pall Mall, a club founded in the early nineteenth century, named after the actor David Garrick, and based on the traditions of the eighteenth century literary society, the Mecca in London for thespians and men of letters, including journalists.

Cronies at the Garrick and Life with Beaverbrook

'A place where actors and men of refinement and education might meet on equal terms; patrons of drama and its professors were brought together; and easy intercourse was promoted between artists and patrons'.

Founders of the Garrick Club, 1831

Thomson had to wait until the end of World War II to achieve his ambition, but after he was elected a member in 1947 the Garrick became his second home for almost half a century until in old age, and when a near invalid, the journey from Hampstead became impossible. The Garrick in the post-war years was renowned as a veritable *Who's Who* of sophisticated and cosmopolitan figures from the worlds of theatre, literature and journalism, and was a popular dining, drinking and social club.

The list of names of those who supported his membership application provided clear evidence that Thomson was firmly established in media and literary circles. They included the successful and popular Scottish playwright, James Bridie; the editor of *The Times*, William Casey; the editor of the *Sunday Express*, John Gordon; the editor of the *Daily Herald*, Percy Cudlipp; the critic and writer, Ivor Brown; and the publisher David Farrer.

'He was always close to his beloved Garrick Club and his cronies there,' his son Peter said. 'There was always a good gathering of chums.'[9]

He was a prominent figure at the Garrick, recalled Chapman Pincher. 'He was always there. On one occasion I spotted George in a little alcove area off to the right as you go in. I was about to go over and say hello when I was stopped by the broadcaster, Robin Day who told me that the area was for members only. Thomson was sitting sprawled, lying across a sofa.'[10] Thomson was elected a Life Member in 1983 and in 1986 at its annual dinner the club honoured Thomson's long service to journalism, literature and the club, and a year later when the author, Kingsley Amis received the same honour, Thomson proposed the toast. [11]

His associations with the Beaverbrook Empire hung heavy throughout his years at the Garrick. Three of his membership supporters, Gordon, Cudlipp and Farrer were or had been employed by Beaverbrook and the toast in his honour in 1986 was delivered by another former *Daily Express* editor, Sir Edward Pickering. Thomson's close connection to Beaverbrook himself was not unhelpful in establishing his social credentials.

Thomson's work for Beaverbrook, which stretched from 1931 until Beaverbrook's death in 1964, was the defining relationship of Thomson's professional career. His entry into Beaverbrook's inner circle was earned when the press baron decided that he valued not only Thomson's populist writing abilities but his political astuteness and strategic thinking. If for Beaverbrook it was always about control, trust and the quality of Thomson's thinking and advice, it required, on Thomson's side, all of the clever, manipulative, and persuasive skills which he used regularly in his dealings with nationalist intellectuals and writers. And as his letters to the nationalist activist, George Dott, attest, Thomson quickly recognised that the deference and respect he accorded Beaverbrook was strengthened if it came tinged with a degree of fear.

On one occasion after he had been out riding in the snow-covered Surrey Hills with Beaverbrook, Thomson said to his friend, Percy Cudlipp: 'It was like the retreat from Moscow. Beaverbrook was Napoleon, I was Marshall Ney'. 'You mean Marshall Yea!' retorted Cudlipp. Thomson, typically, was not offended, admitting later in his own obituary of Cudlipp, that he, the victim of the remark, 'had spread its fame'. [12]

David Farrer, who worked beside Thomson in Beaverbrook's office during the war years, said the riposte, while quick and witty was well wide of the mark. Thomson, he said, was one of the very few in Beaverbrook's entourage who dared to say 'Nay'. He would argue with him and quite often persuade him to change his mind. 'He had a quality of self-reliance, a robust faith in his own judgement, a pragmatic approach to problems, that appealed to all that was best in Beaverbrook.' He came to acquire a unique position in Beaverbrook's esteem and held it right up to the day of his employer's death. Thomson was like an *eminence grise* who knew what Beaverbrook was thinking five minutes before Beaverbrook did – and if he didn't like that thought he would head it off at the past. 'Unlike other Beaverbrook courtiers he was allowed the licence of the jester or a Shakespearean fool to point out the Old Man's lapses from wisdom.' [13]

Thomson's persuasive influence over Beaverbrook enabled him to warn him off what he regarded as unwise and impulsive decisions. In 1942 Beaverbrook threatened Churchill with his resignation from the War Cabinet if he did not make changes to a White Paper on the Ministry of Production. Churchill refused. Thomson listened as Beaverbrook recited the defects of the White Paper and why he was still minded to resign. Thomson agreed with him but observed that it was already too late to change the Paper and Beaverbrook gave way, later writing, 'I then accepted the paper as laid down by the prime minister.' [14]

After the war Thomson would regularly receive telephone calls summoning him to the south of France where Beaverbrook, particularly in his final years, spent a lot of time at his villa, La Capponcina, at Cap d'Ail. 'He kept Mr Thomson near him for most of the day, discussing what was going on in the world, articles in the newspapers, and ideas for the *Express*.' On one occasion despite a rainfall and remonstrations from others about his health, Beaverbrook announced he was going for a walk, calling out as he went, 'Come on George!' Thomson in raincoat followed Beaverbrook in dark-coloured overcoat and black hat. 'It was a most extraordinary sight,' one observer said later. 'The old man threw out ideas and continually cried, What do you think of this? Whaddya think of that? Yes, yes, agreed Mr Thomson, excellent. And he scribbled in his notebook as the rain fell on it.'[15]

His son Peter said he could never understand why his father called Beaverbrook 'sir'. 'I was always slightly astonished that my father was calling someone sir. My father was very clever, but he was maybe not so clever at being dominated by Beaverbrook for so long. I can recall that when Beaverbrook was having trouble with Churchill in the south of France he would ring my father and tell him to come down and help him.' [16]

Farrer rejects the idea that Thomson was dominated by Beaverbrook, recalling that Thomson had warned him that 'the Old Man' loved to dominate and given half a chance would be a bully, but would never respect employees who succumbed to his bullying. 'When you feel affronted or put upon for God's sake answer back,' Thomson advised. The Scot was Beaverbrook's listening post – 'His Master's Ear' – able to give him advice that was listened to, and although Beaverbrook would never admit it, often resulted in a reversal of his original intention.

When Beaverbrook asked Farrer to write a book about the Ministry of Aircraft Production, Thomson made suggestions, offered criticisms and amendments before the redraft was submitted to Beaverbrook. Beaverbrook would inevitably show the new version to Thomson: 'Farrer seems to think,' he would say. Thomson would consider the typescript pages as if he had never seen them before, pause for reflection, and then persuasively, almost diffidently, indicate that perhaps Farrer was right. 'These were Machiavellian tactics, but by and large they worked.'

Beaverbrook was constantly on the telephone to his editors, praising, blaming, criticising, haranguing, and bullying them. 'Thomson, chief leader writer of the *Daily Express*, was not wholly immune, though he was never bullied.' [17]

At only one point was Thomson's association and loyalty to Beaverbrook under threat. Following VE Day on 8 May 1945 he was unsure where his future lay, confessing to Gibb that he was 'disinclined' to go back to Fleet Street in any capacity. 'I feel incapable of the effort that a new start there would involve,' he said. He had effectively worked as a civil service bureaucrat since Beaverbrook had joined the War Cabinet in 1940 and admitted that if the right job, 'really interesting, constructive in administration' was available he would be tempted. But, unusually for someone who always had a high regard of his own abilities, Thomson doubted if could break into the civil service 'magic spiral' at the proper level.[18]

In the event, Thomson could have remained a Government employee: 'the civil service was more than anxious to claim him for their own'. But Beaverbrook offered him the post of Chief Leader Writer on the *Daily Express* with Chief Book Reviewer of the *Evening Standard* thrown in along with the continuance of his advisory role. 'He opted for his old master, preferring perhaps the extremely engaging devil he knew.' Until the end of Beaverbrook's life Thomson continued to draft letters and papers for him, faithfully recording his views for his editorials in the *Daily Express*. When Beaverbrook's fading powers made it impossible for him to dictate, Thomson was often beside him, even when 'he was too tired to ask Thomson to draft a letter'. [19]

Historian, the Guilt of Mary Queen of Scots, and a Scottish Award

Unlike Farrer and others, Thomson, the advisor who was closest to him for three decades, never produced an account of his Beaverbrook years. There are only two possible explanations for this: his respect and loyalty to Beaverbrook, even after death, and the certainty that Thomson would have known that the eminent historian A.J.P. Taylor, a close associate of Beaverbrook, had been given access to his private papers and that his biography would become the standard text on Beaverbrook's life. Taylor's *Beaverbrook* was published in 1972.

Thomson, however, by the 1960s had entered the third and final chapter of his life, one in which he planned to establish his credentials not only as a journalist, but as the successful author of novels, histories and biographies. His personal publishing tribute to Beaverbrook was *The Twelve Days 24 July to 4 August 1914* released in March 1964 only a few months before Beaverbrook's death in June. The book, a detailed account of the events preceding the outbreak of World War I, was dedicated: 'To Lord Beaverbrook, witness and matchless historian of those days, in admiration and affection.' [20]

Beaverbrook himself is likely to have given Thomson the idea for such a book five years earlier on another occasion when he had been summoned to the villa in the south of France to assist Beaverbrook, then eighty, with Churchill, who was his guest. After Churchill retired to his room Beaverbrook started to reminisce about the great events of the twentieth century which he witnessed.

'Thomson listened completely enthralled as the inside story of a pageant of history was unrolled in a manner which the written word would never excel. Thomson realised that here was a very great film script; these figures, these dramas, passed before his eyes as if there was a 'vista Vision' screen at the end of the dining room.' [21]

Among the dramas and the figures Beaverbrook described were the events prior to the outbreak of World War I. Thomson's phrase 'witness and matchless historian' was chosen carefully. Later in the year Thomson travelled to Leeds to receive a scroll and a cheque for £100 when *The Twelve Days* won the first *Yorkshire Post* Book of the Year Award. However, not all of Thomson's books entered the public domain as free of controversy as *The Twelve Days*. [22]

In February 1967 the novelist, Eric Linklater, living in Ross-shire, received a letter from Lady Antonia Fraser, then married to the Tory MP, Sir Hugh Fraser, in which she criticised Thomson's book, *The Crime of Mary Stuart* (1967). Thomson, she wrote, was wrong to claim that Mary Queen of Scots was implicated in the murder of her husband, Lord Darnley, in 1567, that the infamous Casket Letters, allegedly love letters between Mary and her lover, the Earl of Bothwell and which contained proof of her guilt, were genuine. Fraser, then engaged in her own research for her biography, *Mary, Queen of Scots* (1969), could not believe that anyone still regarded the Casket Letters as authentic. 'I read Thomson's book with amazement,' she wrote.

Fraser was preaching to the converted as Linklater had already publicly stated that in attempting to establish proof of Mary's guilt Thomson was 'the latest in a long line to be deluded'. No shred of evidence exists of her guilt and 'the odds are that no evidence ever did exist. The Casket Letters are said to be copies of originals that no one since 1600 has even claimed to have seen,' Linklater said. Thomson, convinced of Mary's complicity in the murder, defended his book arguing that the people of Edinburgh had decided against the Queen in June 1567. 'They did so because they had a native prejudice against any woman who married her husband's murderer.'

The literary tiff conducted through the letters page of *The Times* concerning the guilt or otherwise of a Queen in a sixteenth century

Scottish murder continued for several more days until Thomson reached for the epitaph for Mary from her brother-in-law, Charles IX of France who wrote, 'Ah, the poor fool will never cease until she lose her head. In faith, they will put her to death. It is her own fault and folly. I see no remedy for it!' Thomson appealed: 'There being no dispute regarding Mary's eventual fate, 'could the matter be left there?' [23]

Despite the dissent, Thomson's book received positive reviews: 'It is delightfully written without losing its scholarly precision. He is brilliantly perceptive. No one has read her better'; 'It has the excitement of a whodunit with the added merit that it is also sound historical reporting'. However, although *The Crime of Mary Stuart* was a bestseller, the propaganda battle over Mary's guilt or innocence was won two years later when Fraser's much more sympathetic portrait of her was published. *Mary Queen of Scots* was an international publishing success, the 1969 winner of the James Tait Black Memorial Prize for biography, and established Fraser's reputation as an author, historian and biographer. [24]

Thomson, I suspect, enjoyed the controversy and the publicity the spat had engendered, and despite his conviction about Mary Stuart's guilt, in 1972 following calls for her body to be exhumed from its place at Westminster Abbey he declared that if it should happen she should be reburied 'in the country in which she was born and of which she was Queen'. [25]

He returned to Scottish historical murder mysteries with *A Kind of Justice: Two Studies in Treason* (1970). The first part, *The Skin of the Red Fox*, was an account of the celebrated Appin Murder of 1752 when Red Colin Campbell was shot dead by a member of the rival Stewart clan, an event which was the inspiration for Robert Louis Stevenson's *Kidnapped* and from which he drew his fictional character Alan Breck. The second, *The Gowrie Conspiracy*, was Thomson's interpretation of the alleged plot in 1600 to kidnap and murder James VI – later James I following the Union of the Crowns – which was followed by the deaths of two Perthshire noblemen. Thomson's fascination with Scottish history also led to his first historical novel, *The Ball at Glenkerran* (1982), set in Scotland during and after the 1745 Jacobite rebellion. The book was warmly reviewed although Thomson was most likely pleased to be described in one review as 'a distinguished 82-year-old historian'. [26]

The 'distinguished historian' was a mere 76 years old when, in 1976, he was the recipient of an accolade from the Scottish Arts Council. Almost fifty years after the publication of Thomson's first book, *Caledonia*, at its monthly meeting in Edinburgh the Council – a body whose very existence would have been no more than a pipe-dream to Thomson between the wars – approved a recommendation of a Book Award to Thomson's book, *The North West Passage* (1975). The Council, charitably some might have thought, treated Thomson as a Scots-born author, although he had been a London resident for half-a-century, since 1926. Thomson found himself in the company of some of the biggest names of contemporary Scottish poetry, fiction and prose also given awards. They included the poets Edwin Morgan, Robert Garrioch, Iain Crichton Smith and Flora Garry, the historical novelists Dorothy Dunnett and Elizabeth Byrd, and Alexander Fenton, the author of books on Scottish country life. Perhaps the most interesting recipient of an award was the Ayrshire novelist, William McIlvanney for his book, *Docherty*, the story of a mining family struggling against poverty in the early decades of the twentieth century. McIlvanney's book also won the 1975 Whitbread Prize for Fiction.

The Porpoise Press interwar teams – Thomson and Kerr in the early 1920s and Thomson and Blake in the early 1930s – would have taken great pleasure in the richness, variety, quality and success to be found in modern Scottish literature, particularly the poetry, of the 1970s. Significantly, Thomson's award was for a book which was neither set in or about Scotland. *The North West Passage* recounted the story of the men who had endeavoured to forge a route through the Arctic Ocean to connect the Atlantic and Pacific Oceans. Written as a history of the various attempts through five centuries from Frobisher to Amundsen, the book, complete with Notes on Sources, Bibliography and Index, provided, again, evidence of Thomson's work ethic of undertaking serious research and his ability to translate this into an epic adventure story. [27]

The Arts Council meeting approved the individual awards of £400.00 each recommended to it by its Reading Panel set-up to consider both 'Book and New Writing' categories. Had he been aware, Thomson may have found it both interesting and somewhat ironic that one member of the Reading Panel was Deirdre Chapman, a well known Scottish journalist and columnist, who, as the wife of another journalist, Michael Grieve, was the daughter-in-law of Christopher Grieve, aka, Hugh Mac-Diarmid. MacDiarmid died in 1978, only a year before the Devolution Referendum which many, at the time, believed would establish an Assembly in Edinburgh. He was revered as Scotland's greatest literary figure of the twentieth century but until the end he remained controversial, citing Anglophobia as his recreation in his *Who's Who* entry.

Thomson, even at the height of his interwar anger against the Anglicisation of Scottish society and culture, had never shared MacDiarmid's dislike of the English. Indeed for the last fifty years of his life – albeit from a base in London – there was no greater anglicised Scot than Thomson himself, although he continued to refer to himself as 'an old Scottish home ruler, but no separatist'. [28]

Post-War Nationalism and North Sea Oil

Throughout the war years, despite his full time commitment with Beaverbrook, Thomson maintained his enthusiasm for home rule, and, on occasion, sent new ideas to Gibb. One of his schemes envisaged the establishment of a Scottish Plebiscite Committee to urge the government to hold a referendum on home rule following demobilisation, a plan which, he fancied, might be adopted by Tom Johnston, the Secretary of State for Scotland.

'It could be represented to Johnston as the culmination of his work. If there is to be a plebiscite, it ought obviously to be undertaken by the government.' Thomson's parliament would have full power over all domestic matters, including labour, transport and trade in relation to all internal Scottish industrial and commercial affairs, with Westminster retaining authority in all other areas. It was an agenda he continued to pursue at the end of the war, particularly following the surprise victory of the SNP candidate, Robert McIntyre at the Motherwell by-election in April 1945, believing, wrongly, that it would be repeated at the General Election in July and sensing, again wrongly, that the nationalist cause would benefit from the mood in Scotland that the 'dreadful between-the-wars condition of Scotland' had been ignored by Conservative unionists.

'I feel I must do something for the old country,' he told Gibb. 'It is surely in a hopeful phase of her political fortunes with a fair deal in the reconstruction period and the immediate initiation of a devolutionary process.' Thomson, perhaps influenced by Beaverbrook and the press baron's close links to Churchill, like so many commentators and political insiders at the time totally misread the likely outcome of the General Election, predicting to Gibb that the election would be close and that whoever took office would have only a short period in power: 'the election will be inconceivably squalid and horrible, mainly because no real issue will clearly emerge.' [29]

In the immediate post-war years, as the Labour Government embarked on its massive programme of industrial and welfare reform the campaign for Scottish home rule appeared less relevant than it had during the interwar period. Despite this political reality, feelings of national identity remained buoyant and in 1949 the Scottish Covenant calling for home rule attracted almost two million signatures. The more abiding memory of nationalism from the period came on Christmas Eve, 1950 when four Glasgow University students broke into Westminster Abbey and stole the Stone of Destiny from its place beneath the Coronation Chair. It was recovered three months later from Arbroath Abbey.

It was not until the 1960s, however, that national identity and nationalism as electoral forces converged with mainstream Scottish politics as the post-war boom gradually ebbed, giving way to industrial decline and economic uncertainty. A new and invigorated SNP emerged, abandoned the failed moderate and propagandist policies advocated by Thomson, Gibb and others from the pre-war period onwards and adopted aggressive and competitive strategies of electoral confrontation and competition. [30]

By the 1970s the 'old time Scottish home ruler' was unimpressed and lukewarm about the modern SNP, by then firmly established as a left-of-centre political party. The two General Elections of 1974 provided a major breakthrough with 7 SNP MPs elected in the February election and 11 MPs in October when the party won a record 30.4% share of the vote. The Labour Government was forced by the extent of popular support for the nationalists to bring forward legislation for Scottish devolution.

Thomson, the author of *The Kingdom of Scotland Restored*, the proponent of 'New Nationalism', the nationalist activist who had called for a home rule parliament in Edinburgh, displayed little public enthusiasm for the possibility that this was now within the grasp of the Scottish people. The party he had helped plan and plot into being was no longer to his liking. Thomson and the world had moved on.

Despite the books, articles, commentaries and correspondence, he had physically left Scotland in the 1920s and from the late 1940s all that was left was an emotional pull which he maintained only through Scotland's culture and history – occasional trips to the Edinburgh Festival and a series of books set in the sixteenth, seventeenth, and eighteenth centuries. Politically, he disagreed with the SNP's popular, influential but controversial campaign, 'It's Scotland's Oil', which maintained that the Scots were not benefitting from the economic proceeds of North Sea oil and gas and that this strengthened the arguments for independence. Thomson believed that as Scotland was not a sovereign state, under devolution, England, in strict population terms, would be entitled to eight-ninths of all oil revenues, leaving Scotland with one-ninth, about £220 million in 1977 figures. 'Quite a reasonable sum I would have thought,' Thomson said. He rejected a division based on North Sea territorial water lines as 'unfair to England'. [31]

He showed a similar lack of enthusiasm for the Scottish Office's plan to spend £2.65 million on a home for the proposed Scottish Assembly: 'It is doubtful if the house will be big enough for the purpose or even if it would be used at all.' He would have preferred the Scottish Office to give £1.1 million to the National Gallery of Scotland to prevent the sale of a Duccio painting to an American buyer. 'What a curious sense of values my fellow countrymen seem to have', Thomson said. [32]

233

John Knox and Bishops in the Kirk

In response to the question 'Was your father a regular church goer?' Thomson's son Peter laughed. 'No, not all, you must be joking! My father remained silent about the whole religious thing, He would go to church for weddings and funerals.' Peter and his sister were brought up through the established Anglican faith in the Church of England. 'All of the schools I attended were Church of England schools. I was a choir boy both at prep school and at Charterhouse,' Peter said.[33]

Thomson's children's religious upbringing mirrored his intent that they should enjoy and hopefully benefit from the traditional routes in life embraced by the ambitious upper middle classes of London and the Home Counties. Thomson himself remained at heart the Presbyterian Scot of his youth, essentially in his middle and later years a condition he preferred to keep private. But occasionally he allowed the veil to drop and his deep-seated Calvinism emerged.

In late September 1956 as the situation in the Suez Canal threatened to turn into a full-blown crisis and he wrote blistering commentaries reflecting Beaverbrook's support for Britain's dwindling imperial legacy Thomson claimed editorial space in the *Daily Express* to celebrate the 400th anniversary of John Knox's visit to Geneva and his conversion to Calvinism.

This was, Thomson wrote, a key event in modern history. 'He went back to Scotland and imposed his new creed upon his own people. The Scots have never been the same since. Scotland plus John Knox and the philosophy he brought back with him to Edinburgh added up to a nation more important in the world than its numbers justify. Knox tore down the old feudal Scotland and built a new one. Few nations in history – the Jews by Moses, the Russians by Lenin have been so reshaped by one man'.[34]

Thomson's adulation for Knox represented a rare occasion when he felt compelled to use his executive influence on the *Express* to contemplate things Scottish. But the following year when a major event caused furore in the Church of Scotland Thomson found himself orchestrating on behalf of Beaverbrook – and likely also himself – a campaign in Scotland against Kirk leaders. It followed the publication of a report *Relations between Anglican and Presbyterian Churches* produced by a committee representing the Church of Scotland, the Scottish Episcopal Church, the Church of England and the Presbyterian Church of England. The report became notorious, at least in Scotland, as the 'Bishops in the Kirk' report since its main recommendation – a union between the Church of Scotland and Episcopalian Church – would require Kirk ministers to accept ordination from Episcopalian bishops who would be moderators of local presbyteries.

Ian McColl, a senior editorial executive on the *Scottish Daily Express* – and who was also a Kirk elder and Session Clerk of Sandyford Church in Glasgow – brought the report to the attention of Beaverbrook and Thomson. Beaverbrook, the son of a Presbyterian minister, saw a campaign against 'Bishops in the Kirk' as the rightful defence of both Scotland's and his own Presbyterian heritage. Gallagher wrote later that Beaverbrook insisted that the campaign should draw heavily on John Knox for inspiration, Knox having famously denounced bishops in the Westminster Confession of Faith. According to McColl Beaverbrook declared 'fight, fight at whatever cost even if it means losing circulation'.[35]

From 1957 until 1959, when the General Assembly of the Church of Scotland rejected the report, the campaign in Scotland was run by McColl. The veteran Scottish journalist and commentator, Tom Brown who was the young Religious Affairs reporter on the *Scottish Daily Express* at the time, recalls that Beaverbrook's instructions on the campaign were transmitted to Scotland by Thomson who, Brown states, was known in the office as 'The Lord's representative on earth'. McColl separately described himself as 'the keeper of Lord Beaverbrook's Presbyterian conscience'.[36] Charles Graham, the legendary leader-writer of the *Scottish Daily Express,* was, Brown states, briefed by Thomson on the 'line to take' and 'I know that at least a couple of the Scottish editorials and thundering full-page pieces, particularly on the eve of the debate in the General Assembly came up the line from Thomson in London with the imprimatur – OK'd at Cherkley, Beaverbrook's country home'.

The defeat of the 'Bishops in the Kirk' move was hailed as a great victory for Beaverbrook, not least by the *Express* itself. McColl's reward was, in 1961, the editorship of the *Scottish Daily Express*. Thomson, who not for the first time in his career had been manipulating events from the background, dedicated to Ian McColl his 1970 book, *A Kind of Justice*.[37]

The Old Man in a Hampstead Pub

When Thomson died, aged 96, in 1996, obituaries focused almost exclusively on his association with Beaverbrook; one, while stating that he was 'his master's pen, the obedient leader writer', also noted that his role had previously been compared to that of 'a prostitute', a comparison with which Thomson had said, mischievously, he would not quarrel. He had not been in the least offended, 'freely confessing that he wrote things he did not believe.' A former colleague wrote that he was 'quick-witted in every sense' and during his career with Beaverbrook inspired universal admiration and affection: 'he was courteous, polite, unassuming and puckish.' He was, said *The Times*, 'quiet, shrewd, erudite, politically astute and gifted with an acute sense of humour'.

Scottish newspapers, like their Fleet Street counterparts, also appeared ignorant of Thomson's interwar reputation, his forthright opinions on his fellow Scots, his publishing enterprises, his activities on behalf of Scottish home rule, or the notoriety he had acquired because of his views of Irish Catholic immigrants. *The Herald* newspaper in Glasgow merely recalled that two of his books *Caledonia* and *Short History* published in 1930 'caught the eye of Lord Beaverbrook'. *The Herald's* summary of Thomson's life was that even Scottish interest in him was confined to links with Beaverbrook, as a Fleet Street journalist, and in retirement as the author of histories, biographies and novels. It noted only that Thomson was 'a keen' Scottish nationalist and that at a students' meeting in 1928 he had called for the return of the Stone of Scone to Scotland.' The brief reference to only two of Thomson's Scottish books is only relevant in terms of Beaverbrook's interest in them. Thomson, in the view of *The Herald*, was a 'Scots-born' author with a reputation made in London. The Scottish years are either unknown or ignored. [38]

The historian Michael Fry later introduced some Scottish balance to such incomplete eulogies; calling Thomson a significant writer and *Caledonia* as the book that summed up better than anything else he had read the bitter disillusion of the 1920s.

'That decade when Scots realised not only that a land fit for heroes would never be built but also what was left to them after the terrible sacrifices of war would probably be taken away, too.' Thomson, he wrote, understood that the classical Scottish economy of the nineteenth century was on the way out and that it would fail to make the transition from Victorian individualism to modern multinational capitalism.

'He understands also what it will leave behind, a dependency culture with no future except what it can beg from outsiders.' Fry had assumed that Thomson was long dead and expressed surprise that he had never come across him 'in word or flesh' in the contemporary era. Thomson, he suspected, had chosen anonymity, even as 'ghost writer and general factotum to Beaverbrook'. [39]

In 1995, a year before Thomson's death, Kenneth Roy, journalist and founder of the *Scottish Review*, was taken on a guided tour of Hampstead by Gerald Isaaman, the former editor of the *Hampstead and Highgate Express*. At one point Isaaman said, 'If we hurry you may be able to meet George Malcolm Thomson. You have heard of him?' Roy mistakenly thought Isaaman was referring to George Thomson, the Dundee born former Labour MP, European Commissioner and television bureaucrat. Roy learned that the Hampstead Thomson had been assistant to Lord Beaverbrook and had written leaders for the *Daily Express* when it was Britain's top selling daily newspaper. Roy was intrigued, but the taxi was slow and by the time they reached the Coach and Horses pub Thomson had left. 'Evidently he is a man of regular habits. He leaves his favourite pub every afternoon on the stroke of 1.20. At the age of 96 he is entitled,' Roy wrote afterwards. [40]

When he returned home Roy came across the name in Edwin Muir's autobiography, in the section discussing his time living in Hampstead in the 1930s. 'To my astonishment as I lit on the name, [I found] the old man we had missed in the pub – George Malcolm Thomson, living in the district then, as he is now.' Roy made no connection between the old man he had missed in a Hampstead pub and the man who for a period between the wars was Scotland's most controversial journalist and commentator and whose name today – in Scottish historiography – remains notorious.

Within a year of Roy's flying visit and missed meeting, Thomson was dead, apparently with only one regret. In a birthday speech a few years before his death Thomson said it was his one ambition to live to 101, to have lived in three centuries. 'It's a simple ambition, rather childish,' he said. His son Peter said that despite his unfulfilled ambition at the end his father was happy to go when he did. 'I was very grateful when he went. His quality of life had gone completely.' [41]

CHAPTER 12

Endnote – an assessment

IN 1990 when he was 90, George Malcolm Thomson was awarded the OBE, not for his journalism, or for long service to the newspaper industry, or for his wartime political work with Beaverbrook, but for his authorship of novels, histories and biographies since the 1960s. 'I thought they had forgotten me,' was his immediate response, but he was, nevertheless, proud that his work had been recognised. [1]

With the inevitable exception of his Irish-Catholic references, Thomson's interwar Scottish books had largely been forgotten until in 2006, ten years after his death, a small book of 130 pages written in 1930 brought him unlikely fame. Had he made it past the millennium and entered the ranks of the centenarians he would have been pleased, amused, flattered, but above all astonished to learn that the book had been republished and had sold more copies than it did following its original publication. He would also have enjoyed the irony that the book in question, *Whisky*, had been written by him under the pseudonym of Aeneas MacDonald and that in its modern manifestation it had been accorded the accolade of being a 'classic'. Charles Maclean, Scotch whisky historian, said: 'If I could take one whisky book to a desert island it would be *Whisky*.' Aeneas MacDonald, he added, has been firmly installed in the pantheon of Scottish writers of the twentieth century. [2]

At the 2009 Wigtown Book Festival in south west Scotland, Thomson's book was described as 'a love letter to Scotland's national drink', and 'the first great literary work to be solely inspired by and about whisky.' *Whisky Magazine* called it 'the finest whisky book ever written', an accolade echoed by the *Aberdeen Press and Journal*, 'probably the greatest literary book every written about whisky,' it said.

The modern experts and reviewers were not, however, the first to recognise the qualities of *Whisky*. In 1930, at a time when Prohibition was still in place, Christopher Morley, an American literary figure, made it his 'red hot recommendation' to United States publishers and arranged to have the first chapter printed privately and circulated amongst friends. The impetus for the modern reprint of *Whisky* came from another Scotch whisky expert, Ian Buxton, who took the original book to the Edinburgh publishing house, Canongate. Buxton believed that the book had been largely forgotten except by a tiny group of whisky writers, collectors and enthusiasts. He said: 'We realised its significance as a wonderful piece of writing and the first book about whisky written for the drinker, as opposed to the industry.' [3]

The fact that Thomson wrote such a book, did so under a *nom-de-plume*, and the origin of the name he chose, reveal much about Thomson and the contradictions he embodied as an observer and commentator on Scottish life in the interwar period. One reason suggested for the pseudonym was that as the book was published by the Porpoise Press, Thomson did not want to give the impression that as one of the imprint's founders he was giving priority to his own work. This is unlikely, since by 1930 Thomson had published no significant works for the Porpoise Press under his own name, he no longer had any controlling interest, and his 'condition' books and *Short History* were published by London publishers. A more likely conjecture is Thomson's own ego: that having gained a controversial reputation after *Caledonia* and *Re-Discovery*, he did not want his name associated with a book about whisky; or, alternatively, that he did not want the book's reputation connected to his own notoriety, even if it contained an impressive narrative on the history of whisky. What cannot be disputed is that Thomson abandoned his own name as author of *Whisky* to escape his mother's disapproval. [4]

He dedicated his *Short History* to his mother, safe in the knowledge that she would have approved the subject and content. *Whisky*, in common with most of the books and pamphlets that Thomson wrote under his real name, was a polemic, not as controversial as those dealing with the economic, political and social life of Scotland but still a robust view on the history, geography, distilling and manufacture of whisky, which Thomson wrapped up in a mixture of homage and lecture about the sense of Scottishness one might draw from the heritage of the country's national beverage.

Whisky to Thomson was more than an industry vital to the Scottish economy. It was a cultural icon to be placed alongside golf, porridge, haggis, the kilt, the bagpipes, music hall comedians, and public house jokes. Here Thomson displays a further contradiction, since such representations hardly met with his approval; he regarded them as part of an identity at odds with the harsh realities of modern Scotland. And while he accepted the popular legacies attached to such icons, he found them a strange collection of 'gifts' for Scotland to bequeath to the world.

'They come from a people serious to the point of gloom,' he said, 'a curious list of products for a staid and sober people.' Whisky, however, in Thomson's view, was a class apart since it not only belonged to the Scots but to the world at large. It sat proudly above them all. It had a history. It had, said Thomson, an honoured place in the commissariat that tended to the needs of the Jacobite army during the 1745 rebellion. 'It comforted the kilted soldiery on the mad, memorable raid on Derby and was ministered to the Prince himself when he was a hunted man. He had already tasted it in Culloden House on the eve of the fatal battle.'[5]

It was from the events and players in the Jacobite Army that Thomson specifically chose the *nom-de-plume* of Aeneas MacDonald. If his reason for writing under a pseudonym was related to a family situation in the present, his choice of the name he wrote under was firmly lodged in the 1745 rebellion. Aeneas MacDonald was one of Charles Edward Stuart's earliest and most loyal supporters, one of the Parisian exiles known as the 'Seven Men of Moidart' who accompanied him from France and landed with him near Arisaig in July 1745. MacDonald, described as 'a cautious man' was appointed banker to the Jacobite army and although he was raising funds in the Hebrides in February 1746 and avoided the defeat at Culloden, he was captured, sent for trial and sentenced to death for high treason. He was later pardoned and returned to Paris where he died during the French Revolution. [6]

Thomson's reasons for choosing MacDonald from a host of those close to Edward Stuart remain unknown. MacDonald was by birth a member of Clan MacDonald which rallied to the Prince's banner, but he had spent his life in Paris where had been educated, and, unlike some others, he had no meaningful role in the military campaigns. Buxton

241

argues that a pseudonym is not lightly chosen and that Thomson had adopted a name with 'resonance in Scottish history', that MacDonald's role may have been small but it was pivotal. 'In dressing in Jacobite clothing Thomson consciously takes on an identity entirely sympathetic to his own Scottish Renaissance.'[7]

But the choice of the name is of less importance than Thomson's assessment of Jacobitism itself as a symbol of cultural nationalism and its historic impact on Scottish national consciousness. It is unlikely that Thomson would have sympathised with the political aspiration of the Jacobites to restore the Stuarts to the British throne, but Jacobitism's legend and tradition and its part in maintaining and defining a separate and unique Scottish cultural distinctiveness appealed to his interwar blend of Scottishness and nationalism. Thomson would have agreed with the analysis of Donaldson in 1988 that Jacobitism in its cultural embodiment was one of the forces within Scottish society resisting English cultural hegemony. 'The Scots early achieved a sense of nationhood,' Donaldson wrote, 'and one of the most important moving forces behind it during the eighteenth century was the Jacobite movement.'[8]

The movements of Scottish history in the story of whisky reverberates throughout the book. But it is not just a history or a geographical bible of the spread of whisky making across the highlands, islands and lowlands of Scotland. It is a eulogy to whisky and its place in the annals of modern Scotland, one which Thomson argued had been misplaced by the Scots themselves, by particular groups in the population who shared the responsibility of nurturing and protecting something which was akin to a national treasure. *Whisky* is Thomson's salutation to Scotland's national drink, a book in which he holds up the fate of whisky as almost a mirror image of the decline and decay in the Scottish society he writes about in his mainstream books such as *Caledonia*. Whisky historians like Buxton and MacLean commend it as the book which 'began whisky's renaissance', for the magic of its poetry and prose, for passages of passionate, lyrical beauty, 'a love of whisky permeates his soul. We are transfixed by the soaring spirit and graceful imagination of a true acolyte.'[9]

Social historians, however, are more likely to find greater interest in

Thomson's contemporary views on those who drank, marketed and produced whisky; the people, the groups, he believed, were the enemies of the true stature and importance of whisky and who had 'ruined' its image and reputation. When Thomson considered Whisky and concluded that, in his view, it had lost its shine, its greatness reduced, he reacted as he did with so many aspects of contemporary life in Scotland, and he sought to apportion blame. He blamed men who did not drink for the pleasure of drinking or for the flavour of the bouquet which a whisky may possess, but who drank to obtain a physical change. 'They regard whisky not as a beverage but as a drug, not as an end but as a means to an end,' he wrote.

One detects a degree of self-righteousness and moral judgement from Thomson as he criticises those who drink whisky for the effect, who revel in the intoxication it brings them. It is, perhaps, one view from the book which would have met with the approval of Thomson's teetotal mother. 'Whisky suffers its worst insults at the hands of the swillers, the drinkers-to-get-drunk who have not organs of taste and smell in them but only gauges of alcoholic content,' Thomson wrote. But his disdain was not confined to those mainly poorer classes whose drinking habits matched the picture he painted. Other groups, also, used whisky as a drug, 'It is drunk for all kinds of illegitimate reasons, by journalists to quieten conscience, by inferior poets to whip up rhymes, by commercial travellers to dull the memories of rebuff, and by the timid to avert catarrh.'

Thomson, who in other writings professed admiration for the modern arts of propaganda and public relations, displays his contradictions and inconsistencies by criticising the motives and marketing of the whisky salesmen. 'They bandy no words about the aesthetic aspect of their wares,' he says. They fail to understand the higher qualities of their product and instead promote whisky as some form of medicinal food, as a moral product: 'It does you good'; 'After a hot, tiring day'; 'Now that the cold weather is coming'; and 'The doctor recommends it'. Thomson deplores this, arguing that it plays into the hands of those who look upon whisky at its lowest as little more than the 'mere brute stimulant'.

'They believe that one bottle of whisky resembles another very much as one packet of Gold Flake cigarettes another packet of Gold Flake cigarettes.' Whisky, as Thomson views it, has been downgraded as a product, the tendency has been to abolish it from the table of the connoisseur to the golf club smoke room and the saloon bar. 'It may be,' he states, 'the decline of whisky as a civilised pleasure is linked with the decay of taste in Scotland.' Thomson writes not just as the defender of whisky, but as a whisky snob.

The whisky culture he seeks has standards, his perfection rests somewhere in the past when the gentry and men of letters held whisky in their cellars and 'selected it with as much care and knowledge as they gave to the stocking of claret.' Thomson regrets that such an age has passed that whisky no longer retains a place as one of 'the higher delights of mankind'. He reserves his final condemnation for the industry itself, the distillers, the producers, guilty of seeking easier and more profitable paths 'at the expense of their own commodity'. [10]

The modern regard and praise of *Whisky* and the tributes paid to the quality of Thomson's writing – albeit under the pseudonym of Aeneas MacDonald – represents the perfect irony of his cultural nationalism and the campaign he waged as both a participant artist and commentator in the interwar period. It was the first of only two books he wrote under the imprint of the Porpoise Press – it was followed in 1935 by *Distressed* – but Thomson presents opinions and arguments in *Whisky* which can be judged as a parable of his wider condemnation and warnings regarding threats to Scotland's national and cultural identity. Exaggerated as it was, in the book he both celebrates and mourns a symbol of national beauty, something steeped in culture and history, which he sees as reduced to a debased currency. In Thomson's thesis for *Whisky* read Scotland! The ultimate irony, of course, is that *Whisky* having been re-discovered and the secret of its true authorship revealed it will take a place in Scottish literature not conferred on Thomson's angry condition of Scotland books, from which, if recalled at all, only his mean-spirited attacks on Irish Catholic immigrants arouse critical scholarly attention.

Controversial, Notorious, Machiavellian, Significant and Under-Rated

George Malcolm Thomson was an unlikely candidate for the notoriety of 'best hated man'. He was the product of a god-fearing Presbyterian family, his early instincts and values were those common to the successful professional middle classes of lowland Scotland; proud of their separate Scottish identity but committed to the union and the Empire, and particularly to the Scottish contribution to Britain's imperial greatness. It was a post-Victorian and Edwardian mindset associated with economic and industrial achievement which was, initially, only partly blown off course by the sacrifices of World War I. If one of the legacies of the war was Scottish working class and trade union demands for greater equality and a political voice Thomson's priorities were focused on softer middle class anxieties about English influences on Scottish society, particularly those threatening culture and identity.

Thomson's early sense of national identity, his cultural nationalism, was firmly fixed on rejecting Anglicisation, projecting modern Scottish literature and, ambitiously, calling for the revival – in a modern setting – of the intellectual distinctiveness of the eighteenth century enlightenment.

Thomson was a man of contradictions, contradictions embodied in his contrary views about Scotland as it faced the changes, displacements and confusions of the interwar years. Thomson in his first embodiment was the middle-class conservative, a Protestant unionist, ambitious and optimistic, reflecting the positive aspirations of a newly graduated young man. He was proudly Scottish but believed that the union brought strength and security; and any feelings of nationalism were solely related to concerns that further English influences on Scottish society represented a threat to native culture and identity.

In Thomson's second stage the eager, cultural enthusiast of the early 1920s gave way to the angry and disillusioned writer and journalist of the late 1920s, followed by the reluctant but eventually committed nationalist plotter of the early 1930s, and finally to the resigned and more contemplative commentator of the mid to late 1930s. Thomson, in his first phase, must be considered in the context of his formative years, his middle-class and religious background, his father's passion for journalism and the self reliance reflected in his business activities; his mother's commitment to the United Free Church and her work in the working class communities in Leith; and the society and period in which he was born when Scotland – despite massive social inequalities – was regarded by most Scots as economically successful and not dependent on England, indeed a country that punched above its weight.

The events of the 1920s – industrial slump and economic decline – altered Thomson's political boundaries compelling him to look more widely at the condition of Scottish society and to question the reluctance of the Westminster government to intervene. Thomson responded in the manner of a campaigning journalist in researching the background to the events and issues but as a commentator and prophet when he reached his own conclusions about the consequences. Thomson in his writings identified the historical significance of industrial and economic decline, social dislocation, and the creation of an uncertain, less confident people, a dependent nation, and one he contemptuously and repeatedly called second-rate. His eventual answer is a muted form of political nationalism, home rule, not because he was anti-English – he was and remained opposed to separation – but he believed that it was a means of forcing his fellow Scots to face up to the problems and find their own solutions. The alternative, as he saw it, was the continuation of a second-rate country hooked on a dependency culture which would sap not only national confidence but the Scot's ingenuity and entrepreneurial instincts.

Thomson in his books, pamphlets, broadcasts, and essays was the self-proclaimed oracle on what was wrong with Scotland. He issued advice, warnings, prophesies and remedies like confetti, all of his revelations and predictions underpinned with his repeated narrative of despondency and negativity which charged Scotland with failing to match the modern progress of other small European nations.

Caledonia introduced a new form of criticism into the world of Scottish Letters. He was outrageous, scattering verbal venom with a mixture, of anger and disgust. He was deliberately provocative believing that the intensity and passion of the accusatory language he employed would prove contentious and divisive and provoke reaction. That was his objective. He had barely finished *Caledonia* when he wrote *Re-Discovery*.

He was also intent on building a reputation as an outspoken and controversial journalist, essayist and writer. There are no apparent matters of conscience as he lectured Scotland from London. He decried the fact that so many talented Scots, the best brains, the educated were leaving the country; there is never a sense that Thomson pauses and looks in the mirror, at himself, at his own choices. His decision to loosen his commitment to the Porpoise Press, to leave Scotland and seek professional advancement in London suggests that while, as a journalist, commentator and writer he was committed to expressing through words what he believed was wrong with Scotland and campaigning for political, economic, social and cultural change, he would not be part of it.

As it was for tens of thousands of interwar Scots Thomson's future lay in London. A career in Fleet Street was not one likely to appeal to Scottish poets or the authors of short stories, essays or plays, yet ironically, only a few years earlier, one of the central manifesto objectives of the Porpoise Press was to provide a home-based outlet for the new, younger generation of talented writers who might, otherwise, be tempted to take the high road to London. 'Scotland needs a literary and publishing centre of its own; the Porpoise Press does not direct its appeal to a coterie, but to a nation.' [11]

Such fine words and ideals proved elusive yet no one can question the youthful honesty and ambition with which Thomson and his colleague Kerr launched their publishing project. In the same manner, despite the extent of his anger and disillusion about economic and social decline, Thomson, still in his 20s, was heartfelt and earnest when he considered the condition of Scotland. He was equally genuine when he finally cast aside his doubts and embraced the case for a Parliament in Edinburgh, believing that it would act as a catalyst for the renewal and regeneration of civic and cultural Scotland, that it would strengthen national consciousness and identity.

Thomson wrote and spoke about the crucial themes of the time, and many of these like economic decline, nationalism, dependency, culture and identity continued to dominate much of the political and social landscape of Scotland in the second half of the twentieth century. He understood the history, and accurately diagnosed the causes of decline, and knowingly invited approbation and controversy upon himself by choosing to apportion blame, wielding his pen with abandon as he targeted what he regarded as the defiance, ignorance and complacency of leaders, elites, politicians and industrialists. He also refused to spare the middle and working classes for their defeatism and quick embrace of a culture based, as he saw it, on subsidies and hand-outs. Thomson sensed inferiorism, a second rate nation losing its way in the present and too easily prepared to look backwards to seek assurances about its identity and separateness.

Thomson's anger and pessimism are also manifestations of his shame. Wherever he looks he sees a country in denial. The slums merely reinforce his negative and cynical view of his native country. His lurid language about the slums is not out of place, but writing about the slums is not enough in itself. Thomson rages in books, pamphlets and speeches venting his frustration at the self-righteous reaction and response of the Scottish establishment, particularly his own Presbyterian church.

In his early books there is an emphasis on the Irish Catholic issue, but there are also significant and influential commentaries on economic, political and social conditions. He wrote controversial pamphlets on the Presbyterian churches and the case for home rule and in his third condition book, *Distressed*, he produced a studiously researched, well argued, and evidence-based analysis of the causes of Scotland's decline. In the calmer political atmosphere of the mid-1930s the book received a fairer hearing from the Scottish press than that accorded to *Caledonia* and *Re-Discovery* in the late 1920s. Intellectuals like Helen Cruickshank and Edwin Muir separately called it the best book written about the Scottish interwar condition. Thomson's research and the conclusions he reached were largely confirmed before World War II by the assessments of the Dundee economist James Bowie.

Obituaries, in both London and Scotland, focused on Thomson's role as Beaverbrook's mouthpiece. His contribution to the intellectual debate about the dislocations in Scotland between the wars was unknown, ignored, unimportant, or simply forgotten. In terms of the period he has no seat beside the accepted literary or intellectual giants of the time, MacDiarmid, Muir, Gibbon, Gunn, Linklater or even William Power or George Blake. Thomson, during the interwar period, produced no memorable novel or prose, but he appreciated the greatness in others. He lavished public and personal praise on Gibbon, recognising immediately after reading *Sunset Song* in 1932 that it was a remarkable, modern book written by a unique literary talent. And despite his view that MacDiarmid should stay out of nationalist politics he acknowledged that MacDiarmid's poetry had renewed and inspired a new generation of Scots and that in doing so he was established as the worthy leader of the literary revival. However, not all of Thomson's personal characteristics were as worthy.

David Farrer, his friend and wartime colleague in Beaverbrook's private office, praised Thomson for the Machiavellian and persuasive skills which he deployed in his dealings with Beaverbrook. His correspondence with leading nationalist and intellectual figures confirm that he was prepared to be as manipulative, duplicitous, and mischievous as Thomson believed was required to influence, convince and mould behaviours to achieve the necessary responses and outcomes. He employed double-standards but if there was a strong smell of contradiction and hypocrisy Thomson carried on regardless, displaying an air of superiority and certainty as he sought to convert both Tory unionism and radical nationalism to a diet of moderate home rule.

Studying the controlling and often contradictory tendencies revealed in Thomson's letters is a reminder of the dismissive yet suspicious comment of his fellow undergraduate, Margaret H. Kidd, 'he appeared too clever by half.' Thomson's cleverness, however, was occasionally stretched, particularly when he appeared desperate to ensure that Beaverbrook should not be aware of the extent of his nationalist activities. To George Dott: 'Beaverbrook, of course, does not know that I am a nationalist. It would be very awkward for me if it got back to Beaverbrook that I was claiming to have influenced him.'

Despite his arrogance, certainty, pretensions of intellectual superiority, and awareness of his own cleverness, I suspect that, deep down, Thomson would have been content to be remembered as a controversial and influential journalist and commentator. Thomson lived for a further sixty years after his final condition book was published in 1935, ample time and opportunity for one to revisit the past, for possible reconsideration, even revisionism.

An impenitent historian is one without regret or remorse, unrepentant about his interpretation and analysis of the period he has researched and upon which he has passed judgement. The contemporary historian, even of the polemicist variety as Thomson regarded himself in the 1920s and 1930s, has the additional burden of writing and judging events and developments which he has lived through. Should he also feel compelled and confident enough to predict future consequences on the basis of his own current evaluations and attitudes he may, subsequently, have the opportunity to reflect, reconsider, even repent.

In 1965 Thomson, as journalist and book reviewer, having considered A.J.P. Taylor's *English History: 1914-1945* (1965), concluded that Taylor was firmly in the 'impenitent' line of historians. 'It is the most difficult problem a historian can face,' Thomson wrote, 'to write the history of years he has lived through, years the sequel to which he may guess at but cannot foresee.' It was, said Thomson, like reading the small type in a newspaper through the wrong end of a telescope, 'perspective is the difficulty.' [12]

Thomson wrote polemical contemporary history, at least his version of it, and he, additionally, felt confident enough to foresee and predict the consequences, none more so than the repercussions that would follow for Scotland because of Irish Catholic population growth. If Thomson looked at any part of Scottish society through the wrong end of a telescope in the interwar period, if he had cause to conclude that the sequels he chose not to guess at but to actually foresee required revisionism, he never said.

He cannot escape the charge of sectarianism and racism; that he deliberately set out to engender fear by highlighting and sensationalising the Irish issue. The evidence of his books is sufficient for his conviction as do the words from his personal correspondence demonstrate and substantiate the duplicity and hypocrisy of his subsequent rhetoric in which he denied anti-Irish sentiments while continuing to call privately for anti-Irish measures. These facts undermine his later admission to Tom Gallagher in 1982 that he 'regretted' his anti-Irish outbursts, citing a confusion of thinking with nationalist politics.

Had he reflected further he might also have considered if his constant indictment of Scotland as second-rate and his regular dire warnings of the dangers to national confidence and consciousness that would arise from embracing a culture of dependency served to question the nation's self-worth and embed an inferiority complex. Did his pessimistic role as a prophet of gloom cast him as an intellectual voice presenting to his fellow countrymen a narrative and philosophy of mediocrity?

Such a negative image of Scottishness, of low-self-esteem, has, some scholars argue, been a feature of the Scottish personality since the interwar period. Mitchell has described a view that intellectuals have presented Scotland in such negative light, 'a country which can be exhaustively described in terms of poverty, philistinism, bigotry, repression – a land of no gods or heroes', a society portrayed as deeply divided, having many negative features. This complex area creates negative perceptions of Scottish history and culture, 'which profoundly influence Scots' understanding of themselves and their national identity.' Beveridge and Turnbull argue that this has led to an 'inferiorist' mentality which distorts cultural expression and reinforces Scotland's political subordination, 'inferiorist assumptions are deeply ingrained.' [13]

Dependency and inferiorism has created a form of identity confusion in many Scots, on the one hand arrogant and boastful, on the other imbued feelings of inferiority ranging across political, economic, social and cultural issues. Such modern viewpoints and analysis, although not unanimously supported, have enabled critical voices to project negative images of Scotland and associate these with the nationalist movement. The unionist writer and commentator Allan Massie claims that the twentieth century development of Scottish hostility to the English originated from the resentment festered as Scotland grew comparatively poorer: 'by the second half of the twentieth century awareness of economic decline and inferiority affected the Scottish temper.' [14]

The upshot of this destructive manifestation of dependency and inferiorism was the 'Scottish cringe' displayed perversely through the denial of a lack of self confidence and fear. Thomson was an early voice responsible for creating a language of failure and the sense of inferiority. He accurately foretold the impact on the national character of economic and social decline allied with a culture of defeatism, dependency and complacency. The consequences of such decline, he argued in 1935, could only be answered by 'a reawakened national consciousness', even nationalists might have to lay aside political and economic arguments 'to convince their fellow countrymen that 'nationhood is in itself something worth having'.

Thomson recognised that national sentiment was one of the strongest weapons available to argue and promote Scotland's cause. He contrasted Scotland's position with that of an English region like Durham, contending that while grave economic stress in the north-east of England would be lamentable, alarming and regrettable it would have minor effect on England as a whole. 'If economic decline in Durham were counterbalanced by an enrichment of, say, Middlesex, then the element of grand tragedy would disappear instantly from the scene,' he said. In contrast an adverse economic effect upon Scotland would be a high tragedy with the tension of a spiritual drama. It would be, he said, an attack upon the material existence, the means of life, of a highly differentiated human type, a people, 'whose influence upon the history of Western civilisation, for good or evil, has certainly been remarkable in proportion to its mass. Should such an attack develop its triumph would be a disaster for which there could be no satisfactory compensation.' [15]

By the mid-1930s Thomson's life had moved on from the problems facing Scotland. He, his wife and two children were settled in Hampstead and his career was dedicated to serving the Beaverbrook cause, as both journalist and political advisor. His final interwar book, *Distressed,* and the play *Moonlight Flitting* helped him maintain a small but less contentious profile in Scotland. His name was regularly to be found on a by-line on the main editorial page of the *London Daily Express*, express-ing the views of Beaverbrook on the great national and international developments as Europe drifted towards war. The brief appearance of *Moonlight Flitting* on a London stage in late 1938 exposed and recognised his Scottish background but as his children have confirmed, Scottish identity, culture and politics were not issues discussed in the Thomson household.

Throughout the war years and until the late 1940s Thomson maintained private contact with Andrew Dewar Gibb but in his profess-ional and social life in the environs of Beaverbrook Newspapers and the Garrick Club, Thomson's Scottishness was confined to his accent. Thomson, I believe, did more than accuse his native country of being second-rate; he concluded that his own talents were more likely to flourish in the dynamic London environment. Despite his move south, until he was recruited by Beaverbrook in 1931 Thomson's journalism and literary interests remained focused on Scottish affairs. And as his correspondence reveals, his private and personal interests – at least until the mid-1930s – were concentrated on his programme of what he called 'Unionist-Nationalism'.

He did not consciously abandon Scotland. Life, family, career, events drew him away but one suspects that when he did look backwards he would have been pleased that it had done so. In later life he would have been embarrassed to be reminded that at one point he had attempted to create a group he described as 'the secret league of intellectuals'. He would likely have pleaded youthful enthusiasm – at the time he was aged thirty – adding quickly, that it was in the worthwhile cause of Scottish home rule.

> Scotland, the people, the culture, are the outcome of the interaction of converging forces; the collision of a set of racial and cultural energies within a narrow, well defined geographical and climatic environment. Modified through time by philosophical influences and contacts with other peoples and cultures, it created a human type vigorous in expression and powerful in outline. It is a culture, a political organisation, a church, a philosophy, a tradition, stubbornly sprouting, frequently threatened and firmly defended.

Scotland, like every other true nation, is something whole, something rounded, complete, and therefore it cannot be repeated. It is a unit; it is unique.

George Malcolm Thomson, *Scotland That Distressed Area*

George Malcolm Thomson, 1979

Notes

Introduction

1 George Malcolm Thomson, *The Re-Discovery of Scotland* (London, 1928), Dust-Jacket.

2 L. McN. W., 'A Silly Book about Scotland: A Reply to a Traducer', *Forward* (26 November 1928), p. 3.

3 C.M. Grieve, *Albyn or Scotland and the Future* (London, 1927), pp. 43-44.

4 Sir Robert Rait and George S. Pryde, *Scotland* (London, 1934), p. 141.

5 Agnes Mure Mackenzie, *Scotland in Modern Times 1720-1939* (Edinburgh, 1941), p. 432.

6 Doris N. Dalglish, 'Towards a Nationalist Literature: The Scottish Renaissance', *Times Literary Supplement*, 30 April 1938, Scottish Supplement, p.x.

7 Richard J. Finlay, 'National Identity in Crisis: Politicians, Intellectuals and the 'End of Scotland', 1920-1939', *The Historical Association* (1994), p. 247

8 See: George Malcolm Thomson, *Caledonia, or The Future of Scots* (London, 1927); Thomson, *Rediscovery*.

9 Margery Palmer McCulloch, *Scottish Modernism and its Contexts 1918-1959: Literature, National Identity and Cultural Exchange* (Edinburgh, 2009), p. 95.

10 Liam McIlvanney, 'Literature that Upped the Anti', *Sunday Herald*, 9 April 2000, p.14.

11 Keith Dixon, 'Making Sense of Ourselves: National and Community in Modern Scottish Writing', *Forum for Modern Language Studies*, Vol. 19, No 4 (1993) p. 360.

12 Alf Young, 'The Scotland of Tomorrow, as imagined 75 years ago', *The Herald*, 29 December 2000, p.16.

13 Richard J. Finlay, 'Nationalism, Race, Religion and the Irish Question in Inter-War Scotland', *Innes Review*, Vol. 42, No. 1. (Spring 1991), pp. 53-54.

14 Liam Connell, 'Irish Immigration and Scottish Identity', in *The Irish and Britain*, BAIS Conference, (Salford, 5-7 September 1997).

15 James Mitchell, *Strategies for Self-Government: The Campaigns for a Scottish Parliament* (Edinburgh, 1996), pp. 180-181.

16 Helen B. Cruickshank, *Octobiography* (Montrose, 1976), p. 59

17 Helen B. Cruickshank, Letter to Eric Linklater, 26 October, 1935, NLS. *Eric Linklater Papers*, Acc. 10282, Folder 1.

18 Edwin Muir, Review, 'Scotland: That Distressed Area', by George Malcolm Thomson, originally published in *Criterion*, Vol. 15 (January 1936), pp. 330-332; in Andrew Noble, ed., *Edwin Muir: Uncollected Scottish Criticism* (London, 1982), p. 115.

19 George Scott-Moncrieff, 'The Scottish Renaissance of the 1930s', in Karl Miller, ed., *Memoirs of Modern Scotland* (London, 1970), p. 73

20 Letter to Alexander Gray, 13 June 1929, *J. Leslie Mitchell: Lewis Grassic Gibbon'*

Papers, NLS, MS 26109, Folder 4, quoted in Hanne Tange, 'Lewis Grassic Gibbon and the Scottish Renaissance', Paper, Association of Scottish Literary Studies Conference (Aberdeen, 9-10 June 2001). http://www.arts.gla.ac.uk/ScotLit/ASLS/Conference2001.html

21 Christopher M. Grieve, 'An Outstanding Year', *Daily Record, 3* November, 1931.

22 George Malcolm Thomson, Pamphlet, *The Kingdom of Scotland Restored* (London, 1931).

23 Alistair McCleery, *The Porpoise Press 1922-39* (Edinburgh, 1988).

Chapter 1

1 J.M. Reid, Scotland's Progress: The Survival of the Nation (London, 1971), p. 12.

2 G.R. Blake, *Scotland of the Scots* (London, 1918), p. 9.

3 Richard Finlay, 'Changing Cultures: The History of Scotland since 1918', in Ian Brown, Thomas Owen Clancy, Susan Manning and Murray Pittock, eds., *The Edinburgh History of Scottish Literature* Volume 3 (Edinburgh, 2007), pp. 1-10.

4 J.M. Reid, *Scotland Past and Present* (Edinburgh, 1968), pp. 43-44.

5 R. J.M. Finlay, 'National Identity', in Michael Lynch, ed., *Oxford Companion to Scottish History* (Oxford, 2001), pp. 443-444.

6 John Foster, 'The Twentieth Century, 1914-1979', in R.A. Houston and W.W.J. Knox, eds., *The New Penguin History of Scotland From the Earliest Times to the Present Day* (London, 2001), pp. 417-493, p. 431

7 J.G. Kyd, 'Scotland's Population', *The Scottish Historical Review*, Vol. 28, No. 106 (October 1949), pp. 98-100

8 Malcolm Smith, Democracy in a Depression: Britain in the 1920s and 1930s (Cardiff, 1998), p. 1.

9 D.W. Parsons, The Political Economy of British Regional Policy (London, 1986), p. 46.

10 Angus Calder, *Scotlands of the Mind* (Edinburgh, 2002), pp. 112-114.

11 J.P. Priestley, *English Journey* (London, 1934).

12 Edwin Muir, *Scottish Journey* (London, 1935), p. 243

13 Edwin Muir, *An Autobiography* (London, 1987), pp. 232, 237.

14 George Malcolm Thomson, *Scotland: That Distressed Area* (Edinburgh, 1935), p. 107.

15 Andrew Dewar Gibb, *Scotland in Eclipse* (London, 1930), p. 112.

16 George Blake, *The Heart of Scotland*, First Edition (London, 1934), p. 112.

17 Alan Riach, 'Hugh McDiarmid', in *The Edinburgh History of Scottish Literature*, Vol. 3, p. 81.

18 Reid, *Scotland Past and Present*, p. 165; *Scotland's Progress*, p. 176.

19 J.H. Burns, 'Stands Scotland Where it Did?' *History*, Vol.70, No. 228 (February 1985), p. 47.

20 George Hewitt, 'Reformation to Revolution', in Ian Donnachie and Christopher Whatley, eds., *The Manufacture of Scottish History* (Edinburgh, 1992), pp. 16-17.

Chapter 2

1 Andrew Fletcher of Saltoun, 'Account of a Conversation concerning a Right Regulation of Governments for the Common Good of Mankind', cited in

Christopher Harvie, *Scotland and Nationalism*, p.7.

2 John S. Gibson, *The Thistle and the Crown: A History of the Scottish Office* (Edinburgh, 1985), pp. 182-183.

3 Anthony P Cohen, 'A Scottish View of Some Rites, Rights and Wrongs', *American Ethnologist*, Vol. 23, No. 4 (Nov., 1996), p. 805.

4 See Colin Kidd, Union and Unionisms: Political Thought in Scotland, 1500-2000 (Cambridge, 2008), p. 288; Richard J. Finlay, Independent and Free: Scottish Politics and the Origins of the Scottish National Party 1918-1945 (Edinburgh, 1994), p. 130.

5 Various Reports, *The Scotsman*, 2 August 1899, pp. 5, 6,7,8,9 and 10.

6 George Malcolm Thomson, 'A Holiday as the World Changed', *Daily Express*, 4 August 1964, p. 4.

7 'Edinburgh Bankruptcy Court', *The Scotsman*, 14 November 1900, p. 5.

8 'Service Volunteers', *The Scotsman*, 4 March 1901, p. 8.

9 Archives of Junction Road United Free Church, NAS, CH3/728/90.

10 Rev. James Mr. Scott, Minister, Junction Road United Free Church, Annual Report, July, 1912, NAS, CH3/728/90.

11 Band of Hope Rules, Junction Road United Free Church Records, NAS, CH3/728/89.

12 George Malcolm Thomson to Neil Gunn, 14 November 1930, 16 January 1931, NLS, Neil Gunn Papers, Dep. 209, Box 20.

13 Daniel Stewart's College, *The Scotsman*, 27 July, 1915, p. 7; 26 July, 1917 p. 7.

14 George Malcolm Thomson, 'School Notes', *Daniel Stewart's College Magazine* (December 1916), p. 22, (July 1917), pp. 90-91

15 George Malcolm Thomson, First Matrics, Da 34, *Centre for Research Collections* Edinburgh University (1919).

16 George Malcolm Thomson, A Short History of Scotland From the Earliest Times to the Outbreak of The Great War (London, 1930), p. 298.

17 Thomson, *Caledonia*, pp. 60-62.

18 McCleery, *Porpoise Press*, pp. 17-19.

19 Roderick Watson Kerr, 'Princes Street Porpoise', *The Broughton Magazine*, 1957 Jubilee Edition, No. 49, 1 (Summer 1957), p. 11.

20 Alistair McCleery, Interview with George Malcolm Thomson, 31 August, 1983, cited in McCleery, *Porpoise Press*, p. 18.

21 Watson Kerr, 'Princes Street Porpoise', p. 11.

22 Alistair McCleery, Interview with Dame Margaret H. Kidd, 2 February, 1984, cited in McCleery, *Porpoise Press*, p. 18.

23 Kerr, 'Princes Street Porpoise', p. 11.

24 McCleery, *Porpoise Press*, p. 27

25 Edinburgh Evening News, March 1923, quoted in McCleery, *Porpoise Press*, p. 27; 'A Porpoise Production', *Glasgow Evening News*, 14 June, 1923, p. 4

26 Kerr, 'Princes Street Porpoise', p. 11.

27 R. Watson Kerr, *Annus Mirabilis or The Ascension O' Jimmie Broon*, Broadsheet Number 10 (Edinburgh, May 1924).

28 Jackie McGlone, 'Woman artist who sacrificed herself on the altar of domesticity', *The Herald*, 8 June 1991, p.16

29 'Edinburgh Group Exhibition', *The Scotsman*, 3 December 1921, p. 8.

30 Interview with Peter Thomson, 19 Holly Hill, Hampstead, London, 22 February 2011.

31 McCleery, *Porpoise Press*, pp. 40-44.

32 McCleery, *Porpoise Press*, p. 11.

33 Thomson, *Distressed*, p. 5-6.

34 T.C. Smout, 'Scotland 1850-1950', in F.M.L. Thompson, ed., *The Cambridge Social History of Britain 1750-1950 Vol. 1 Regions and Communities* (Cambridge, 1990), pp. 209-210.

35 Thomson, *Distressed*, p. 7.

36 Thomson, *Short History*, pp. 299-300.

37 Margery Palmer McCulloch, ed., *Modernism and Nationalism Literature and Society in Scotland 1919-1939: Source Documents for the Scottish Renaissance* (Glasgow, 2004), p. xiii

38 Reid, *Scotland's Progress*, pp.13-14.

39 Finlay, 'National Identity in Crisis', p.243.

40 Thomson, *Caledonia*, p. 62.

41 George Malcolm Thomson, 'George Blake', *The Bookman* (July 1928), pp. 200-202.

42 See George Malcolm Thomson, Correspondence with Andrew Dewar Gibb, September, October, December 1930; 2 October 1933, NLS, Gibb Papers, Dep. 217, Box 1, 2.

43 See Thomson, *The Kingdom of Scotland Restored* (London, 1931)

44 George Malcolm Thomson to Neil Gunn, 30 March 1930, NLS, Gunn Papers, Dep. 209, Box 20, Folder 8.

45 McCleery, *Porpoise Press*, pp. 64-65

46 Thomson to Gunn, 26 September 1930.

47 Thomson to Gunn, 10 October 1930.

48 George Blake and Porpoise Press, Faber and Faber Archives, FVM 48, quoted in McCleery, *Porpoise Press*, pp. 71-73

49 'Blake and Porpoise Press'. Faber Archives, FVM 48, quoted in McCleery *Porpoise Press*, p. 85.

50 'Five Scottish Books: History and Economic Problems', *The Scotsman*, 26 September 1935, p. 13.

51 Thomson, *Distressed*, p. 107.

52 Thomson, *Distressed*, p. 122.

53 William Dunbar, 'Lament for the Makars', John Small, ed., *The Poems of William Dunbar* (Edinburgh 1893), quoted in Thomson, *Distressed*, p. 122.

Chapter 3

1 George Malcolm Thomson, *Moonlight Flitting*, Scottish Theatre Archive, Special Collections, Glasgow University, STA Bw 6, Record No. 13519, Acc. No. 139, Act 1, pp. 16-18

2 'Play of a Glasgow Slum', *The Scotsman*, 23 November 1938, p. 13.

3 'Curtain Theatre Company', *Scottish Theatre Archive*, Special Collections, Glasgow University, GB 247 STA By 1.

4 See 'Moonlight Flitting', *The Times*, 5 November 1938, p. 10; 'Play of a Glasgow Slum', p. 13.

5 Thomson, *Moonlight Flitting*, Act I, pp. 22-23.

6 Thomson, *Moonlight Flitting*, Act III, p. 20.

7 George Blake, *The Shipbuilders* (Edinburgh, 1993), pp. 256-257, 1st pub. (1935).

8 See George Blake Papers, NLS, Acc. 11930/32.

9 Agnew Mure Mackenzie, 'The Shipbuilders', *Times Literary Supplement*, 14 March 1935, No. 1728, p. 158.

10 Thomson, 'George Blake', pp. 200-202.

11 Thomson, *Caledonia*' pp. 39, 43

12 Thomson, *Re-Discovery*, pp. 95, 97.

13 Thomson, *Re-Discovery*, p. 84, *Caledonia*, p. 44.

14 Thomson, *Re-Discovery*, p 86.

15 Thomson, *Re-Discovery*, pp. 4, 5.

16 Thomson, *Re-Discovery*, pp. 16-17.

17 Thomson, *Caledonia*, pp. 8-10, 44.

18 Thomson, *Re-Discovery*, pp. 31-34.

19 Thomson, *Caledonia*, p. 45.

20 George Malcolm Thomson, *Will the Scottish Church Survive?* Porpoise Pamphlet, (Edinburgh, 1930), pp. 30-31

21 Thomson, *Caledonia*, pp. 53, 56.

22 Thomson, *Scottish Church Survive*, pp. 30-31.

23 Thomson, *Scottish Church Survive*, p. 16.

24 Thomson, *Scottish Church Survive*, pp. 21, 22, 23, 37.

25 Thomson, *Scottish Church Survive*, p. 26.

26 Junction Road United Free Archives, NAS, CH3/728/90.

27 http://www.nls.uk/about-us/what-we-are/nls-history

28 George Malcolm Thomson, 'The Scottish Advocate', *Library Review*, Vol. 3, No. 3 (1931), pp. 111-114

29 Thomson, *Caledonia*, pp. 8, 44, 45, 47, 48, 49, 50, 51, 52, 53, 67, 68.

30 Thomson, *Short History*, pp. 211, 212.

31 Thomson, *Short History*, pp. 295, 296.

32 Thomson, *Caledonia*, pp. 63-64.

33 Thomson, *Short History*, p. 296.

34 Thomson, *Re-Discovery*, pp. 72-73.

35 Thomson, *Re-Discovery*, pp. 71-73.

36 Thomson, *Caledonia*, pp. 68, 69, 70.

37 George Gladstone Robertson with Roderick Grant, *Gorbals Doctor* (London, 1970), p. 39.

38 Robertson, *Gorbals Doctor*, p.40.

39 Thomson, *Caledonia*, p. 18-19.

40 William Bolitho, *Cancer of Empire* (London, 1924).

41 Thomson, *Re-Discovery*, pp. 108-109

42 Thomson, *Caledonia*, pp. 18-22

43 Thomson, *Re-Discovery*, p. 108; See also Report of Baldwin speech in Stirling, *The Scotsman*, 26 January 1926, quoted in Gabrielle Ward-Smith, 'Baldwin and Scotland: More than Englishness', *Contemporary British History*, Vol. 15, No. 1 (Spring 2001), p. 64.

44 'Baldwin on Housing', *The Scotsman*, 2 October 1925, p. 6.

45 Thomson, *Re-Discovery*, p. 109-11.

46 'Alien Immigration: Effect on Glasgow Slums', *The Scotsman*, 24 November 1925, p. 6.

47 'Glasgow's Reputation: Unfair Criticism', *The Scotsman*, 28 November 1925, p. 7.

48 'Social Conditions: Dr White on the Position of the Church's Problem', *The Scotsman*, 17 February 1926, p. 8.

49 Muir, *Scottish Journey*, p. 87.

50 Muir, *An Autobiography*, pp. 91-92.

51 Muir, *Scottish Journey*, pp. 119,-123.

52 Letter to Alexander Gray, 13 June 1929, *J. Leslie Mitchell 'Lewis Grassic Gibbon' Papers*, NLS, MS 26109, Folder 4, quoted in Hanne Tange, 'Lewis Grassic Gibbon and the Scottish Renaissance', paper delivered at Association of Scottish Literary Studies, Conference,(Aberdeen, 9-10 June 2001). http://www.arts.gla.ac.uk/ScotLit/ASLS/Conference2001.html

53 Lewis Grassic Gibbon, 'Glasgow', in Grassic Gibbon and MacDiarmid, *Scottish Scene*, pp. 117-119

54 John Boyd Orr, *As I Recall: The 1880s to the 1960s* (London, 1966), pp. 42-44.

55 Sir John Orr, 'Scotland As it Is', in Alexander Maclehose, The *Scotland of Our Sons* (Glasgow, 1937), p. 81.

56 Orr, 'As it Is', pp. 80-83.

57 'Conditions in Glasgow Slums', *Scottish Board of Health Annual Report 1926*, HMSO, Cmd. 2881 (Edinburgh, 1927), pp. 49-50.

58 James Stewart, David Kirkwood, Debate on the Report, Scottish Board of Health, *House of Commons*, HC Deb, 21 July 1927, Vol. 209 cc. 599-653.

59 Walter Elliot, HC Debate 15 July 1930, Vol. 241 cc1215-33.

60 Thomson, *Re-Discovery*, pp. 103, 104, 112, 113.

61 Walter Elliot, Housing (Glasgow), HC Deb 18 December 1936, vol. 318 cc2862-2886.

62 Stephen Constantine, *Social Conditions in Britain* 1918-1939 (London, 1983) p. 41.

63 John Boyd Orr, *Infant Mortality in Scotland*, Department of Health (Scotland), HMSO (1943), quoted in Foster, 'The Twentieth Century, 1914-1979', pp. 431-432.

64 RA Cage, 'Infant Mortality Rates and Housing', in Anthony Cooke, Ian Donnachie, Ann MacSween and Christopher Whatling, eds., *Modern Scottish History 1707 to the Present Vol. 4: Readings 1850 to the Present* (Edinburgh, 1998), pp. 134-135.

65 Thomson, *Caledonia*, pp. 18-19.

Chapter 4

1 Thomson, *Caledonia*, p. 10.

2 T.M. Devine, *Scottish Nation* (London, 2006), pp. 318, 629.

3 Thomson, *Caledonia*, p. 10.

4 Thomson, *Re-Discovery*, p. 107.

5 Thomson, *Caledonia*, pp. 10-15.

6 1921 Census, quoted in 'Irish Menace', *The Scots Independent*, Vol. 1, No. 2 (December 1926), pp. 1-2.

7 Quoted in James Edmund Handley, *The Irish in Modern Scotland* (Cork, 1947), p. 305-306.

8 *Glasgow Herald* (20 March, 1929), quoted in Steve Bruce, Tony Glendinning, Iain Paterson and Michael Rosie, eds., *Sectarianism in Scotland,* (Edinburgh, 2004), p. 43.

9 See Graham Walker, Intimate Strangers: Political and Cultural Interaction between Scotland and Ulster in Modern Times (Edinburgh, 2004), p. 65.

10 Thomson, *Re-Discovery*, p. 84.

11 Handley, *The Irish in Modern Scotland*, p. 306.

12 Thomson, *Re-Discovery*, p. 42-43, 50-51.

13 Irish Menace', *Scots Independent*, pp. 1-2.

14 See Devine, *Scottish Nation*, p. 498-499; Callum G. Brown, 'Religion and Secularisation', in Dickson and Treble, *People and Society in Scotland,* p. 71.

15 See Hugh MacLeod, 'Protestantism and British National Identity 1815-1945', in Peter Van Der Veer and Hartmut Lehman, eds., *Nation and Religion: Perspectives on Europe and Asia* (Princeton, 1999), p. 56.

16 The Menace of the Irish Race to our Scottish Nationality, Report to the General Assembly,1923', quoted in Callum G. Brown, *Religion and Society in Scotland since 1707* (Edinburgh, 1997), p. 192-193.

17 See MacLeod, 'Protestantism and British National Identity', p. 56; Rev. Duncan Cameron, Report, *Stirling Observer*, 13 December 1927, quoted in Brown, 'Religion and Society', p. 192-193.

18 Handley, The Irish in Modern Scotland, p.302.

19 'Alien Immigration: Effect on Glasgow Slums', *The Scotsman*, 24 November 1925, p. 6.

20 George Wingate, 'Proceedings of the Glasgow Philosophical Society', Vol. 54 (1927), p. 41, quoted in James D. Young, *The Rousing of the Scottish Working Class* (London, 1979), p. 220.

21 Alan G. Ogilvie, ed., *Essays in Regional Geography* (Cambridge, 1928), p. 450.

22 E.J. Russell, 'Introduction', *Essays in Regional Geography*, p. xxx.

23 *Glasgow Herald*, 29 May 1922, p. 25, quoted in Stewart J. Brown, 'Outside the Covenant: The Scottish Presbyterian Churches and Irish Immigration, 1922-1938', *Innes Review*, Vol. 22, No. 1 (Spring 1991), pp. 19-20.

24 *Stirling Observer*, December 13 1927, quoted in Brown, *Religion and Society in Scotland*, p.192-193.

25 Thomson, *Caledonia*, p. 70.

26 T.B. Macaulay, Leopold von Ranke, 'The Ecclesiastical and Political History of the Popes during the Sixteenth and Seventeenth Centuries', translated by S. Austin, (London, 1840), *Edinburgh Review* 72, (October 1840), pp. 227-258, in *Lord Macaulay's Essays and Lays of Ancient Rome*, (London, 1893), pp. 547-569.

27 Thomson, *Caledonia*, pp. 70, 73, 75, 76, 79, 81, 82, 94.

28 'The Irish in Scotland: An Inquiry into the Facts', *Glasgow Herald,* 20, 21, 22, 23, 24, 25 March 1929.

29 Handley, The Irish in Modern Scotland, p. 315.

30 J.C. Dunlop, 'Glasgow Herald articles entitled Irish in Scotland', 20-25 March 1929, SRO, HH. 1. 557, quoted in Brown, 'Outside the Covenant', p. 35.

31 HC Deb, 24 November 1932, vol. 272 cc235-360.

32 See Thomson, *Caledonia*, p. 10.

33 HC Deb, 24 November 1932, vol. 272 cc235-360.

34 Bruce, Glendinning, Paterson and Rosie, *Sectarianism in Scotland*, pp. 46-47.

35 Lord Scone, Vagrants: HC Deb, 12 June 1934, vol. 290 c1520.

36 H.A.L. Fisher, Foreword, Rait and Pryde, *Scotland*, pp. v-vii.

37 Andrew Dewar Gibb, *Scotland in Eclipse* (London, 1930)

38 See Tom Devine, 'No Headline Present', *The Herald*, 19 July 1998; Andrew Noble, 'Blarney, Dogma, Hatred and Fear', *The Herald*, 7 December 1996; Keith Dixon, 'Conservative Scottish Nationalism During the Interwar Period: The Ideas of Andrew Dewar Gibb and George Malcolm Thomson', *Etudes Ecossaise*, Grenoble, No. 4 (1997), pp. 211, 220.

39 See Appointments, *The Times*, Saturday 26 May 1934, p. 14; 'New Professor of Law, Glasgow A Scottish Nationalist', *The Scotsman*, 26 May, 1934, p. 12.

40 George Malcolm Thomson to Andrew Dewar Gibb, 31 October 1930, NLS, Gibb Papers, Dep. 217, Boxes 1-2.

41 Andrew Dewar Gibb to Stanley Baldwin, 23 June 1930, NLS, Gibb Papers, Dep. 217, Box 1.

42 Gibb, *Scotland in Eclipse*, pp. 53, 54, 55, 56, 57, 59.

43 Handley, *The Irish in Modern Scotland*, p. 316.

44 Tom Gallagher, *The Uneasy Peace Religious Tension in Modern Scotland* (Manchester, 1987), p. 168; Gallagher Interview with George Malcolm Thomson, 26 March 1928, quoted in Gallagher, *Uneasy Peace*, p. 170.

45 Various letters George Malcolm Thomson to Andrew Dewar Gibb, 1930-1935, NLS, Gibb Papers, Dep. 217, Boxes 1, 2.

46 George Malcolm Thomson to Neil M. Gunn, 13 March 1930; 15 August 1930, NLS, Gunn Papers, Dep. 209, Box 20,

47 See George Malcolm Thomson to George Dott, Letter, 1 August 1930, NLS, Dott Papers, Acc. 5927/1 Folder 1.

48 Thomson, 30 March 1930, Gunn Papers.

49 Thomson, *Short History*, pp. 281-283.

50 Thomson to Gunn, 13 March 1930, Gunn Papers.

51 George Malcolm Thomson, 'National Party's Position', *The Scotsman*, 22 October 1929, p. 7

52 Thomson to Gunn, 15 March 1930, NLS, Gunn Papers,

53 George Malcolm Thomson to George Dott, 1 August 1930, Dott Papers.

54 Graham Walker, 'Varieties of Scottish Protestant Identity', in T. M. Devine and R.J. Finlay, eds., *Scotland in the Twentieth Century* (Edinburgh, 1996), p. 254.

55 George Malcolm Thomson to Andrew Dewar Gibb, 8 March 1934, NLS, Gibb Papers, Dep. 217, Box 1.

56 Thomson to Gibb, 5 April 1933, Gibb Papers.

57 Thomson to Gibb, 18 December 1933, Gibb Papers.

58 Thomson to Gibb, 8 March 1934, Gibb Papers.

59 'Nationalist Claim Scottish Problems', *The Scotsman*, 5 June 1937, p. 16; *Scots Independent*, July 1937, p. 3, quoted in Richard J. Finlay, *Independent and Free: Scottish Politics and the Origins of the Scottish National Party, 1880-1945*(Edinburgh, 1994), p. 193.

60 Dr Duncan Lamont, *Scots Independent*, (July 1937), p. 3, quoted in Finlay *Independent and Free*, p. 193.

61 John MacCormick, *The Flag and the Wind* (London, 1955), pp. 50, 51, 52, 53, 117.

62 Liam Connell, 'Irish Immigration and Scottish Identity', *The Irish and Britain*, BAIS Conference, Salford (5-7 September 1997). http://www.nationalismproject.org/links/article.htm

Chapter 5

1 Thomson, *Caledonia*, p. 58.

2 Thomson, *Caledonia*, p. 60.

3 L.M.'N.W., 'A Silly Book,' p. 3.

4 'C. M. Grieve to George Ogilvie', 30 January 1928, in Catherine Kerrigan, ed., *The Hugh MacDiarmid-George Ogilvie Letters* (Aberdeen, 1988), pp. 130-132.

5 Today and Tomorrow Series, Annex, in Grieve, *Albyn*, p. 17.

6 Kerrigan, 'Grieve to Ogilvie', p. 131.

7 Grieve, *Albyn*, pp. 10-12, 16-17.

8 C.M. Grieve, 'The Truth about Scotland', *The New Age*, Vol.42, No. 2 (10 November 1927), p. 17.

9 Grieve, *Albyn*, pp. 43-44.

10 Grieve, 'Truth about Scotland', p. 16.

11 Jack Brand, *The National Movement in Scotland* (London, 1978), pp. 77-78.

12 See Alan Riach, ed., *Hugh MacDiarmid Albyn Shorter Books and Monographs* (Manchester, 1996), p. 357.

13 Thomson, *Re-Discovery*, p. 80-81.

14 F, Marian McNeil, 'The New Burns', *Scots Independent* (December 1930), quoted in McCulloch, 'Modernism and Nationalism', pp. 122-124.

15 HC Deb, 20 December 1934, vol.296 cc1513-8; HL Deb, 19 December 1934, vol. 95 cc617-48. HC Deb, 20 December 1934, vol. 296 cc1513-8.

16 Wal Hannington, *The Problem of the Distressed Areas* (London, 1937), p. 18.

17 HC Deb, 29 March 1935, vol. 299, cc 2247-54.

18 See Thomson, *Distressed*.

19 Helen B. Cruickshank, Letter to Eric Linklater, 26 October 1935, NLS, Eric Linklater Papers, Acc 10281/1.

20 'History and Economic Problems', T*he Sc*otsman, 26 September 1935, p. 13.

21 Thomson, *Distressed*, p. 3, 7, 22-25.

22 Thomson, *Distressed*, p. 26.

23 Andrew Dewar Gibb, 'Whither Scotland? The Empire and Scottish Emigration', *BBC National Programme*, 21 Oct. 1937, NLS Gibb Papers, Acc. 9188, No. 6.

24 Thomson, *Distressed*, pp. 29-32.

25 Thomson, *Distressed*, p. 32, 59, 64.

26 Scotland Lags Behind in Trade Revival', *Financial Times*, 29 February 1936, p. 9.

27 Thomson, *Distressed*, p. 64-65.

28 William Ferguson, *Scotland 1689 to the Present Day* (Edinburgh, 1968), pp. 373-374.

29 C.A. Oakley, *Scottish Industry Today* (Edinburgh, 1937).

30 Earl of Elgin, preface, in Oakley, *Scottish Industry Today*, pp. ix-x.

31 James A. Bowie, *The Future of Scotland: A Survey of the Present Position with some Proposals for Future Policy* (Edinburgh, 1939).

32 Bowie, *Future of Scotland*, p. 133, 134.

33 George Blake, *The Heart of Scotland* (London, 1934), p. 112.

34 Walter Elliot, Memorandum, 'The State of Scotland', 18 December 1937, SRO, DD 10/175 quoted in R.H. Campbell, 'The Scottish Office and the Special Areas in the 1930s', *The Historical Journal* Vol. 22, No. 1 (Mar., 1979), pp. 182-183.

35 'New Scots Play, A Malcolm Thomson Drama, Curtain Theatre', *Glasgow Herald*, 2 October, 1936.

Chapter 6

1 George Malcolm Thomson to George Dott, 24 January 1930, NLS, Dott Papers, Acc. 5927, Folder 1.

2 Thomson to Dott, 24 January 1930.

3 William Power, *Should Auld Acquaintance... An Autobiography* (London, 1937), pp. 229-230

4 George Blake, *Annals of Scotland* (London, 1956), p. 32

5 Hugh MacDiarmid, *Lucky Poet: A Self Study in Literature and Political Ideas* (London, 1943), p. 278

6 Colin Walkinshaw, *Scots Tragedy* (Edinburgh, 1935), p. 179

7 Thomson to Dott, 1 August, 1930, NLS, Dott Papers, Acc. 5927/1.

8 A.J.P. Taylor, *Beaverbrook* (London, 1972), p. 142.

9 Beaverbrook, *Men and Power 1917-1919* (London, 1956), p. 267.

10 H.D. Lasswell, 'The Person: Subject and Object of Propaganda', *Annals of the American Academy of Political and Social Science*, Vol. 179, p. 189, quoted in Richard Taylor, *Film Propaganda Soviet Russia and Nazi German* (London, 1979), p. 26.

11 Harold D. Lasswell, 'The Theory of Political Propaganda', *The American Political Science Review*, Vol. 21, No. 3 (Aug., 1927), pp. 627-631.

12 Noam Chomsky, *Media Control The Spectacular Achievements of Propaganda* (New York, 2002), pp. 14-15.

13 Thomson to Dott, 1 August, 1930.

14 Thomson, *Re-Discovery*, pp. 67-70.

15 George Malcolm Thomson to Neil Gunn, 30 March 1930, NLS, Gunn Papers, Dep. 209, Box 20, Folder 8.

16 See Regional Comparison of Licence Holding in Mark Pegg, *Broadcasting and Society 1918-1939* (London, 1983), pp. 12-16.

17 George Malcolm Thomson, 'If I were Dictator of Scotland', BBC Scottish Region, 19 October 1929, extract from *The Listener*, 8 January 1930, p. 67.

18 Thomson, *Re-Discovery*, pp. 8, 16-17, 20.

19 'Edinburgh and Glasgow, A Broadcast Comparison', *The Scotsman*, 16 March 1931, p, 7.

20 'Edinburgh as Conference Centre', *The Scotsman*, 20 June 1931, p. 11.

21 George Malcolm Thomson to Andrew Dewar Gibb, 15 August, 1930, NLS, Gibb Papers, Dep. 217, Box 1.

22 Scottish Unionist Conference, December, 1929, quoted in Gerald Warner, *The Scottish Tory Party A History* (London, 1982), pp. 191-192.

23 Rait and Pryde, *Scotland*, p. 154.

24 Thomson to Dott, 1 August 1930

25 Thomson to Dott, 8 August, 1930, NLS, Dott Papers, Acc. 5927, Box 1, Folder 1.

26 Thomson, to Gunn, 8 August 1930.

27 H.V. Morton, *In Search of Scotland* (London, 1929), pp. 50-52.

28 Thomson to Gibb, 11 August 1930.

29 Thomson to Gibb, 11 August 1930, Thomson to Dott, 8 August 1930.

30 Thomson to Gunn, 15 August 1930.

31 Thomson to Gibb, 30 December, 1932.

32 Thomson to Gunn, 15 August 1930.

33 Moray McLaren, *Return to Scotland: An Egoist's Journey* (London, 1930), p. 11.

34 Thomson to Gibb, 15, August 1930.

35 Thomson to Dott, 8 August 1930,; Thomson to Gibb, 15 August, 31 October, 11 December 1930.

36 Thomson to Dott, 24 January 1930; Thomson to Gunn, 30 March 1930; Thomson to Gibb, date obscured, 1930.

37 Thomson to Gunn, 15 August 1930; Thomson to Dott, 8 August 1930; Thomson to Gibb, 11 December 1930.

38 Compton Mackenzie to T.H. Gibson, (date obscured), NLS, Gibson Papers, Acc. 6058, Box 1, Folder 3.

39 Thomson to Gunn, 13 March 1930, 30 March 1930.

40 Thomson to Gibb, 19 September 1930, 20 April 1931.

Chapter 7

1 Colonel P.J. Blair, Letter to Andrew Dewar Gibb, 7 November 1928, NLS, Gibb Papers, Dep. 217, Box 1.

2 Winston Churchill to Andrew Dewar Gibb, Treasury Chambers, Whitehall, 27 May 1929; Stanley Baldwin to Andrew Dewar Gibb, 10 Downing Street, 23 May 1929, NLS, Gibb Papers, Dep. 217, Folder 6.

3 Thomson to Gibb, 15 August, 13 September, 31 October 1930, Gibb Papers.

4 Gibb, *In Eclipse*, pp. 176, 177, 179, 180, 190, 191.

5 George Malcolm Thomson, *The Kingdom of Scotland Restored* (London, 1931)., Introduction, pp. 6-8, 9-10, 11-12, 12-14, 15.

6 Thomson to Gibb, 11 August, 26 August, 11 December 1930, 20 April 1931, Gibb Papers.

7 John McCormick to Neil Gunn, 11 March 1931, NLS, Gunn Papers, Dep. 209, Box 15, Folder 1.

8 Margery Palmer McCulloch, 'William Power (1873–1951)' *ODNB* (Oxford 2004); William Power, *Should Auld Acquaintance... An Autobiography* (London, 1937), p. 68.

9 William Power, *My Scotland* (Edinburgh, 1934), p. 214; Power, *Should Auld Acquaintance*, pp. 128-129.

10 Thomson, *Will the Church Survive?* p. 37-38.

11 A. Muir, 'John White' (London, 1958), quoted in I.G.C. Hutchinson, ''Scottish Unionism Between the Wars', in Catriona M.M. Macdonald, ed., *Unionist Scotland 1800 – 1997* (Edinburgh, 1998), p. 82.

12 McCulloch, 'William Power', ODNB; Power, *My Scotland*, pp. 300-301.

13 MacCormick, *Flag in the Wind*, p. 76.

14 Thomson to Gibb, 1933 (date obscured), Gibb Papers.

15 See Brand, *National Movement*, pp. 216-217; Connell, 'Irish Immigration and Scottish Identity'; Kidd, *Union and Unionisms*, pp. 289-290.

16 John H. Young, A History of the Cathcart Conservative and Unionist Association 1918-1993 (Glasgow, 1993), p. 27; John Kevan McDowall, Scottish Biographies 1938 (Glasgow, 1938), p. 464.

17 Thomson to Gibb, 11 July 1932, NLS, Gibb Papers, Acc. 9188, No. 6.

18 Kevan McDowall, 'Cathcart Unionists and Imperial Policy', *Glasgow Herald*, 22 June 1932, p. 8; J. Kevan McDowall, 'Cathcart Unionists and Imperial Policy', *Glasgow Herald*, 24 June 1932 p. 8.

19 J. Kevan McDowall, 'Home Rule Statement Welcomed by Prominent Scots', *Daily Record*, 20 July 1932, p. 1-2.

20 'Scotland and Home Rule, Unionists who believe in Devolution', *Daily Record*, 17 June 1932, p. 1; 'A Great Day for Scots People, Premier Adopts Our Plan', *Daily Record*, 19 July 1932, p. 1.

21 *Scottish Daily Express*, 6 August 1932, p. 1, quoted in, Brand, *National Movement*, pp. 214-215; *Scottish Daily Express* 7 September 1932, p. 1, quoted in, Young, *Cathcart Conservative*, p. 26.

22 See Brand, *National Movement*, pp. 216-217.

23 Thomson to Dott, 20 October, 24 October 1931, NLS, Dott Papers, Acc. 5927/1 Folder 1.

24 Thomson to Gibb, 11 July 1932, Gibb Papers, Acc. 9188, No. 6.

25 Richard Finlay, 'Pressure Group or Political Party? The Nationalist Impact on Scottish Politics, 1928-1945', *Twentieth Century British History*, Vol. 3, No. 3 (1992), pp. 275-276.

Chapter 8

1 Home Rule for Scotland?' Editorial, *The Times*, 10 November 1932, p. 11.; Alexander Johnston, Federation of British Industries, Scottish Office, 'Scottish Home Rule', *The Times*, 18 November 1932 p. 10.

2 'Scottish Home Rule Opposition Body Formed', *The Times*, 15 November 1932, p 15.

3 'Conditions in Scotland', *The Scotsman*, 25 November 1932, p. 8.

4 George Buchanan, 'Debate on the Address', HC Deb 24 November 1932, vol. 272, cc 235-360.

5 John Buchan, 'Debate on the Address', *HC Deb*, 24 November 1932, vol. 272 cc 235-360; Sir Reginald Coupland, *Welsh and Scottish Nationalism: A Study*

(London, 1954), p. 403; Janet Adam Smith, *John Buchan: A Biography* (Oxford, 1985), p. 322.

6 Christopher Harvie, 'Second Thoughts of a Scotsman on the Make', *The Scottish Historical Review,* Volume 70, 1: No.188 (April 1991), p. 51; Buchan, 'Debate on the Address', 262, 266.

7 Kate Macdonald, John Buchan A Companion to the Mystery Fiction (North Carolina, 2009), pp. 49-50.

8 John Buchan to Andrew Dewar Gibb, 2 November 1927, NLS, Gibb Papers, Dep. 217, Box 1.

9 John Buchan. 'Speech at Edinburgh University Unionist Association', (n.d. ca. 1903-1935) John Buchan Papers 7214, National Library of Scotland from Queens University Archives, Ontario, Microfilm, Mf. MSS. 312. J.B.Papers Box 16, quoted in Margaret Beaumont Bolter, 'John Buchan: The Antonyms of Scottish Nationalism', (Undergraduate Thesis, Department of History, Mount Holyoke College, South Hadley, MA, 2005), p. 135.

10 Quoted in Smith, *John Buchan,* p. 184.

11 Power, *Should Auld Acquaintance,* p. 129; Smith, *John Buchan,* p. 184.

12 Brand, *National Movement,* p. 90.

13 In January 1933 Cleghorn Thomson wrote to Reith and reminded him of the background to his original appointment. Ref. David Cleghorn Thomson to Sir John Reith, Handwritten Letter, 28 January 1933, BBC WAC L1/421/4.

14 W.H. McDowell, *The History of BBC Broadcasting in Scotland 1923-1983* (Edinburgh, 1992), p. 19; See Adrienne Scullion, 'BBC Radio in Scotland, 1923-1939: Devolution, Regionalism and Centralisation', *Northern Scotland,* Vol. 15 (1995), pp. 63-93; Pegg, *Broadcasting and Society,* pp. 22-23.

15 BBC Board of Governors, 'Extract from Board Meeting', 8 June 1932, BBC WAC L1/421/2.

16 Note for Postmaster General, 'Staff Private', 16 December 1936, BBC WAC L1/421/4.

17 BBC WAC R/13/369/2. 1928-38; 'BBC Change, Disagreement on Scottish Policy, Director Resigns, "Insuperable Obstacles", No Successor Yet', *The Scotsman,* 11 April 1933, p. 6.

18 David Cleghorn Thomson to Val H. Goldsmith, Letter, 8 April 1933, BBC WAC R/13/369/2, 1928-38.

19 Val. H. Goldsmith to David Cleghorn Thomson, Letter, 10 April 1933, BBC WAC R/13/369/2, 1928-38.; David Cleghorn Thomson to Val. H. Goldsmith, Letter, 11 April 1933, BBC WAC R/13/369/2, 1928-38.

20 *The Scotsman,* 11 April 1933, p. 6.

21 David Pat Walker, *The BBC in Scotland: The First Fifty Years* (Edinburgh, 2011), pp. 69, 81-82.

22 Lindsay Wellington, Internal Circulating Memo, 'The Present Situation in the Scottish Region', 31 October 1932, BBC WAC, R/13/369/2, 1928-38; J.M. Rose-Trump, Director Talks to Sir John Reith, Director General, 'Report on Visit to Scotland', 29 March 1933, BBC WAC, R/13/369/2, 1928-38.

23 BBC Programme Board, 19 October 1933, BBC WAC, R34/600/5, BBC WAC R51/418 quoted as footnote in Thomas Hajkowski, 'The BBC and National Identity in Britain, 1922-1954', PhD Thesis, North-Western University (2005), pp. 196.

24 John Reith, 'State Control of Broadcasting', *The Times,* 29 July 1930, p. 12.

25 Harvie, *Scotland and Nationalism,* p. 110.

26 David Cleghorn Thomson, 'Remarkable Attack on Middle-Aged Respectability', *Scottish Daily Express*, 29 April 1933, p. 15.

27 Power, *Should Auld Acquaintance*, p. 182-184.

28 Editorial, 10 December, 1930 The *Listener*, Vol. 4 (July 2 1930 to December 30 1930), p. 967; 'The Scottish Orchestra', Editorial, *The Gramophone*, Vol. 18, No. 314 (November 1940), p. 6.

29 Cleghorn Thomson, *Scotland in Quest of Her Youth*, Introduction, p. 1.

30 David Cleghorn Thomson to Major W. Gladstone Murray, Letter to Head Office, 8 February 1933, BBC WAC, L1/421/4.

31 Lachlan MacNeill Weir, *The Tragedy of Ramsay MacDonald* (London, 1938), p. 533.

32 Hajkowski, 'BBC and National Identity', pp. 195-196.

Chapter 9

1 Andrew Dewar Gibb to the Duke of Montrose, 30 August, 1930, NLS, Gibb Papers, Dep. 217, Box 2.

2 Sir Alexander MacEwen, *The Thistle and the Rose: Scotland's Problem Today* (Edinburgh, 1932), p. 20.

3 Sir Alexander MacEwen, *Nationalism in Practice*, NLS, MacEwen Papers, Acc. 6113.

4 MacCormick, *Flag in the Wind*, p. 66; John MacCormick, *Scots Independent* (July, 1932), p. 131, quoted in Richard J. Finlay, '"For or against?" Scottish Nationalists and the British Empire, 1919-39', *The Scottish Historical Review*, Vol. 71, Nos. 191-2 (Apr.-Oct., 1992), pp.184-206; 'A Scots Parliament, Scottish Party Decision', *Glasgow Herald*, 2 December 1932, p.6.

5 Neil Gunn to Andrew Dewar Gibb, 28 July 1933, NLS, Gibb Papers, Dep. 217, Folder 6.

6 Andrew Dewar Gibb to Neil Gunn, 29 July 1933, NLS, Gunn Papers, Dep. 209, Box 15.

7 Sir Alexander MacEwen to Andrew Dewar Gibb, 17 October 1933, NLS, Gibb Papers, Dep. 217, Box 1, Folder 2.

8 Neil Gunn to Eric Linklater, 25 October 1933, NLS, Linklater Papers, Acc. 10282/1.

9 Gunn to Gibb, 20 December 1933, Gibb Papers, Dep. 217, Folder 6; Thomson to Gibb, 2 October 1933, NLS, Gibb Papers, Dep. 217/Box 1.

10 MacCormick, *Flag in the Wind*, p. 86; D.N. McIver, 'The Paradox of Nationalism in Scotland', in Colin H. Williams, ed., *National Separatism* (Cardiff, 1982), p. 122-123.

11 Finlay, *Independent and Free*, pp. 156-158.; MacCormick, *Flag in the Wind*, p. 35.

12 Hugh MacDiarmid, *Daily Telegraph Magazine*, 9 February 1968, quoted in Iain McLean, 'The Rise and Fall of the Scottish National Party', *Political Studies*, Vol. 18, No. 3 (Sept., 1970), p. 357.

13 H.J. Hanham, *Scottish Nationalism* (London, 1969), p. 165; Kidd, *Union and Unionisms*, pp. 292-293; Finlay, *Independent and Free*, pp. 163-165.

14 Thomson to Gibb, 31 August 1934, NLS, Gibb Papers, Dep. 217, Box 1.

15 Andrew Dewar Gibb, *Scottish Empire* (London, 1937), pp. 310-311; Gibb, 'Case for Nationalism', 24 April 1936; Andrew Dewar Gibb, *Whither Scotland*,

Empire Emigration, BBC Scottish Region Broadcast, 21 October 1937, in NLS, Gibb Papers, Dep. 217, Box 2, Folder 4.

16 Andrew Dewar Gibb, Speech Notes, *SNP Conference*, Edinburgh, 27 May 1939, in NLS, Gibb Papers, Dep. 217, Box 4.

17 Rait and Pryde, *Scotland*, p. 155.

18 Ferguson, *Scotland 1689 to the Present*, p. 379.

19 H. M. Begg and J.A. Stewart, 'The Nationalist Movement in Scotland', *Journal of Contemporary History*, Vol. 6, No. 1 (1971), p. 139.

20 Ewen A. Cameron, 'The Politics of the Union in an Age of Unionism', in T.M. Devine, ed., *Scotland and the Union 1707-2007* (Edinburgh, 2008), p. 127.

21 McDowall, *Scottish Biographies*, p. 464.

22 Ewen A. Cameron, '*Gibb, Andrew Dewar* (1888–1974)', *ODNB*.

23 Interview with Peter Thomson, Holly Hill, Hampstead, 22 February 2011.

24 Moray McLaren, memo to Andrew Stewart, Scottish Regional Programme Director, c.c. Scottish Regional Director, 'Talks on Nationalism', 29 January 1936, BBC WAC, R13/369/1-3) Departmental: Regions, Scotland 1926-54; Andrew Stewart memo to Moray McLaren, 30 January 1936, *BBC WAC*, R13/369/1-3) .Departmental: Regions, Scotland 1 926-54.

25 Sir John Reith to Andrew Dewar Gibb, Note to File, undated, *BBC WAC*, R/51/341/1; J.M. Rose-Trump, Director Talks, 'Scottish Nationalism', Internal Circulating Memo, 4 December, 1935, *BBC WAC*, R13/369/1-3) Departmental: Regions, Scotland 1926-54.

26 Andrew Dewar Gibb, 'The Case for Scottish Nationalism', in *Three Nations - A Historical Survey*, BBC National Programme, 24 April, 1936, extract, *The Listener*, 6 May 1936, pp. 865-867.

27 Andrew Dewar Gibb, 'The Case for Scottish Nationalism', in *Three Nations - A Historical Survey*, BBC National Programme, 24 April, 1936, extract, *The Listener*, 6 May 1936, pp. 865-867.

28 Thomson to Gibb, 10 November 1937, 10 March 1939, NLS, Gibb Papers, Acc. 9188/No. 6.

29 George Malcolm Thomson, 'There will be no War', *Daily Express*, 18 June 1938, p. 10; Richard Boston, 'Beaverbrook's Sharpest Pen', *The Guardian*, 23 May 1996, p. 17.

Chapter 10

1 Helen B Cruikshank, 'Spring in the Mearns, for Lewis Grassic Gibbon', in Cruikshank, *Octobiography*, pp. 91-92.

2 George Malcolm Thomson to Helen B. Cruikshank, Letter, August 1932, Notes on Lewis Grassic Gibbon, University of Stirling Library, *Helen B. Cruikshank Papers*, MS2, Folder 7.

3 Cruickshank, 'Notes on Lewis Grassic Gibbon'; 'New Fiction, Sunset Song', *The Scotsman*, 31 October 1932, p. 2.

4 George Malcolm Thomson to Lewis Grassic Gibbon, Letters, 21 August 1932, 23 July 1933, 14 November 1934, quoted in Ian S. Munro, *Leslie Mitchell: Lewis Grassic Gibbon* (Edinburgh 1966), pp. 74, 117-118, 183.

5 Cruikshank, *Octobiography*, p. 87.

6 Thomson to Gibbon, 23 July 1933, quoted in Munro, *Lewis Grassic Gibbon*, pp. 117-118.

7 Lewis Grassic Gibbon, 'Glasgow', in *Scottish Scene*, pp. 116, 118,119.

8 Lewis Grassic Gibbon to Neil Gunn, 2 November 1934, NLS, Gunn Papers, Dep. 209, Box 17, Folder 2.

9 Ian Carter, 'Lewis Grassic Gibbon, "A Scots Quair", and the Peasantry', *History Workshop*, No. 6 (Autumn 1978), p. 181; 10 Douglas F. Young, 'Mitchell, (James) Leslie (1901–1935)', *ODNB* (2004).

10 Hanne Tange, 'Lewis Grassic Gibbon and the Scottish Renaissance', Paper, Association of Scottish Literary Studies (Aberdeen, 9-10 June, 2001). http://www.arts.gla.ac.uk/ScotLit/ASLS/Conference2001.html

11 Lewis Grassic Gibbon, *Grey Granite*, in *A Scots Quair*, Seventh Impression (London, 1967), p. 408.

12 Helen B. Cruickshank to Eric Linklater, Letter, 26 October 1935, NLS, Linklater Papers, Acc. 10281, Folder 1.

13 Compton Mackenzie, *Daily Mail*, 13 September 1932, quoted in, Young, 'Mitchell', ODNB (September 2004).

14 James Barke, 'The Scottish National Question', *Left Review*, No. 14 (Nov 1936) pp. 739-44; James Barke to Lewis Grassic Gibbon, 12 December, 1932 Mitchell Library, Glasgow, James Barke Papers, Box 4.; Lewis Grassic Gibbon to James Barke, 21 January 1933, Barke Papers, Box 4.

15 Moira Burgess, 'Barke, James William' (1905–1958)', *ODNB* (2004); James Barke, *Major Operation* (London, 1936); Barke, 'The Scottish National Question', pp. 739-740.

16 Robert McLennan, 'The National Question and Scotland', *Communist Review*, Vol. 4, No. 10 (October 1932), p. 505.

17 Helen Crawfurd, 'The Scottish National Movement', *Communist Review*, Vol. 5, No. 2 (February 1933), pp. 84-85.; Editor, Communist Review, in Crawfurd, 'National Movement', p. 84.

18 Oliver Bell, 'The Scottish National Movement', *Communist Review*, Vol. 5, No. 4 (April 1933), pp. 195-197.

19 James D. Young, 'Marxism and the Scottish National Question', *Journal of Contemporary History*, Vol. 18, No. 1 (January 1983), pp. 141-163; 21 Neil M. Gunn, 'Scotland a Nation', *Left Review*, Vol. 2. No. 14 (November 1936), pp. 735-738.

20 Margery Greenshields McCulloch, 'Scottish and International Themes in the Work of Edwin Muir and Neil M. Gunn', PhD Thesis, University of Glasgow (January 1982), pp. 244-246.; Muir, 'Review: Distressed Area', p.330-332.

21 Muir, *Scottish Journey*, (Edinburgh, 1980), first published 1935, pp. 231-234.

22 Cicely Hamilton, *Modern Scotland as seen by an Englishwoman* (London, 1937) pp. 100-101.

23 Edwin Muir, *Scott and Scotland: The Predicament of the Scottish Writer* (London 1936), p. 181-18.

24 Muir, *Autobiography*, p.113.

25 Thomson, *Kingdom of Scotland Restored*, Introduction; Blake, *Heart of Scotland, p. 112.*

26 Edwin Muir, 'Review, The Heart of Scotland', *The Spectator*, No. 5549, 2 November 1934, p. 676, in Noble, *Edwin Muir Uncollected Scottish Criticism*, Chapter 3, The Problem of Scotland, pp. 111-114.

27 Hamilton, *Modern Scotland*, p. 219.

28 John Orr, 'As it is', in Alexander Maclehose, *The Scotland of our Sons* (Glasgow, 1937), pp. 64-66.

29 Maclehose, *Scotland of our Sons*, p. 25; 32 Thomson, *Distressed*, p. 107.

30 John R. Allan, *Summer in Scotland* (London 1938), pp. 30-32.

31 Earl of Elgin, in Oakley, *Scottish Industry Today*, preface, p. ix.

32 George Bruce, *To Foster and Enrich: The First Fifty Years of the Saltire Society* (Tillicoultry, 1986), pp. 12, 14, 24.

33 John Fowler, 'A Past that's always Ahead of them', *The Herald*, 22 April 1966, p. 14

34 Lord Cullen of Whitekirk, Executive Summary, Report of the Saltire Commission, *Saltire Society* (2011), p. 1.

35 Agnew Mure Mackenzie, 'The Saltire Society: Its Background and Purpose' *Aberdeen University Review* (1943), pp. 236-242; Scottish Culture Objects of the Saltire Society', *The Scotsman*, 2 September 1937, p. 11.

36 Agnes Mure Mackenzie, 'Saltire Society Rousing Scotland', *The Scotsman*, 3 October 1938, p. 13; Dr James Bowie, 'Scottish Industry Why it is Not More Developed', *The Scotsman*, 28 October 1938, p. 8.

37 Robert Hurd, *Scotland Under Trust* (London, 1939), preface, p. xi.

38 'Scottish Renaissance: Mr George Thomson at PEN Dinner', *The Scotsman*, 19 October 1950, p. 3.

Chapter 11

1 Telephone Interview with Chapman Pincher, 25 October 2010; Telephone Interview with Gerald Isaaman, 8 August 2011.

2 George Malcolm Thomson, *A Kind of Justice Two Studies in Treason* (London, 1970).

3 Telephone Interview with Peter Thomson, 20 September 2010; 4 Telephone Interviews with Peter Thomson and Mrs Anne Ettlinger, 20 September 2010.; Interview with Peter Thomson, Holly Hill, Hampstead, 22 February 2011.

4 Rosslyn Mitchell, 'I Must Take Up the Challenge', *What's Wrong With Scotland?* BBC Scottish Region, 12 November 1929, extract, *The Listener*, 8 January 1930, pp. 70-71; Donald Carswell, 'Scotland has Failed in the Art of Living', in *What's Wrong With Scotland?* 29 October 1929, extract, *The Listener*, 8 January 1930, p. 68.

5 Will Y. Darling, 'What Scotland Wants is Scotsmen', in *What's Wrong with Scotland?* BBC Scottish Region, 22 October 1929, extract, *The Listener*, 8 January 1930, pp. 67-68; 'Lads O' Pairts "Stay in Scotland Slogan" National Movement', *The Scotsman*, 23 October 1929, p. 7.

6 J.M.Barrie, *What Every Woman Knows* (1906); 8 T.W. H. Crosland, *The Unspeakable Scot* (London, 1902), pp. 47, 60, 192-194.

7 Thomson, *Caledonia*, pp. 44, 47, 59, 60.

8 Interview with Peter Thomson, 22 February 2011.

9 Interview with Peter Thomson, 22 February 2011.

10 Telephone Interview with Chapman Pincher, 25 October 2010.

11 Garrick Club Archives.

12 George Malcolm Thomson, 'Percival Thomas James Cudlipp (1905-1962)' ODNB.

13 David Farrer, *G – For God Almighty: A Personal Memoir of Lord Beaverbrook*

(New York 1969), p. 26; Richard Boston, 'Beaverbrook's Sharpest Pen', *The Guardian*, 23 May 1996, p. 17.

14 Beaverbrook quoted in A.J.P. Taylor, *Beaverbrook* (London, 1972), p. 512.

15 C.M. Vines, *A Little Nut-Brown Man: My Three Years with Lord Beaverbrook* (London, 1968), p. 230.

16 Interview with Peter Thomson, 22 February 2011, Holly Hill, Hampstead.

17 Farrer, *G – For God Almighty*, pp. 27, 48, 109, 110, 151.

18 Thomson to Gibb, 22 May and 2 June 1945, NLS, Gibb Papers, Dep. 217,Box1

19 Farrer, *G – For God Almighty*, p. 151; Vines, *A Little Nut-Brown Man*, p. 274.

20 George Malcolm Thomson, *The Twelve Days 24 July to 4 August 1914* (London, 1964).

21 Farrer, *G – For God Almighty*, pp. 168-169.

22 William Hickey, 'Detailed', *Daily Express*, 4 December 1964, p. 3.

23 Lady Antonia Fraser to Eric Linklater, 21 February 1967, NLS, Linklater Papers, Acc. 10282/4; Eric Linklater, 'Queen in the Dock', Letters to the Editor, *The Times*, 21 February 1967, p. 11.; George Malcolm Thomson, 'Queen in the Dock', Letters to the Editor, *The Times*, 24 February 1967, p. 13; Thomson, 'Queen in the Dock', Letters to the Editor, *The Times*, 3 March 1967, p. 13.

24 Queen in the Dock', Review The Crime of Mary Stuart, *The Times*, 9 February 1967, p. 14; 'The Crime of Mary Stuart Mary Queen of Scots', Review, *Daily Express*, 9 February 1967, p. 6.

25 George Malcolm Thomson, 'Mary Queen of Scots', Letters to the Editor, *The Times*, 15 June 1972, p. 19.

26 Graham Lord, 'Pick of the Fiction', *Sunday Express*, 16 May 1982, p. 6.

27 Scottish Arts Council, Council Meeting, 22 January 1976, NAS, *SAC1/9/53*; George Malcolm Thomson, *The North West Passage* (London, 1975).

28 George Malcolm Thomson quoted in George Hutchison, 'Devolution and the Great North Sea Oil Enigma', *The Times*, 5 February 1977, p. 17.

29 George Malcolm Thomson to Andrew Dewar Gibb, 11 November 1942, 22 May and 2 June 1945, NLS, Gibb Papers, Dep. 217, Box 1.

30 B.A. Farbey, C.R. Mitchell and K. Webb, 'Change and Stability in the Ideology of Scottish Nationalism', *International Political Science Review*, Vol 1, No. 3 (1980), pp. 405-424.

31 Thomson in Hutchison, 'Devolution and North Sea Oil', p. 17.

32 See George Malcolm Thomson, 'Art Heritage in Scotland', Letters to the Editor, *The Times*, 8 July 1976, p. 17.

33 Interview with Peter Thomson, 19 Holly Hill, Hampstead, London, 22 February 2011

34 George Malcolm Thomson, 'A Man Called John Knox', *Daily Express*, 27 September 1956, p.6

35 Tom Gallagher, Interview with Ian McColl, 14 February 1989, quoted in Graham Walker and Tom Gallagher, eds., *Sermons and Battle Hymns; Protestant Popular Culture in Modern Scotland*, (Edinburgh 1990), p. 195

36 Gallagher, Interview with Ian McColl.

37 Interview with Tom Brown, 12 April 1013.

38 ' George Malcolm Thomson', Obituary, *The Economist*, June 1986, p. 86;

Boston, 'Beaverbrook's Sharpest Pen', *The Guardian*, p. 17; 'George Malcolm Thomson', *The Herald*, 23 May 1996, p. 22.

39 Michael Fry, 'Second-Hand Thoughts and Second-Rate Minds', *The Herald*, 29 May 1996, p. 16.

40 Kenneth Roy, 'Kenneth Roy's Britain', *The Observer*, 10 December 1995, p. 10.

41 Boston, 'Beaverbrook's Sharpest Pen', *The Guardian*, p. 17; Interview with Peter Thomson, 22 February 2011.

Chapter 12

1 Boston, 'Beaverbrook's Sharpest Pen', *Guardian*, p. 17.

2 Canongate Books Publicity, Aeneas MacDonald, *Whisky*, Reprint, Canongate Books (Edinburgh, 2006); Charles Maclean, Foreword, 'Whisky', *p. v-vi*

3 *Wigtown Book Festival Official Programme*, October 2009, p 16. http:// www.bladnoch.co.uk/pdfs/festival2009.pdf.
David Broom, *Whisky Magazine*. issue57 12007242.html
Martha Allison, *Press and Journal*, 10 October 2009.
Quoted in *Whisky Magazine*. http://www.whiskymag.com/magazine/issue57/ 12007242.html.
Ian Buxton, Interview, Frank R. Shaw, 'A Highlander and his Books A Chat with Ian Buxton', Electric Scotland, 5 June, 2007. http://www.electricscotland.com/ familytree/frank/buxton.htm

4 See Thomson to Gunn, 14 November 1930, NLS, Gunn Papers, Dep. 209, Box 20.

5 Aeneas MacDonald, *Whisky* (Porpoise Press, 1930), pp. 21, 35.

6 See 'Moidart, Inverness-shire', in John Keay and Julia Keay, eds., *Scotland* (London 1994), p 701. (Charles Edward Stuart stayed at Kinloch-Moidart House after landing at Arisaig in August 1745. Seven beech trees planted near the House represent his loyal companions, the Seven Men of Moidart who landed with him); See Bruce Lenman, 'The Jacobite Diaspora 1688-1746: From Despair to Integration', *History Today*, Early Modern (16th-18th C) England France, Vol. 30, Issue 5.
http://www.historytoday.com/bruce-lenman/jacobite-diaspora-1688-1746-despair-integration.

7 Buxton, *Whisky*, Reprint 2006, Introduction, pp. xx-xxi.

8 William Donaldson, *The Jacobite Song Political Myth and National Identity* (Aberdeen, 1988), p. 113.

9 Buxton, *Whisky*, (Reprint 2006), Introduction, pp. vii-viii.

10 MacDonald, *Whisky*, pp. 9, 13, 14, 15, 16, 22.

11 Manifesto Report, *The Scots Pictorial*, quoted in McCleery, *Porpoise Press*, pp.19-20.

12 George Malcolm Thomson, 'He's as Impenitent as ever, A.J.P. Taylor Looking at our Times', *Daily Express*, 21 October 1965, p. 10.

13 James Mitchell, *Strategies for Self-Government The Campaign for a Scottish Parliament* (Edinburgh, 1996), pp. 28-30; Craig Beveridge and Ronald Turnbull, *The Eclipse of Scottish Culture: Inferiorism and Intellectuals* (Edinburgh, 1989), abstract, pp. 112-113.

14 Allan Massie, *The Thistle and the Rose: Six Centuries of Love and Hate between the Scots and the English* (London, 2005), p. 293.

15 Thomson, *Distressed*, pp 120-122.

Selected Reading

George Malcolm Thomson Books, Pamphlets, 1919-1939

Caledonia or *The Future of The Scots* (London, 1927).

The Re-Discovery of Scotland (London, 1928).

A Short History of Scotland: from the Earliest Times to the Outbreak of the Great War (London, 1930).

Will the Scottish Church Survive? (Edinburgh, 1930).

The Kingdom of Scotland Restored (London, 1931).

Scotland: That Distressed Area (Edinburgh, 1935).

Whisky (Edinburgh, 1930); Whisky, Reissue (Edinburgh, 2006) as Aeneas MacDonald.

Essays, Broadcasts, Plays

'School Notes', Daniel Stewart's College Magazine (December 1916, July 1917).

'Epistle to Roderick Watson Kerr', Porpoise Press Broadsheets (June 1926).

'George Blake', *The Bookman* (July 1928).

'If I Were Dictator of Scotland', BBC Scottish Region Broadcast, What is Wrong with Scotland, 19 October 1929, Reproduced, *The Listener*, 8 January 1930.

'The Scottish Advocate', *Library Review*, Vol. 3, No. 3 (1931).

'Moonlight Flitting', Curtain Theatre Company, at Lyric Theatre, Glasgow (October 1937); Scottish Theatre Archive, Special Collections, University of Glasgow, Call No. STA Bw 6, Rec. 13519.

Correspondence

George Malcolm Thomson to Andrew Dewar Gibb 1930-1945, NLS, Letters, Gibb Papers, Dep. 217, Acc. 9188.

George Malcolm Thomson to Neil M. Gunn 1930-1934, NLS, Letters, Gunn Papers, Dep. 209.

George Malcolm Thomson to George Dott 1930-1934, NLS, Letters, George Dott Papers, Acc. 5927/1.

Obituaries

The Economist, London, 1 June 1996.

The Herald, Glasgow, 23 May 1996.

The Guardian, 23 May 1996.

The Times, London, 21 May 1996

Interview

Son, Peter Thomson, 19 Holly Hill, Hampstead, London, 22 February, 2011.

SELECTED BOOKS, PAMPHLETS, ESSAYS

Pre 1939

Allan, J.R., *Summer in Scotland* (London, 1938).

Barke, James, 'The Scottish National Question', *Left Review*, Vol. 2, No. 14 (November 1936).

Bernays, Edward, *Propaganda* (New York, 1928).

Blake, George, *The Shipbuilders* (Edinburgh, 1935).

Blake, George, *The Heart of Scotland* (London, 1934).

Blake, G.R., *Scotland of the Scots* (London, 1918).

Bolitho, William, *Cancer of Empire* (London, 1924).

Bowie, James A., *The Future of Scotland: A Survey of the Present Position with some Proposals for Future Policy* (Edinburgh, 1939).

Crawfurd, Helen, 'The Scottish National Movement', *Communist Review*, Vol. 5, No. 2 (February 1933).

Gibb, Andrew Dewar, *Scotland in Eclipse* (London, 1930).

Gibb, Andrew Dewar, *Scottish Empire* (London, 1937).

Gibbon, Lewis Grassic and Hugh MacDiarmid, *Scottish Scene or An Intelligent Man's Guide to Albyn* (London, 1934).

Grieve, C. M. *Albyn or Scotland and the Future* (London, 1927).

Grieve, C. M., 'The Truth about Scotland', *The New Age*, Vol. 42, No. 2, 10 (November 1927).

Gunn, Neil M., 'Scotland a Nation', *Left Review*, Vol. 2. No. 14 (November 1936).

Hamilton, Cicely, *Modern Scotland as seen by an Englishwoman* (London, 1937).

Hannington, Wal, *The Problem of the Distressed Areas* (London, 1937).

Hurd, Robert, *Scotland Under Trust* (London, 1939).

Kerr, R. Watson, *Annus Mirabilis or the Ascension O' Jimmie Broon*, Broadsheet

Number 10 (Edinburgh, May 1924).

Lasswell, Harold D., 'The Theory of Political Propaganda', *The American Political Science Review*, Vol. 21, No. 3 (August 1927).

Lasswell, Harold D., *Propaganda Technique in the World War* (London, 1938).

MacEwen, Alexander Malcolm, *The Thistle and the Rose: Scotland's Problem Today* (Edinburgh, 1932).

Mackenzie, Agnes Mure, *Scotland in Modern Times 1720-1939* (Edinburgh, 1941).

Mackenzie, Agnes Mure, 'The Saltire Society: Its Background and Purpose', *Aberdeen University Review* (1943).

McLaren, Moray, *Return to Scotland: An Egoist's Journey* (London, 1930)

McLennan, Robert, 'The National Question and Scotland', *Communist Review*, Vol. 4, No. 10 (October 1932).

Maclehose, Alexander, *The Scotland of our Sons* (Glasgow, 1937).

Muir, Edwin, *Scottish Journey* (London, 1985), orig. pub. (London, 1935).

Muir, Edwin, *Scott and Scotland: The Predicament of the Scottish Writer* (London, 1936).

Oakley C. A., *Scottish Industry Today* (Edinburgh, 1937).

Power, William, *Scotland and the Scots* (Edinburgh, 1934).

Power, William, *My Scotland* (Edinburgh, 1934).

Power, William, *Should Auld Acquaintance. . . An Autobiography* (London, 1937).

Rait, Robert and George S. Pryde, *Scotland* (London, 1934).

Thomson, David Cleghorn, *Radio Is Changing Us: A Survey of Radio Development and its Problems in our Changing World* (London, 1937).

Thomson, David Cleghorn, ed., *Scotland in Quest of Her Youth* (Edinburgh, 1932).

Walkinshaw, Colin, *The Scots Tragedy* (Edinburgh, 1935).

Weir, Lachlan MacNeill, 'A Silly Book about Scotland: A Reply to a Traducer', *Forward* (26 November 1927).

Post 1939 Books

Beaverbrook, Lord, *Men and Power 1917-1919* (London, 1956).

Beaverbrook, Lord, *The Divine Propagandist* (London, 1962)

Beveridge, Craig and Ronald Turnbull, *The Eclipse of Scottish Culture: Inferiorism and the Intellectuals* (Edinburgh, 1989).

Brand, Jack, *The National Movement in Scotland* (London, 1978).

Bold, Alan, *MacDiarmid: Christopher Murray Grieve: A Critical Biography* (London, 1990).

Boyd Orr, John, *As I Recall* (London, 1966).

Brown, Callum G., *Religion and Society in Scotland since 1707* (Edinburgh, 1997).

Brown, Ian, Thomas Owen Clancy, Susan Manning and Murray Pittock, eds., *The Edinburgh History of Scottish Literature* Volume 2 (Edinburgh, 2007).

Bruce, George, *To Foster and Enrich: The First Fifty Years of the Saltire Society* (Tillicoultry, 1986).

Bruce, Steve, Tony Glendinning, Iain Paterson and Michael Rosie, *Sectarianism in Scotland* (Edinburgh, 2004).

Calder, Angus, *Scotlands of the Mind* (Edinburgh, 2002).

Constantine, Stephen, *Social Conditions in Britain 1918-1939* (London, 1983).

Coote, Colin, *A Companion of Honour: The Story of Walter Elliot* (London, 1965).

Cowan, Edward J. and Finlay Richard J., *Scottish History: The Power of the Past* (Edinburgh, 2002).

Cruickshank, Helen B., *Octobiography* (Montrose, 1976).

Devine, T.M., *The Scottish Nation 1700-2007* (London, 2006).

Devine, T.M., ed., *Scotland and the Union 1707-2007* (Edinburgh, 2008).

Devine, T.M., and R. J. Finlay, eds., *Scotland in the Twentieth Century* (Edinburgh, 1996).

Dickson, A. and J.H. Treble, eds., *People and Society in Scotland Vol. III, 1914-1990* (Edinburgh, 1992).

Donaldson, William, *The Jacobite Song: Political Myth and National Identity* (Aberdeen, 1988).

Farrer, David, *G - For God Almighty: A Personal Memoir of Lord Beaverbrook* (New York, 1969).

Ferguson, William, *Scotland 1689 to the Present* (Edinburgh, 1968)

Finlay, Richard J., *Independent and Free: Scottish Politics and the Origins of the Scottish National Party 1918-1945* (Edinburgh, 1994).

Finlay, Richard J., *Modern Scotland 1914-2000* (London, 2004).

Gallagher, Tom, *Glasgow The Uneasy Peace: Religious tension in Modern Scotland, 1819-1914* (Manchester, 1987).

Gibson, John S, *The Thistle and the Crown: A History of the Scottish Office* (Edinburgh, 1985).

Gilbert, Bentley B. *British Social Policy 1914-1939* (London, 1970).

Glen, Duncan, *Hugh MacDiarmid and the Scottish Renaissance* (Edinburgh, 1964).

Handley, James Edmund, *The Irish in Modern Scotland* (Cork, 1947).

Hanham, H.J., *Scottish Nationalism* (London, 1969).

Houston, R.A. and W.W. J. Knox, eds., *The New Penguin History of Scotland: From the Earliest Times to the Present Day* (London, 2001).

Harvie, Christopher, *Scotland and Nationalism: Scottish Society and Politics 1707-1994* (London, 1994).

Harvie, Christopher, *No Gods and Precious Few Heroes: Scotland 1914-1980* (Edinburgh, 1981).

Kerrigan, Catherine, ed., *The Hugh MacDiarmid-George Ogilvie Letters* (Aberdeen, ????)

Kidd, Colin, *Union and Unionisms: Political thought in Scotland, 1500-2000* (Cambridge, 2008).

Lynch, Michael, *Scotland: A New History* (London, 1991).

McCleery, Alastair, *The Porpoise Press 1922-39* (Edinburgh, 1988).

MacCormick, John, *The Flag in the Wind: The Story of the National Movement in Scotland* (London, 1955).

McCrone, David, *Understanding Scotland the Sociology of a Nation*, 2nd ed. (London, 2001).

McCulloch, Margery Palmer, ed., *Modernism and Nationalism: Literature and Society in Scotland 1919-1939 Source Documents for the Scottish Renaissance* (Glasgow, 2004).

McCulloch, Margery Palmer, *Scottish Modernism and its Contexts 1918-1959 Literature, National Identity and Cultural Exchange* (Edinburgh, 2009).

Macdonald, Catriona M.M., *Unionist Scotland 1800-1997* (Edinburgh, 1998).

Macdonald, Kate, *John Buchan: A Companion to the Mystery Fiction* (North Carolina, 2009).

McDowell, W.H., *The History of BBC Broadcasting in Scotland 1923-1983* (Edinburgh, 1992).

Massie, Allan, *The Thistle and the Rose: Six Centuries of Love and Hate between the Scots and the English* (London, 2005).

Miller Karl, ed., *Memoirs of Modern Scotland* (London, 1970).

Miller, William L., ed., *Anglo-Scottish Relations from 1900 to Devolution* (Oxford, 2005).

Mitchell, James, *Strategies for Self-Government: The Campaigns for a Scottish Parliament* (Edinburgh, 1996).

Muir, Edwin, *An Autobiography* (London, 1987).

Munro, Ian S., *Leslie Mitchell: Lewis Grassic Gibbon* (Edinburgh, 1966).

Noble, Andrew, *Edwin Muir: Uncollected Scottish Criticism* (London, 1982).

Pegg, Mark, *Broadcasting and Society 1918-1939* (London, 1983).

Reid, J.M., *Scotland Past and Present* (Oxford, 1959).

Reid, J.M., *Scotland's Progress: The Survival of the Nation* (London, 1971).

Riach, Alan, ed., *Hugh MacDiarmid: Albyn Shorter Books and Monographs* (Manchester, 1996).

Robertson, George Gladstone MD, with Roderick Grant, *Gorbals Doctor* (London, 1970).

Scannell, Paddy and David Cardiff, *A Social History of British Broadcasting, Vol. 1, 1922-1939: Serving the Nation* (Oxford, 1991).

Skidelsky, Robert, *Politicians and the Slump: The Labour Government of 1929-1931* (London, 1967).

Smith, Anthony D., *National Identity* (London, 1991).

Smith, Janet-Adam, *John Buchan: A Biography* (London, 1965).

Smith, Malcolm, *Democracy in a Depression Britain in the 1920s and 1930s* (Cardiff, 1998).

Smout, T.C. and Sydney Wood, *Scottish Voices 1745-1960* (London, 1990).

Smout, T.C., *A Century of the Scottish People 1830-1950* (Glasgow, 1986).

Stevenson, John, *Social Conditions in Britain Between the Wars* (London, 1977).

Taylor, A.J.P., *Beaverbrook* (London, 1972).

Thompson, F.M.L., ed., *The Cambridge Social History of Britain 1750-1950 Vol. 1 Regions and Communities* (Cambridge, 1990).

Thorpe, Andrew, *Britain in the 1930s: The Deceptive Decade* (Oxford, 1992).

Vines, C.M., *A Little Nut-Brown Man: My Three Years with Lord Beaverbrook* (London, 1968).

Walker, David Pat, *The BBC in Scotland: The First Fifty Years* (Luath Press, 2011).

Walker, Graham, *Intimate Strangers: Political and Cultural Interaction between Scotland and Ulster in Modern Times* (Edinburgh, 1995).

Webb, Keith, *The Growth of Nationalism in Scotland* (Glasgow, 1977).

Young, John H., *A History of the Cathcart Conservative and Unionist Association 1918-1993* (Glasgow, 1993).

Post 1939 Essays & Articles

Aldcroft, Derek H., 'Economic Growth in the Inter-War years: A Reassessment', *The Economic History Review*, Vol. 20, No. 2 (August 1967).

Begg, H.M. and J. A. Stewart, 'The Nationalist Movement in Scotland', *Journal of Contemporary History*, Vol. 6, No. 1 (1971).

Brown, Stewart J., 'Outside the Covenant': the Scottish Presbyterian Churches and Irish Immigration, 1922-1938', *Innes Review*, Vol. 42, No. 1 (Spring 1991).

Campbell, R.H. 'The Scottish Office and the Special Areas in the 1930s', *The Historical Journal*, Vol. 22, No. 1 (March 1979).

Cohen Anthony P., 'A Scottish View of Some Rites, Rights and Wrongs', *American Ethnologist*, Vol. 23, No. 4 (Nov., 1996).

Connell, Liam, 'Irish Immigration and Scottish Identity', *BAIS Conference, The Irish and Britain, Salford* (September 1997).

Devine, T.M., 'The Break-Up of Britain? Scotland and the End of Empire', *Transactions of the Royal Historical Society*, 16 (2006).

Devine, T.M., 'In Bed with an Elephant; Almost Three Hundred Years of the Anglo-Scottish Union', *Scottish Affairs*, No. 57 (autumn 2006).

Dixon, Keith, 'Conservative Scottish Nationalism during the Interwar Period: The Ideas of Andrew Dewar Gibb and George Malcolm Thomson', *Etudes Ecossaises*, Grenoble, No. 4 (1997).

Finlay, Richard J., 'National Identity in Crisis: Politicians, Intellectuals and the "End of Scotland", 1920-1939', *The Historical Association* (1994).

Finlay, Richard J., 'Controlling the Past: Scottish Historiography and Scottish Identity in the 19th and 20th Centuries', *Scottish Affairs*, No. 9 (autumn 1994).

Finlay, Richard J., '"For or against?" Scottish Nationalists and the British Empire, 1919-39', *The Scottish Historical Review*, Vol. 71, Nos. 191-2 (Apr., Oct. 1992).

Finlay, Richard J., 'Pressure Group of Political Party? The Nationalist Impact on Scottish Politics 1928-1945', *Twentieth Century British History*, Vol. 3, No. 3 (1992).

Finlay, R., 'The Rise and Fall of Popular Imperialism in Scotland 1850-1950', *Scottish Geographical Magazine*, 113, No. 1 (1997).

Finlay, Richard J., 'Nationalism, Race, Religion and the Irish Question in Interwar Scotland', *Innes Review*, Vol. 42, No. 1 (Spring 1991).

Hajkowski, Thomas, 'The BBC and National Identity in Britain 1922-1954', PhD Thesis, Northwestern University, Illinois (December 2005).

Harvie, Christopher, 'Second Thoughts of a Scotsman on the Make: Politics, Nationalism and Myth in John Buchan', *The Scottish Historical Review*, Vol. 70, 1: No. 188 (April, 1991).

Kyd, J.G., 'Scotland's Population', *The Scottish Historical Review*, Vol. 28, No. 106 (October, 1949).

McLean, Iain, 'The Rise and Fall of the Scottish National Party', *Political Studies*, Vol. 18, No. 3 (Oxford 1970).

Scullion, Adrienne, 'BBC Radio in Scotland, 1923-1939: Devolution, Regionalism and Centralisation', *Northern Scotland*, Vol. 15 (1995).

Tange, Hanne, 'Lewis Grassic Gibbon and the Scottish Renaissance', Paper, (Association of Scottish Literary Studies, Conference, Aberdeen, June 2001).

Ward-Smith Gabrielle, 'Baldwin and Scotland: More than Englishness', *Contemporary British History*, Vol. 15, No. 1 (Spring 2001).

Young, James D. 'Marxism and the Scottish National Question', *Journal of Contemporary History*, Vol. 18, No. 1 (Jan., 1983).

Index